Character
Design
Today

Character Design Today

©2007 PIE BOOKS
All rights reserved. No part of this publication may be reproduced in any form or by any means, graphic, electronic or mechanical, including photocopying and recording by an information storage and retrieval system, without permission in writing from the publisher.

PIE BOOKS
2-32-4, Minami-Otsuka, Toshima-ku, Tokyo 170-0005 Japan
Tel: +81-3-5395-4811   Fax: +81-3-5395-4812
e-mail: editor@piebooks.com   sales@piebooks.com
http://www.piebooks.com/

ISBN978-4-89444-634-2 C3070   Printed in Japan

Contents

Special Interview — 004
特集：佐野研二郎インタビュー

Editorial Note 012

サービス
Service — 013
通信事業　Telecommunications / インターネットサービス　Internet Service /
生命保険業　Life Insurance / 銀行　Bank etc.

製造
Manufacture — 057
食品メーカー　Food Manufacturer / 飲料メーカー　Beverage Manufacturer /
総合家電メーカー　Household Appliance Manufacturer /
自動車メーカー　Auto Manufacturer / おもちゃメーカー　Toy Manufacturer etc.

レクリエーション
Recreation — 105
ミュージアム　Museum / イベント事業　Event Industry /
レジャープール施設　Swimming Pool / スポーツ事業　Sports Industry etc.

流通・販売
Commerce & Retail — 119
コンビニエンスストア　Convenience Store / 商業施設　Commercial Facility /
外食産業　Food Service Industry / 家電販売　Electrical Household Retailer /
百貨店　Department Store etc.

公共機関・団体
Public Institution & Organization — 143
地方自治体　Local Government / 業界団体　Trade Organization /
交通　Transportation / 生活協同組合　Cooperative etc.

クリエイティブ
Media & Creative — 179
テレビ局　TV Station / 出版　Publication / 新聞社　Newspaper Company /
ラジオ局　Radio Station / デザイン会社　Design Firm etc.

Concept & Profile of Characters 225

Index 227

Character Design Today, Special Interview

特集：佐野研二郎 インタビュー

Feature: Interview with Kenjiro Sano

日光江戸村『ニャンまげ』、TBS『ブーブ』、KDDI『au LISMO!』など、
人々の記憶に残るキャラクターを生み出すアート・ディレクター、佐野研二郎氏。
彼がデザインしたキャラクターは、一度見ると忘れられないインパクトを与える。そして、とても愛らしい。
これまでに制作したキャラクターのケーススタディをもとに、長く愛されるキャラクターづくりの秘訣を伺った。

Kenjiro Sano is an art director who has created many memorable characters,
such as Nyan-mage (Edo Wonderland in Nikko), BooBo (TBS), au LISMO (KDDI).
The characters he has designed have an unforgettable impact even if they are seen just once.
They are also quite adorable. Along with case studies of the characters he has designed in the past,
we also ask him about the secrets of making his long-loved characters.

【Mr. Cプロフィール】
本書のために、佐野氏が考案したキャラクター。
キャラクター＝コピーライトという発想のもと、デザインされた。
木登りをしてみたり、北極に行ってみたり、浜辺を散策したり、とても行動的。ときどき高くジャンプする。

<Mr. C Profile>
This is a character that Sano has thought up for this volume. It is based on the idea that Character is equivalent to Copyright. It tries to climb trees, travel to the North Pole, or strolls along the beach, making him a pretty active. Sometimes he jumps up high.

■ ラフ案・初期　The First Design Drafts

■ ラフ案・中期　The Second Design Drafts
■ ラフ案・後期　The Latter Design Drafts

商品やブランドに人格を与える

商品やブランドを体現するときは、「たとえばいい人なのか、カッコいい人なのか、はたまたカワイイ人なのか」のように人格をつけることから始めるんです。というのも、人に例えるとすごく表現しやすくなる。自分の場合は、「キャラクターを作るぞ！」というよりは、分かりやすさや伝わりやすさを考えたときに、キャラクターを立てることを手法のひとつと考えているといったほうがよいでしょうか。それと単にキャラクターとして存在させるだけでなく、"人格のあるシンボルマーク"になることを意識していますね。

子供がマネして描けるくらいシンプルでいい

周囲への分かりやすさや伝わりやすさを考えたとき、子供がマネして描けるくらいシンプルであることがいちばん大切だと思っています。実際、自分でイラストを描くことも多いんですが、"イラストレーションを描いている"というより、あくまでも"アイコン"という点を意識して"デザインすること"を最優先しています。また、例えば、表情をつけなかったり、色数をあえて絞ったりすることで、見た人が話題にしやすいポイントや気になる罠を仕掛けることも重要です。

この本のために制作した『Mr.C』も、その例のひとつ。"顔はないのに、なんで手足は毛むくじゃら？"というように、ほどよい突っ込みが出るくらいがいいんです。ちなみに、『Mr.C』は、キャラクター＝コピーライトという発想から生まれたデザイン。顔のデザインは最初から固まっていましたが、手足を何パターンか作り、最終的に今のものにおとしこみました。

仕事の依頼があったときは、必ず「予習」していくようにしています。自分の中で感じたものを走り書きでもいいので、とりあえず形にしてみる。詳しい内容を聞いてからだと、考えすぎて逆に自由な発想ができなくなることもあると思うんです。予習してからいくと、その場で意見をすり合わせることもできるので、スムーズに進むことが多いですね。

Giving Personality to a Product or Brand

Fleshing out a product or brand, starts by creating some personality. It is either a good person, or stylish, or cute. With that, it is very easy for users to guess what is being expressed. With me, rather than deciding I am going to make a character, instead I use characters as one means of achieving clarity and communicability. A character does not existing merely for the sake of being a character. Rather, it is the symbol of a personality.

The Character needs to be simple enough for children to copy and draw

When considering clarity or communicability, the most important thing is to have the character be simple enough so that even children can copy and draw it. In fact, I draw a lot of characters. But rather than drawing an illustration, I keep in mind that ultimately I am drawing an "icon" and I make designing my priority. Also, by not giving the character an expression, or by limiting the number of colors used, it becomes easier for people to talk about it. There's something that snares the user's attention. This is critical.

The character that was created for this book, "Mr. C" also follows these rules. Even though it lacks a face, why are its arms and legs hairy? Provoking that sort of moderate reaction is good, I've found. By the way, "Mr. C" came about from the concept of Character being equivalent to Copyright. From the beginning, the design of the face was fixed but I made many different versions of the legs and arms. The result of which is how the character appears now.

Whenever I am commissioned for a project, without fail I do my "preparations". Even if it is something that has just come to me that I jot down quickly, I go ahead and give it shape. After hearing the details of the project, I wind up thinking too much and my creativity loses its flexibility sometimes. Instead, most of the time the project progresses smoothly when I've prepared and can give my opinion on the spot.

Case Study 01
KDDI『au LISMO!』ができるまで
The Making of the KDDI [au LISMO!]

■ラフ案　Design Drafts

■採用案　Adopted Design

最初のラフは、オリエンの段階で。そのとき既に、「LISTEN」→「リス」というアイデアが浮かんでいたという。ラフ案の中には、クマのようなシルエットのものや、オンラインサービスということから、デジタルを意識したデザインも。最終的に、オレンジ色のauロゴに対して補色対比的なグリーンを使用した、シルエットがかわいい『リスモ』が誕生した。

The initial draft done at the the orientation meeting. By that time, the idea of substituting "listen" for risu had already occurred to him. The draft concept incorporates a bear-like silhouette with a digital sense that expresses the idea of on-line service. In the end, he used green as a compliment to the orange of the au logo, and the cute "LISMO" silhouette was born.

散漫な情報やイメージを束ねる役割

　僕にとってキャラクターは"しるし"のようなもの。いうなれば、アイコンと同じなんです。同時にそのキャラクターなりアイコンは、分散している情報やイメージを束ねる役割を果たすものだと考えています。KDDIが提供する『リスモ』は、"ケータイで音楽を"というテーマでイチからスタートしたプロジェクト。新サービスというだけでなく、複雑さもカバーする意味合いを込めアイコンを立てることの必要性を感じました。「キャラクターを作ろう」という発想よりは、道路標識のようにシンプルで分かりやすいものが適しているんじゃないかなと思ったんです。新しいサービスを分かりやすく伝えるため、"ナビゲーター"としてのアイコンとして誕生させました。

The Role of Bundling Together Loose Information or Image

For me, a character is like a "sign". It is the same as an icon. Also, as an icon the character has the role of binding together a lot of disparate information or images. LISMO from KDDI is a project that began with the theme of listening to music with your mobile phone. Rather than just conveying the idea of a new service, I felt it needed to be an icon that also had "complexity". Instead than thinking, "Let's make a character," I found that something simple and clear—like a street sign—was the most appropriate. To easily communicate the new service, we created an icon that would serve as a "navigator".

■ 展開例　Application Examples

シンプルで愛情がわくもの

　僕は移動中や打ち合わせ中にノートに思いつくままにイラストを描くことが多いんですが、むしろその場で描けるくらいのものがいいと考えていますね。『リスモ』の場合は、立ち上げのオリエンの段階で"LISTEN"→"リス"の絵が生まれたのがすべての始まり。それに幅広い世代を越えて愛着を持ってもらうには、可愛いすぎて子供っぽくなるのは的はずれな気がした。だから目や鼻、表情を作らなかったのも理由のひとつ。さらに、見た人が「どうして顔がないんだろう」と気になるのと同時にシルエットにも意識が働いて、印象深いものになることも意図しているんですよ。

Simple and Adorable

I often doodle in a notebook when I am traveling or when I am in meetings. Something that can be drawn on the spot like that is the most successful. In the case of "LISMO", everything began at the initial orientation meeting. That is where I set down risu (meaning squirrel in Japanese) for "listen". Though it had broad appeal for different generations and was likeable, it was too cute and would come off as being childish, I felt. That was one of the reasons why the final design does not have eyes, nose, or a facial expression. That makes people think, "Why doesn't it have a face?" At the same time, the idea of using a silhouette was meant to leave a strong impression.

Case Study 02

ベネッセコーポレーション中学講座事業部
『中学サキドリ! ENGLISH』ができるまで
The Making of the Benesse Corporation Middle School Lesson Division "Middle School SAKIDORI! ENGLISH"

■ラフ案　Design Drafts　　　　　　　　　　　　■採用案　Adopted Design

『中学サキドリENGLISH』という教材のタイトルをから、トリをキャラクター化。書店に並んだときのことを考え、色づかいもポップで楽しい雰囲気に。POPやしおりなども作成し、イメージの統一を図った。

From the title of the educational material "Middle School SAKIDORI! ENGLISH," the tori (meaning "bird" in Japanese) is converted into a character. Visualizing the book in bookstores, the use of colors and pop feel give it a fun atmosphere. Making point-of-purchase displays and bookmarks, I planned to maintain consistency with the brand image.

ターゲットに響く、重要なシズルを考える

『中学サキドリENGLISH』というタイトルは、あらかじめ決まっていたこともあって、キャラクターにするなら"トリ"がいいかなと漠然と思っていました。ターゲットは中学進学を控えた小学6年生で、"中学生になる前に英語に触れておこうね"というのが教材の目的。表紙も中面も1色だったり、少し難しそうな感じがする既存の教材が多いなかで、これは中ページも表紙もカラーで、そのうえ編集も分かりやすかったんです。スタンダード・ハイレベルの2種類があるけど、どちらにしても入門編だし、ストイックにしても意味がない。それに何よりもここで外しちゃいけないのは、「英語って難しそうだな」と思っている小学6年生に"取っ付きやすくする"というのが重要なシズルだと考えたんです。

Resonating with the Target User, Considering the Important Sizzle

The title "Middle School SAKIDORI! ENGLISH " was decided from the onset of the project, so I thought that if there were a character a bird would be good. It was a pretty straightforward thought process. The target was 6th grade students waiting to start middle school, to whom this educational material aimed to communicate the message, "Before starting middle school, study a little English". It is common for such material to have covers and interior spreads that are monochromatic and feel like they are slightly difficult. Since a lot of educational material like that already exists, I decided to make the cover and interior in color. Thanks to this, executing the layout wasn't such a challenge. Even though there are two levels, Standard Level and High Level, both are

■ 展開例　Application Examples

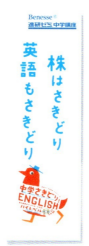

キャラクターは、"やさしいナビゲーター"

　形やテイストなど変遷を遂げましたが、最終的に出来上がったカラフルなものは書店に並んだときにもポップで元気に見えるし、楽しい感じがしますよね。お母さんが購入することも想定して、"ウチの子でもできるんじゃないか"という安心感を与えられたらいいな、とも考えました。タイトルを頭の上や下に置くのではなく、キャラクターと一体化させたのは、よりシンボル感が増すと思ったから。キャラクターを"一緒に頑張ろうね"という、やさしいナビゲーターに位置づけることを目的として、誕生しました。

introductory and there was no reason for making it serious. But more importantly, what is indispensable is the important sizzle that makes 6th graders who think English looks difficult to instead think it's easy to pick up.

Characters are "Friendly Navigators"

Despite the changes in form and taste, the resulting item was a colorful addition to bookstores. It had a pop feel, energetic visual impact, and also had a fun attitude. The assumption was that a mother would buy this, thinking, "Even my child can do this". Providing a feeling of ease is something I also took into consideration. The title doesn't go above or below but is part of the character, which increases its effective symbolism. The goal was to create a friendly navigator that would communicate, "Let's try this together."

Case Study 03

グラクソ・スミスクライン
『ハナッペ / ズキンちゃん』ができるまで
The Making of GlaxoSmithKline "Hanappe" and "Zukin-chan"

■未採用案　Rejected Design

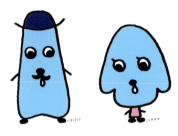

『ハナッペ』は"鼻タレ"を可愛らしくアレンジしたもの。子どもが親しみを感じるように、クマをモチーフにし、『ハナパパ』と『ハナママ』は、最終的には使用しないことに。

The character "Hanappe" is nasal drip redone in a cute manner. To appeal to children, I used a bear as a motif. In the end dropped "Hanapapa" and "Hanamama" from the scheme.

■採用案　Adopted Design

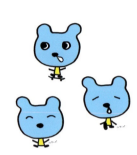

■ラフ案　Design Drafts

■採用案　Adopted Design

『ズキンちゃん』は、偏頭痛に悩まされる女の子。赤いズキンをかぶり、赤いスカート・赤い靴を履いている。普段は元気だが一旦ズキンズキンと頭痛に襲われると、ほかのことが何もできなくなってしまう。プレゼン時に、ラフ案も見せながら、最終案までデザインが変化して行く過程を説明した。

"Zukin-chan" is for girls who suffer from migraines. She is wearing a red hood, a red skirt and red shoes. Usually she is full of energy but now her head is throbbing with a headache and she is unable to do anything else. ("Hood" and "throb" are both zukin in Japanese.) When I made the presentation, I showed the progression of the design, developing from its draft to completion.

ネガティブさを感じさせない安心感のあるキャラクター

『ハナッペ』は小児用の花粉症の薬、『ズキンちゃん』は小児用の頭痛薬のキャラクター。薬局で売られる薬ではなく、医者が処方箋を出す薬にまつわるキャラクターなので、小児科でポスターとして貼られたり、病院で配布されるパンフレットに登場します。なにかとシリアスになってしまうシーンで、アイコン的なものがあればお母さんも子供も親しみやすく、安心できるかなと思って制作しました。これはたくさん描いた分だけ、ボツも多かった事例。でも"ノリで一回作って検証する"作業ってとても大事なんです。感性と理性のタームを変えて作り上げると、理屈を越えたよいものが出来上がるはず。これ、僕の持論です。

A Character that Communicates Ease without a Negative Feeling

"Hanappe" is character for a young children's hay fever medicine, and Zukin-chan is a character for small children's headache medicine. This is not an over-the-counter drug. It is medicine that is prescribed by a doctor so the character involved here appears on posters at the pediatrician's office and pamphlets that are distributed at hospitals. In such a serious situation, an icon with which a mother and child can feel some familiarity will have a soothing effect. I kept this in mind when making the character. I drew a lot of characters for this but this is an example being many rejects. Nonetheless, the process of making something based on "feeling" and then validating it is very important. Making something that changes the terms of feeling and reason helps surpass logic and making something good. That's my philosophy.

Other Works

Esquire『ホーホーくん』 Esquire "HO HO-kun"

「現代の目利き101」という特集であるため、「ホウホウ」と頷く「ホーホーくん」を作成することを考案。知性の象徴でもあるフクロウをモチーフにした。

For the "Contemporary Connoisseur 101" feature story of the magazine, I thought up the character HO HO-kun, who nods his head while saying, "ho ho". I used the owl as a symbol of intellect.

ジョン・F・ケネディーセンター（WASHINGTON, D.C.）
「日本展 / JAPAN! / CULTURE＋HYPER CULTURE」『MOMO』
John F. Kennedy Center (Washington, D.C.) "Japan! Culture + Hyper Culture" "MOMO"

ワシントンD.C.で開催される大規模な日本展のキャラクター。日の丸を様々な色の円で構成することにより、日本のカルチャーの多様性を表現。ピンクの猿『MOMO』が決定案で、ほかは代案。

This character was part of the large-scale exhibition about Japan that was held at the John F. Kennedy Center in Washington, D.C. Using the circular of the "Hinomaru" (the sun symbol of the Japanese flag) in various colors, I was able to express the multifaceted nature of Japanese culture. The pink monkey "MOMO" was the final version while the others were alternates.

長く愛されるキャラクターづくりの秘訣

　自分が『ニャンまげ』（1998年に登場した『日光江戸村』のキャラクター）を手がけていた頃、たまたま伊豆でバスに乗ったら、運転手さんが携帯電話にニャンまげのストラップを付けていたのを目にしたんです。当時はストラップってあまり制作されることがなかったんだけど、それを見て単純に面白いな、建築的だなと感じたんですね。それこそちょっと変わった、こんなトリッキーなキャラクターでも勝手に広がっているんだなって。そのとき、今後は様々なメディアを串刺しにし、時間軸を越えることができるキャラクターが必要だと思ったんです。とはいいつつも、商品やブランドの体現であることが大前提。だから、それらがもつシズル感と合致していないと、いくらキャラクターを作っても機能しないし、長くは続かないような気がしますね。あらゆる角度からいろんなエッセンスで商品やブランドのことを考えると、やるべきことがたくさんあることに気づくのではないでしょうか。

The Secret of Making Characters that are Long-loved

At the time I was involved with the "Nyan-mage" (a character debuted in 1998 for the Edo Wonderland in Nikko), I just happened to be riding a bus in Izu, and I saw that the driver had a Nyan-mage on the strap of his mobile phone. At that time, it was not so common to produce straps for mobile phones, but seeing that I thought it was interesting, and it felt like someyhing that exsisted beyond its original motive. For that reason, it was a little different and even with such a tricky character it had broad appeal. From that time on, I looked sharply at various media and I thought there was a need for characters that could surpass the time axis. Even still, the embodiment of the product or the brand takes precedence over all else and the sizzle feeling must dovetail with it. Otherwise no matter what character you make it won't function and won't have longevity. Considering the various fundaments of a product or brand from all angles, you'll more than likely realize there many things that you must do.

PROFILE
1972年東京都生まれ。1996年多摩美術大学グラフィックデザイン科卒業、博報堂入社。現在、博報堂 / HAKUHODODESIGN クリエイティブセンター、アートディレクター。商品開発やシンボルマーク、キャラクターデザインをはじめとして広告デザイン、TVCM、店頭POPまで幅広いアートディレクションを手掛ける。著書に『佐野研二郎のWORKSHOP』（誠文堂新光社）など

PROFILE
B. 1972, Tokyo. In 1996, graduated from the Tama Art University with a major in Graphic Design and joined Hakuhodo. Currently, he is an art director at the Hakuhodo's HAKUHODODESIGN Creative Center. Beginning with product development, symbol and character design, he is involved in a broad range of art direction, including advertising design, television commercials, and in-store point-of-purchase displays. His book "Kenjiro Sano's Workshop" was published by Seibundo Shinkosha.

Special Interview 011

Editorial Note

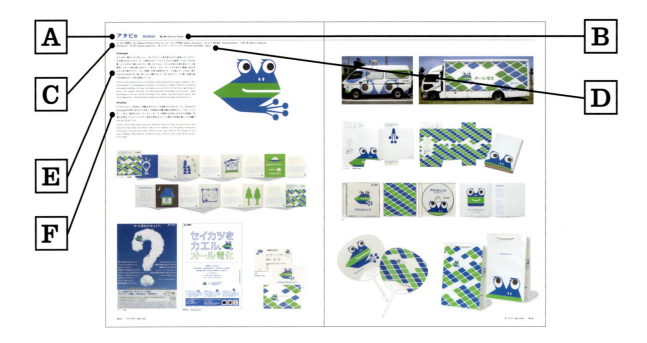

A　キャラクター名　Character's Name

B　クライアント業種・業態・商品のカテゴリー
（商品名もしくは使用目的）
Client's Type of Business and Industry, Product Category
(Product Name and/or Utilization of Character)

C　Creative Stuff　制作スタッフ
CL: Client　クライアント
CD: Creative Director　クリエイティブ・ディレクター
AD: Art Director　アート・ディレクター
D: Designer　デザイナー
P: Photographer　フォトグラファー
I: Illustrator　イラストレーター
DF: Design Firm　デザイン会社
SB: Submitter　作品提供者

D　制作国　Country from which submitted

E　キャラクターのコンセプト　Concept of the Character

F　キャラクターのプロフィール　Profile of the Character

All other production titles are unabbreviated.
上記以外の制作者呼称は省略せずに掲載しています。

Please note that some credit information has been omitted at the request of the submitter.
作品提供者の意向によりデータの一部を記載していない場合があります。

The "kabushiki gaisha (K.K.)" and "yugen gaisha (Ltd.) portions of all names have been omitted.
各企業名に付随する、"株式会社、(株)" および "有限会社、(有)" は表記を省略させていただきました。

The company and product names that appear in this book are published and / or registered trademarks.
本書に記載された企業名・商品名は、掲載各社の商標または登録商標です。

アタビe　Atabie　電力業　Electric Power

CL, SB: 沖縄電力　The Okinawa Electric Power CO., Inc　　CD: 山門茂樹　Shigeki Yamakado　　AD, D, I: 鈴木直之　Naoyuki Suzuki　　P: 奥口 睦　Makoto Okuguchi
CM Director: 中村 剛　Takeshi Nakamura　　DF: タイクーングラフィックス　TYCOON GRAPHICS　　Japan

Concept

カエルは、卵からおたまじゃくし、そして大人へと姿を変えながら成長していくすごい生き物であることから、オール電化のモチーフとしてカエルを選択。デザイン化する際、カエルのもつ親しみやすさ、優しさとともに、カエルが自らの姿を変えていく革新性、スピード感を盛り込みたいと考えた。また、カエルが心地よい環境に溶け込んでしまう様子をイメージし、背景にも同じ配色のパターンを施した。これは、海のみなもやきらめく光、青い空にうかぶ雲のかたち、生い茂るグリーンの葉、空間を抜ける気持ちのいい風を表現している。

The frog was selected as a symbol of all electric living for its remarkable metamorphosis from egg to tadpole to terrestrial adult. In designing the character we wanted to imbue it with the endearing and gentle qualities of a frog, its innate power to reform its own body, and sense of speed. And imaged after the frog blending with its pleasant environment – light sparkling on the sea, clouds floating in blue skies, luxuriant green leaves, and wind blowing by – both frog and background feature the same colored pattern.

Profile

「アタビe」という名前は、沖縄方言でカエルを意味する「あたびー」と、ElectricやEnergyのEを掛け合わせて命名。大好物は沖縄の郷土料理のチャンプルーとラフテー。安心・便利なIHクッキングヒーターで、料理のお手伝いをするのが得意。旺盛な好奇心と人なつっこさで、身近な視点からオール電化の快適な暮らしを沖縄のみんなに伝えている。

Atabie derives his name from the Okinawa word "Atabi" for frog and "e" of electric and energy. His favorite dishes are his mama's chanpuru (Okinawan stir-fry) and raftee (stewed pork), and with an IH cooktop he can enjoy helping. This friendly curious imp introduces the comforts of all electric living to people in Okinawa from users' viewpoint.

リーフレット　Leaflet

チラシ　Flyer

新聞広告　Newspaper AD

名刺　Business Card

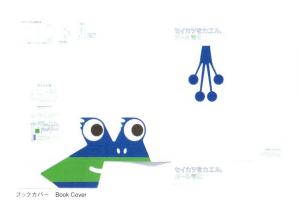

ブックカバー　Book Cover

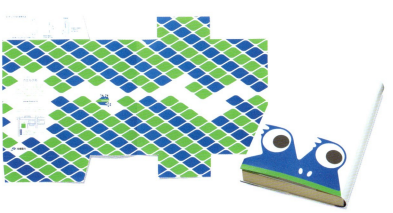

CD

火ぐまのパッチョ Higuma no Paccho   エネルギー事業 Energy Industry

CL: 東京ガス Tokyo Gas Co., LTD.   CD: 澤本嘉光 Yoshimitsu Sawamoto   AD, I: 田中 元 Gen Tanaka   D: 勝又祐子 Yuko Katsumata / 矢野仁志 Hitoshi Yano / 岡本紀子 Noriko Okamoto
Producer: 宮嶋貴子 Takako Miyajima   DF: ワークアップたき WORK UP TAKI   SB: 電通 DENTSU INC.   Japan

Concept
東京ガスは、コンロをはじめとする豊富な商品ラインナップを持っているため、それらを紹介していくためのキャラクターを必要としていた。タレント等をキャラクターにするよりも、もっとキャンペーンのコンセプトに近く、オリジナリティのあるものが良いと考え、「ガス・パッチョ!」のコピーから「火ぐまのパッチョ」というくまのキャラクターを開発。あえて手描き感を残し、温かな味のあるテイストとなるよう意識した。

Tokyo Gas needed a character to introduce its rich lineup of small kitchen stoves and other household products. Feeling it would be better to develop a character with originality in keeping with the campaign concept than to use a popular personality, Higuma no Paccho plays off of the company's Gas Paccho! slogan. A hand-drawn quality was consciously retained in striving to effect a sense of warmth.

Profile
火ぐまの国の王子様。ガスのチカラで、パッと明るく、チョっと豊かな未来の暮らしを人間界に伝えていくのが「パッチョ」の役目。火曜日生まれで、趣味は料理。食いしん坊でちょっと怠け者。小柄で親しみやすい。よく見ると顔が「火」で、からだはガスの炎の色をしている。

The prince of higuma (a play on the words "fire" and "brown bear") country. Paccho's role is to bring a burst of light and a bit of richness to the world of humans. He was born of Tuesday (the day of fire in Japanese) and his hobby is cooking. He's a gourmand, a tad lazy, small in stature, and endearing. While not obvious, his face is the character for fire, and his body, the color of a gas flame.

TVCM

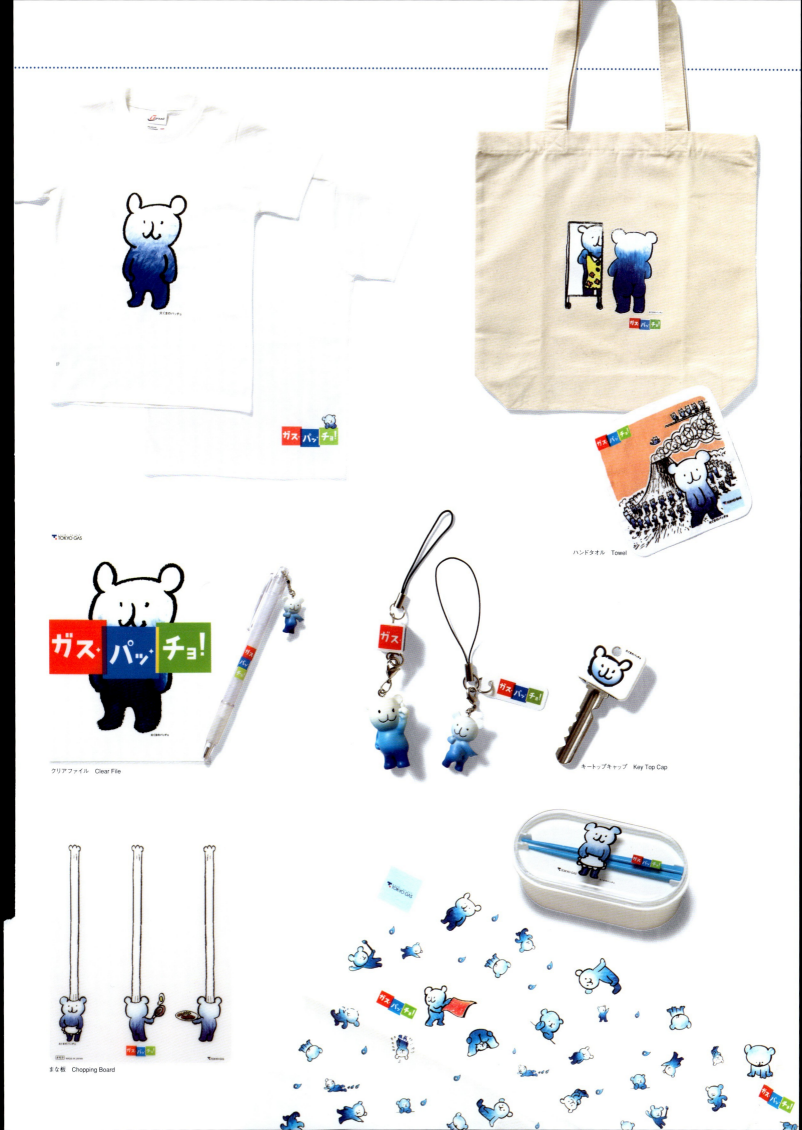

≫火ぐまのパッチョ　Higuma no Paccho

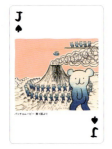

トランプ　Cards

プカ、ポカ、ピカ　PUKA, POKA, PIKA　　エネルギー事業　Energy Industry

CL: 東京ガス　Tokyo Gas Co., Ltd.　　AD: 鈴木不二絵　Fujie Suzuki　　D: 川村省一　Shoichi Kawamura　　SB: 東京ガス がすてな〜に ガスの科学館　Tokyo Gas Co., Ltd. GAS SCIENCE MUSEUM　Japan

Concept
目に見えないガスというものを、子供たちを含めた多くの人々に身近に感じ、親しんでもらうため、ガスが生み出す「炎」「熱」「電気」をキャラクタライズ。愛らしいボディフォルムと豊かな表情は、ガスの温かもりと優しさを表している。それぞれ胸のアイコン、頭の形、ボディカラーで3つの特徴を差別化し、表現した。

The flame, heat, and electricity generated by gas, which is itself invisible, were characterized to make gas a more familiar entity to a broad spectrum of people including children. Their charming body forms and the rich expressions convey the warmth and gentleness of gas. The icons they display on their chests together with their colors and head shapes differentiate and express their distinctive characteristics.

Profile
しっかり者のプカ(青)・癒し系のポカ(橙)・活発なピカ(黄)は、東京ガスが運営する「がすてな〜に ガスの科学館」のキャラクター。リーダーで液体〜気体に自在に変化可能な青色のプカは、天然ガス・LNG・都市ガス・ガスの炎、だいだい色のポカはガスが作り出す熱(温冷)、黄色のピカはガスが作り出す電気を象徴している。

Characters for the Tokyo Gas Science Museum: sturdy and steady Puka, healing Poka and vivacious Pika. Blue Puka symbolizes the flame of natural gas, LNG, and city gas, which change freely from a liquid to gaseous state; orange Poka personifies heat generated by gas; and yellow Pika gas-generated electricity.

ステッカー　Sticker　　ポストカード　Postcard

ハンドタオル　Towel

クリアファイル　Clear File

リーフレット　Leaflet

ヒーラン　Hiiran　電力業　Electric Power

CL, SB: 中部電力　CHUBU Electric Power., Inc　　CD: 立辺一行（ADKボーイズ）　Kazuyuki Tatebe (ADK BOYS)　　I: とみぞうちゃん　TOMIZOUCHAN　Japan

Concept
オール電化を推奨するためのキャラクター。火を使わないことの先進性をより印象的にPRするため、タレントに対する「悪役」としてこの怪獣キャラが生まれた。目の前にモノがあると火を吐いてしまうが、まったく悪意はなく、ただ無邪気に火を使ってしまう、というおとぼけキャラ。愛想がなくふてぶてしい表情をしているが、すぐにいじけてしまうため、どことなく哀愁漂うマヌケキャラになっている。

A campaign character advocating all electric living. A monster beast was developed to play the role of the "bad guy" as an impressive means of promoting the advanced nature of flameless cooking and heating. He breathes fire on whatever stands before him, not maliciously, but through his inadvertent use of fire. He's gruff and brazen in expression but cowers immediately; he's a blockhead with a touch of sadness.

Profile
人に優しく、地球に優しく、自分にはもっと優しく!!　がモットー。身長53cm。焦げた食べ物が好き。現在彼女募集中。常にトレンドを意識している。誉められることに弱くて単純で、ちょっとさみしがり屋。人から注目されると舞い上がって張り切るが、都合が悪くなると、子供のフリをする小心者。

His motto: people-friendly, Earth-friendly, and more so, me-friendly. Height: 53cm. Likes burnt foods. Currently looking for a girlfriend. Always trend-conscious. He's simple-minded, a glutton for flattery, and tends to get lonely. When people are watching, he works like a beaver, but when things don't go right he acts like a child.

パンフレット　Pamphlet

親カバ、子カバ OYA-kaba, KO-kaba　　通信事業 Telecommunications

CL, SB: KDDI　CD: 藤曲厚司 Kouji Fujimagari　AD, I: 寄藤文平 Bunpei Yorifuji　AD: 里見佳音 Kaoto Satomi　D: 酒井 希 Nozomi Sakai　CW: 中里耕平 Kouhei Nakazato
Planner: 松本 巖 Takeshi Matsumoto　Japan

Concept
ジュニア携帯のキャラクター。auカラーのオレンジを基調としたキャラクターで、常に心配していることを表すため、瞳をウルウルさせている。ママのアイコンとしてかわいいエプロンを着せた。

The character for au's children's cellphone. au orange in color, her teary eyes reflect her perpetual state of worry. She wears a pretty apron as a symbol of motherhood.

Profile
かなりの心配性で我が子の安全が気になってしょうがない。子どもを見守るためなら、たとえ電柱の上、水の中？！ 子供のこととなると自分の安全はすっかり忘れていたりする。好きな四字熟語は「安全第一」。特技は気をもむこと。生年月日は聞かないで（♥）。

OYA-kaba (mama hippo) is a worrywart, perpetually concerned about the wellbeing of her little one. She'll even risk her own safety atop a telephone pole or in the water for the sake of her child. Her favorite saying is "safety first". Her special talent is fretting. Her birth date is a secret.

パンフレット　Pamphlet

新聞広告　Newspaper AD

ドコモダケ　Docomodake　通信事業 Telecommunications

CL, SB: エヌ・ティ・ティ・ドコモ　NTT DoCoMo. Inc.　CD: 黒須美彦　Yoshihiko Kurosu / 垣内美香　Mika Kakiuchi / 原田睦子　Mutsuko Harada　Japan

Concept
ドコモダケは「ドコモだけ＝DoCoMo only」の施策を分かりやすく伝えるために開発されたキャラクター。あまり自慢げにしゃべらないように口が×になっていたり、ぼんやりとどこを見ているかわからない感じを表現するために目が離れていたりする。またそれ以外にも個々の特徴として、バーバドコモダケがラベンダー色のおしゃれ染めをしていたり、お年頃のムスメドコモダケの口の×印がリボンになっていて、恋をすると色が変わったりと、年齢にあった仕様にデザインされている。

Docomodake (dake meaning "only" or "mushroom" in Japanese) were developed as an easy-to-understand means of conveying Docomo's unique billing plan. They have all sorts of unusual traits such as their mouths becoming Xs to prevent them from boasting, or their eyes disengaging when they space out. Other characteristics reflect their ages: granny tints herself a chic lavender;and the coming-off-age daughter wears a ribbon on her X and changes color when she fall in love, and suchlike.

Profile
チチ、ハハ、ジージ、バーバ、ムスメ、チュウガク、ショウガクの家族7人とムスメドコモダケの彼、カレシドコモダケ。喜びや愛の表現として転がることが多く、良き日には輪になって踊る習性がある。また、飛ぶこともできる。ただし、重い物を持ったり走ったりすることは苦手。

The seven-member Docomodake family – Papa, Mama, Grandpa, Grandma, Daughter, Jr. High, and Elementary – and Daughter's beau Boyfriend Docomodake. They mostly roll around expressing joy and love, and on good days have the peculiar habit of turning into wheels and dancing. They can also fly, but can't run of carry heavy objects.

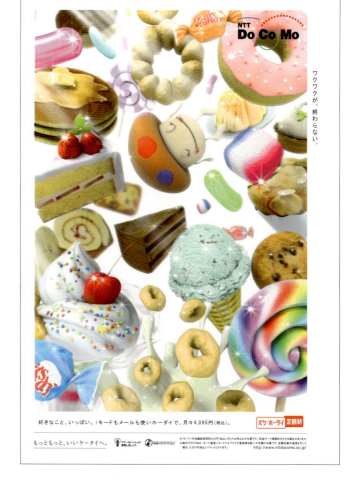

雑誌広告　Magazine AD

ノベルティー　Novelty

カレンダー　Calendar

TVCM

ノベルティー　Novelty

ウェブサイト　Website

サービス　Service　023

家デンくん　Ieden-kun　通信事業 Telecommunications

CL: NTT東日本　NTT East　CD: 大宮エリー　Eri Omiya　AD, I: 池田享史　Takafumi Ikeda　D: 近藤ちはる　Chiharu Kondo　CW: 倉成英俊　Hidetoshi Kuranari　DF: ウルトラグラフィックス　Ultra Graphics
SB: 電通　DENTSU INC.　Japan

Concept
"固定電話（家の電話）から携帯電話の通話料が安くなる"というNTT東日本の新サービスのキャラクター、家デンくん。幅広い層への理解を必要としたため、わかりやすく、愛されるキャラクターを目指し、家・数字・携帯電話をビジュアルに落とし込んだ。店頭ポスターやノベルティ、請求書同封シール、家の電話にも貼ることができるシールなど各媒体でさまざまな展開を行った。

Ieden-kun is a character for NTT East's new service that lets users "call mobile phones for less". Because it needed to communicate to a broad segment of the public, the aim was to create a charming, readily understood character, thus the house, number, and mobile phone form the visuals. Applications for various media including store posters and novelties, and stickers sent with phone bills that could be stuck on telephones were developed

Profile
家デンくんのログセは、「0036！」
Ieden-kun's pet phrase is "0036!".

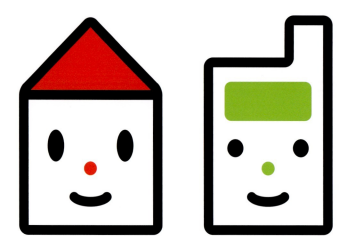

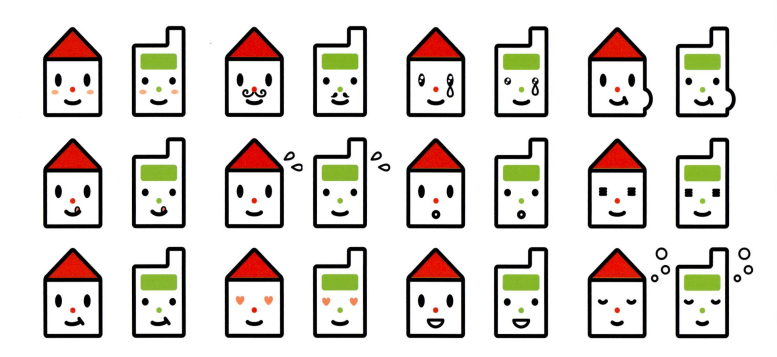

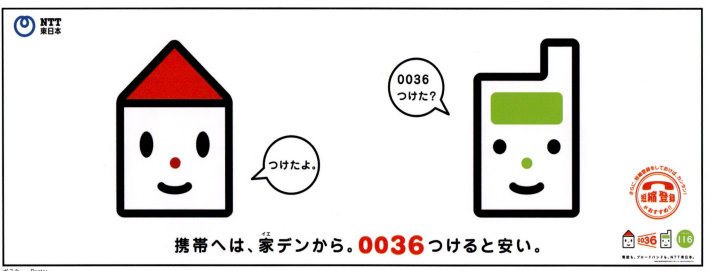

ポスター　Poster

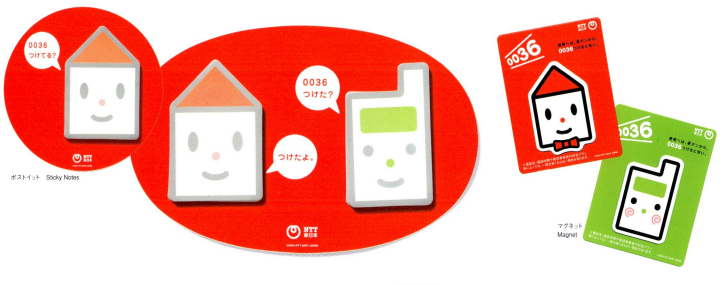

ポストイット　Sticky Notes

マグネット　Magnet

マウスパッド　Mouse Pad

ハンドタオル　Towel

クリアファイル　Clear File

サービス　Service　025

困らない君 Komaranai-kun　教育事業 Educational Industry

CL: ベネッセコーポレーション Benesse Corporation　AD, I: 池田享史 Takafumi Ikeda　D: 近藤ちはる Chiharu Kondo　DF: ウルトラグラフィックス Ultra Graphics　SB: デザインサービス design service　Japan

Concept

ベネッセコーポレーションの通信教育講座「中学で困らないシリーズ」のキャラクター。講座の顔として、困らないクンを設定。各教科の表紙で登場、活躍させることにより、自ら解きたくなる、楽しい問題集の雰囲気作りを目的とした。ほかにも消しゴムくん、コンパスさんなど文房具類をキャラクタライズした。

The campaign character for Benesse Corporation's correspondence course, Junior High without Trouble Series. The course mascot is Komaranai-kun. He appears on the cover of each subject, creating a fun atmosphere in a problem-solving collection where by making him work, the user wants to solve the problems him or herself. Stationery items such as Mr. Eraser and Miss Compass were also characterized.

Profile

中学生になってもひと安心。困らないクンが、小学6年生の勉強をナビゲート!

Worry-free even in junior high! Komaranai-kun guides sixth graders through their studies.

ステッカー　Sticker

マーカーセット　Marker Set

問題集　Teaching Materials

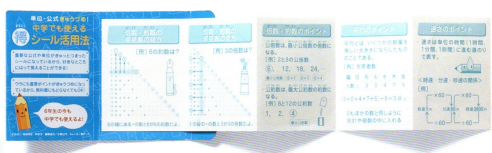

サービス　Service

代ゼミ君　Yozemi-kun　予備校 Cramming School

CL: 代々木ゼミナール yoyogi zeminar　CD: 宮下敏浩 Toshihiro Miyashita　AD, D, I: えぐちりか Rika Eguchi　D: 国分未緒 Mio Kokubun / 三谷 健 Ken Mitani
CW: 角田 武 Takeshi Tsunoda / 志伯健太郎 Kentaro Shihaku　DF: たき工房 Taki Corporation　SB: 電通 DENTSU INC.　Japan

Concept

何年も親しまれてきた、頭に電球のついた代々木ゼミナールのキャラクター「代ゼミ君」。Vネックのセーターだった洋服はパーカーに、イラストのタッチもがらりと変えて現代風にリニューアルした。

Yozemi-kun is the long-familiar mascot character with the lightbulb on his head for the yoyogi zeminar prep school. In undergoing an update to give him a more contemporary look, his V-neck sweater was changed to a parka and even the style in which he was illustrated changed.

交通広告　Traffic AD

クイックマ Quickuma

インターネットインフラ事業（検索サイト「9199.jp」） Internet Infrastructure (Search Engine Website "9199.jp")

CL: GMOインターネット GMO Internet, Inc.　CD: 高瀬真尚 Masanao Takase　AD: 秋山具義 Gugi Akiyama　D: 加藤博明 Hiroaki Katou　DF, SB: デイリー・フレッシュ Dairy Fresh　Japan

Concept
「クイック検索＝早い」ということから足の長いクマをモチーフとし、スピーディーな検索エンジンであることを表現した。
A bear with long legs (= speedy) was chosen as a motif to express the fact that 9199 (read kuikku in Japanese) is a fast search engine.

Profile
検索サイト『9199.jp』のために生まれたキャラクター。
A character created for the search engine website 9199.jp.

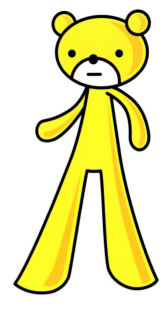

カレンダー　Calendar

サービス　Service

ナップ nap   音楽配信サービス Music Distribution Service

CL: ナップスタージャパン Napster Japan, Inc.　CD: 古川祐也 Yuya Furukawa　AD: 田中元 Gen Tanaka / 沓掛光宏 Mitsuhiro Kutsukake / 室井友希 Yuki Muroi　D: 木田智子 Tomoko Kida / 永元景子 Keiko Nagamoto　CW: 高木基 Moto Takagi / 小山佳奈 Kana Koyama　AE: 三神秀臣 Hideomi Mikami　PR: 仲田繁野 Shigeno Nakata　Agency, SB: 電通 DENTSU INC.　DF: plug　Japan

Concept

アメリカで人気を博す音楽配信サービス「ナップスター」と「タワーレコード」が「ナップスタージャパン」を設立し、日本上陸。その際のシンボルマークに本国で活躍しているキャラクターを使用した。タワーレコードの基本色となっているイエローを地色に敷いている。

The massively popular music file-sharing service Napster and Tower Records established Napster Japan, and with its launch, a character was used as the symbol mark for activities in Japan. The Tower Records' base color, yellow, forms the backdrop to the logo.

Profile

出身、年令、性別など全て不詳だが、音楽が好きである事は間違い無い。

Country of origin, age, sex are all unknown, but is without a doubt a music freak.

缶バッジ　Badge

ステッカー　Sticker

ショップバッグ　Shop Bag

030　サービス Service

ハットトリックス ハンバード Hat-tricks Hanbird

インターネットサービス（インターネットゲームサイト「ハンゲーム」）
Internet Service (Internet Game "Hangame")

CL: NHN Japan　CD, AD, D: 青木克憲　Katsunori Aoki　I: あべ たみお　Tamio Abe　CW: 中崎裕之　Hiroyuki Nakazaki　DF, SB: バタフライ・ストローク　butterfly・stroke inc.　Japan

Concept

広告キャンペーンに使用するため、アイコン性の高いキャラクターにすることを意識して制作。また、CMやポスターのみならず、アバターやゲームなどに使われることも踏まえ、汎用性の高いものを目指した。頭上の鳥がボケて、その下の人間がツッこむという漫才風の遊びを盛り込んだ、楽しいコミュニケーションキャラクターに仕立てた。

Because the character was to be used in an advertising campaign, it was consciously produced to be highly iconic. And to be able to use it not only in commercials and posters, but also as an avatar and in games, the aim was to make him banal in nature. In this way the bird overhead makes some dimwitted statement, irking the person below to create a playful, manzai-like communication character.

Profile

頭にさまざまなものを載せたパンクなキャラクター、ハットトリックスシリーズのひとつ。インターネットゲームサイト「ハンゲーム」のキャラクター、ハンバードは、インターネット科ゲームポータル亜目のおしゃべり鳥。ハンゲーム好きな人の頭上に生息し、おしゃべりや、時には鋭いツッこみを繰り出す。

One of the "hat tricks" series of punk characters with various things on their heads. A character for the Internet game website Hangame, Hanbird is a talkative bird of the Game Portal suborder of the Internet species of birds. He dwells on the heads of Hangame freaks chattering, and sometimes poking fun.

交通広告　Traffic AD

TVCM

ティッシュ　Tissue

ケーぶるちゃん　Cable-chan

放送・ケーブルテレビ事業　Broadcasting & Cable TV Services

CL: ケーブルウエスト　Cable West Inc.　　AD: 葛本尊宏　Takahiro Kuzumoto　　I: 吉井 宏　Hiroshi Yoshii　　DF, SB: ズームデザイン　ZOOM Design Inc.　　Japan

Concept
会社名と事業内容をダイレクトに訴求する「ケーブル」という言葉から「フレンチブルドッグ」をモチーフに、陽気で明るいキャラクター作りを目指した。

To create a direct link between the character and the company name and nature of their services, a French bull dog (caBLE/BULLdog) was chosen as the motif. The aim was to make him a bright and cheerful character.

Profile
某大学の人工知能研究室が開発していたAIプログラムがネットワークを通じて逃げ出し、独自の進化を遂げた謎の犬型生命体。ネットワーク環境の良い場所を好み、現在はケーブルウエストのサービスエリア内に潜伏中。人間の言葉を話すが、語尾に必ず「〜ワン」という犬訛りが入ってしまう。

A mysterious canine creature who set loose on the Internet and was evolved from an artificial intelligence program developed in the ai research lab of an unnamed university. He likes places with good network environments, and is hiding out in the Cable West service area. He speaks the human language with a dog accent ending everything he says with "wan"(dog's bark).

ポスター　Poster

まぐまぐちゃん Magmag-chan　情報サービス業 Information Services

CL, SB: まぐまぐ Magmag, Inc.　AD: 吉田尚玄 Yoshida Takamichi　Japan

Concept

シンプルで分かりやすく、楽しいキャラクターである一方で、謎めいた部分も持ち併せたキャラクター設定を行った。性別は不明、頭に付いた3色の飾りも耳なのか羽なのか、もしくはツノなのかを曖昧にすることなどで、親しみやすいがひと筋縄ではいかないキャラクターであることをアピールし、ユーザーに印象づけることを狙いとしている。

Set to be a simple, easy-to-understand, fun character and yet possess an enigmatic side at the same time. By making vague aspects such as Magmag-chan's sex and looks, for example, the tricolored elements on his head—Are they ears? Feathers? Or perhaps horns?—the aim was to impress and to appeal to users with a character that's endearing yet hard to deal with.

Profile

メールマガジン配信サービス「まぐまぐ!」の看板キャラクター、まぐまぐちゃん。「まぐまぐ!」が運営するさまざまなジャンルに合わせて、七変化を繰り広げている。

Magmag-chan is the mascot character of Magmag!, the email magazine delivery service, who transforms to reflect the many different genres the site offers.

会社案内　Company Brochure

ピザーラくんとトッピングス PIZZA-LA KUN & TOPPINGS

宅配・外食サービス Delivery & Food Service

CL, SB: フォーシーズ Fourseeds corporation　CD: 斎藤和典 Kazunori Saito　AD, I: 安達 翼 Tsubasa Adachi　CW: 藤本宗将 Muneyuki Fujimoto　DF: アドブレーン ADBRAIN Inc.
Agency: 電通 DENTSU INC.　Japan

Concept
ピザーラのピザに使用している食材の豊富さを伝えるため、とにかくたくさんのキャラクターを登場させた。食材の個性やおいしさを子どもにも感じてもらえるよう、手づくりの温かみや親しみのあるデザインに。ピザーラくんとトッピングスが合体することで様々なピザを作ることができ、さらに次々と新しい仲間が加わっていくという仕組みで楽しさを演出。グッズ展開した時にも「集める楽しみ」ができるよう工夫した。デビュー当初から約50種類いたキャラクターは、現在も増え続けている。

Introducing a great many characters was important to show the rich variety of ingredients used in PIZZALA pizzas. To help kids sense their characteristics and deliciousness they are rendered in warm and friendly handmade designs. New characters are increasingly introduced in a scheme by which the various toppings combine with PIZZALA-KUN to make all sorts of pizzas. They have been developed into novelties that customers can enjoy collecting. The character count is currently 50, and rising.

Profile
主人公ピザーラくんはピザの化身。実は8つ子で、イザという時は8人が合体して1枚の丸いピザになるらしい。食材仲間のトッピングスを引っ張るリーダー格。性格はおっとりマイペースだが誰とでも相性がよく、包容力のある人気者。みんなで力を合わせ、おいしいピザで世の中を幸せにするのが目標。

PIZZALA-KUN is a pizza slice incarnate. An octuplet, he and his siblings form a pizza for eight. He acts as the leader of his band of foodstuff friends. He's calm and keeps at his own pace, but tolerant, gets on with everyone, and is therefore popular. His goal is to join forces with his friends to make the world happy with yummy pizza.

ポスター　Poster

チーズくん cheese-kun
宅配・外食サービス Delivery & Food Service

CL, SB: ピザハット〈日本ケンタッキー・フライド・チキン〉 Pizza Hut (Kentucky Fried Chicken Japan., Ltd.)　I: 長尾 隆 Takashi Nagao　DF: ロボッチ Robotti　Japan

Concept
「ピザハット＝チーズが美味しい」という印象をキャラクタライズした。そこで誰にでも分かるよう、また、親しんでもらえよう『チーズくん』とネーミングした。眠たげな表情や色をイエローにすることで、チーズがトロッと溶けた感じを表現。さらに、チーズには多くの種類が存在することからサブキャラクターとしてチーズくんのファミリーを制作。設定をピザの具にし、溶けたチーズを表した。すべてのキャラクターは、ピザハットの商品や素材が動き出したイメージになっている。

The aim was to characterize the impression that "Pizza Hut = good taste". Hence the name cheese-kun, which is easy for everyone to understand and become familiar with. His sleepy look and yellow tone express the sense of melted cheese. And because there are many varieties of cheese, his family members were created as sub-characters. Being pizza ingredients, suggest melted cheese. All of the characters express the image of Pizza Hut products or ingredients coming alive.

Profile
イタリア南部出身のマイペースな男の子。チーズの美味しさを伝えるため日本にやってきた。イタリアで生活していたころは週に2回、鉄窯サロンに通い、モテる存在だったとか。苦手なものは直射日光とネズミ。現在アメリカでチーズ研究員として大学院に在学中の兄（チェダーチーズ）が一人いる。

A boy from southern Italy who lives at his own pace. He came to Japan to convey the good taste of cheese. Back in Italy he went to the iron stove salon twice a week and was popular with the ladies. He hates direct sunlight and mice. His older brother (Cheddar Cheese) is a grad student in the US researching cheese.

ノベルティー Novelty

CD

ぐっぴょん Guppyon
インターネットポータルサイト Internet Portal Site

CL, SB: エヌ・ティ・ティ レゾナント NTT Resonant Inc.　Japan

Concept
子どもの知的好奇心を満たし、学校教育の場や家庭で役立つサイト「キッズgoo」のキャラクター。失敗をしながら成長していく子どもたちと同じ目線に立った、等身大のキャラクターとして、子どもたちが親しみを覚えられるような性格づけとした。

The character for the website "Kids goo", which fulfills a child's intellectual curiosity and is useful at school and home. Growing up and making mistakes along the way, he takes the same perspective as children, and as a life-sized character, has been designed to be memorable to children for his endearing personality.

Profile
キッズgooに住む「ぐっぴょん」は、元気でやる気満々だけれど少しマヌケなキャラクター。キッズgooの中のあらゆるところに登場する。

Guppyon, who lives on Kids goo island, is an energetic and highly motivated character, but missing a few screws upstairs. He appears in all sorts of places on Kids goo.

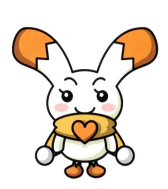

トップアンドファミリー　TOP & FAMILY　クレジットカード業　Credit Card

CL: 東急カード　TOKYU CARD INC.　CD: 高木克也　Katsuya Takagi　AD: 福島 寛　Hiroshi Fukushima　D, I: 吉田千城　Tateki Yoshida　D: 千葉剛道　Takemichi Chiba / 田宮生恵　Ikue Tamiya / 松尾 聡　Satoshi Matsuo　P: 坪谷靖史　Yasushi Tsuboya / 松永 睦（パイナップルアソシエイツ）　Mutsumi Matsunaga（Pineapple Associates）　CW: 高木克也　Katsuya Takagi / 高木葉介　Yosuke Takagi　DF: バードランド　Bird Land Co.　SB: 東急エージェンシー　Tokyu Agency Inc.　Japan

Concept

毎日色んなところで、色んな使い方ができるTOP＆カードの魅力を様々なカタチで伝えていくため、個性的なキャラクターが集まった「家族」という設定に。カードをより身近に感じてもらうため、キャラクターは「お財布」をモチーフとした。さまざまな場所で展開される「TOP＆カードのある楽しい生活」を通して、絆を深めていくこのファミリーの様子を見た人が、少しでも共感し、TOP＆カードの魅力に気づいてくれたら……という願いが込められている。

A "family" of rather idiosyncratic characters designed to convey the many attractions of the TOP& card with its myriad uses at all sorts of places every day. The wallet motif was chosen to give the card a friendly, familiar quality. The concept contains the hope that viewers will empathize with the growing rapport of this family through the many ways they indulge in the "pleasures of life with a TOP& card" and thereby become aware of the appeal of the TOP& card.

Profile

東急沿線に住む仲良しファミリー。デパ地下好きのPa-Pa、お買い物好きのMa-MaとNe-Ne、頭のチャックの位置にこだわりがある甘えん坊のBo-Ya、チャックはあるが自分では開けられないWankoの5人家族。TOKYUポイントを上手に貯めて使いながら、毎日楽しく暮らしている。

A happy family of five living along and making good use of the Tokyu railway line: Pa-Pa, who likes department store basements, Ma-Ma and Ne-Ne who love shopping, the slightly spoilt Bo-Ya who's particular about the position of the zip on his head, and Wanko, who has a zipper but can't open it himself.

©TOP & FAMILY

リーフレット　Leaflet

ポスター　Poster

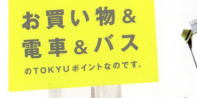

ポスター　Poster

こつりん。 Cotsurin. 生命保険業 Life Insurance

CL, SB: 三井生命保険 MITSUI LIFE INSURANCE COMPANY LIMITED　CD: 今永政雄 Masao Imanaga　AD: 青木謙吾 Kengo Aoki　D: 今村 浩 Hiroshi Imamura　Agency: 電通 DENTSU INC.　Japan

Concept
三井生命の「こつこつきちんと」というメッセージを体現するため、こつこつきちんと育つ苗木をモチーフにキャラクターを開発。「派手に、華々しく」ではなく、「地道に、こつこつと」した印象を大切に、かわいらしいがでしゃばり過ぎないキャラクターを目指した。社内用ポスターからストラップまで、さまざまな用途で使用しやすいよう、色数と構成要素を極力シンプルに抑えて作成した。

The character of a seedling that grows up straight and sure was developed to convey the MITSUI LIFE INSURANCE COMPANY message of "working hard and properly". The aim was a character not showy and brilliant, but rather hard-working and honest, that gave a charming but not too assertive impression. The number of colors and elements were kept to a minimum to facilitate use on a wide variety of applications from in-house posters to mobile phone straps.

Profile
「こつりん。」は、三井生命のCMで軽快な「こつこつミラクル♪」のCMソングに合わせて、あなたのために、みんなのために、地球のために「こつこつきちんと」頑張るキャラクター。

Cotsurin. is a tenacious little character who accompanied by the MITSUI LIFE INSURANCE COMPANY jingle, "hard-working miracle", works hard and properly for you, for everyone, for the planet.

こつりん。　　ちびこつりん。

携帯用クリーナー　Mobile Phone Cleaner

ポスター　Poster

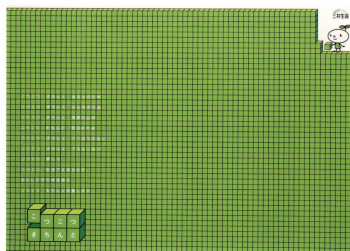

ぶら下がり子パンダ　Burasagari Kopanda　　航空会社　Airline

CL: 全日本空輸　All Nippon Airways Co., Ltd.　CD: 佐々木 宏（シンガタ）Hiroshi Sasaki (Shingata Inc.)　AD: 副田高行（副田デザイン制作所）Takayuki Soeda (SOEDA DESIGN FACTORY)
D: 小野勝也（小野デザイン）Katsuya Ono (Ono Design)　CW: 一倉 宏（一倉広告制作所）Hiroshi Ichikura / 坂本和加（一倉広告制作所）Waka Sakamoto
Pr: 西澤恵子（トレードマーク）Keiko Nishizawa (tRADEMARK)　Agency: シンガタ　Shingata Inc.　Agency, SB: 電通　DENTSU INC.　Japan

Concept

まず最初に、ANAが中国線就航20周年を記念して飛ぶ特別機全体を、一頭のパンダに見立てた「FLY!パンダ」を制作するところからスタートした。機体の「FLY!パンダ」を親パンダと見立て、その子どもとして開発したのが「ぶら下がり子パンダ」。日本と中国の空を高速で飛ぶ親パンダに必死にしがみついている子パンダを、機体のみならず機内の様々なアイテムにも展開し、パンダづくしの特別機に仕上げた。

"日本と中国、これからもっと行ったり来たり"の時代を、より明るいものにしたい、という思いが込められている。

The first step of this campaign involved a development of "Fly! Panda" design which was applied to ANA special airplanes used in celebration of the 20th anniversary of regular flight service between Japan and China to look like a gigantic mother panda. Then, Burasagari Kopanda, a child panda disparately clinging to the speeding mother's body, was developed and applied to a variety of promotional items as well as on the aircraft. The design was devised with the hope for a brighter future where the distance between Japan and China would be more shortened. The name "Fly! Panda" was chosen from the public entries.

ポスター　Poster

紙ナプキン　Paper Napkin　　スナック　Snack

割り箸　Chopsticks

紙コップ　Paper Cup

バッジ　Badge

抱き枕　Pillow

タネタネフレンズ tanetanefriends 資産運用会社 Asset Management Company

CL, SB: 三菱UFJ投信 Mitsubishi UFJ Asset Management Co., Ltd　I: 木原庸佐 Yosuke Kihara　Contents Planner: 浅田幸男 Yukio Asada　Japan

Concept
三菱UFJ投信のキャラクター。地球のどこかにある「生命感」に満ちたムアム王国に住み、「未来」「夢」「好奇心」「温かさ」のあるものを応援するのが好きという設定。そのコンセプトが自然に感じられるデザインにすることを心がけた。新聞など説得媒体向けには高品質を漂わせる「立体デザイン」、商品ビデオ向けには躍動感のある「3DCGデザイン」、WEBの「投信マンガ」には「平面デザイン」と、3通りのデザインを使い分けることにより、キャラクターとしての活力と奥行きを表現している。

Used by Mitsubishi UFJ Asset Management, the tanetanefriends inhabit the lively kingdom of Muam, and are keen supporters of anything to do with the future, dreams, curiosity, and friendliness. The design work was divided into three types: three-dimensional to add an upmarket note for newspapers and other persuasive media; dynamic 3DCG design for product videos, and two-dimensional design for the asset management comic strip on the Web, to express the vitality and depth of the characters.

Profile
タネタネフレンズには、いつも晴れ晴れしい顔で頼りになる「はれタネくん」、元気で行動派の「やっタネくん」、小さい体でよく気が利く、紅一点の「コマメちゃん」、のんびりしていて癒し系の「ドッシリくん」、親分肌の「そだっタネくん」、頭脳明晰で発明好きな「みのっタネくん」の6体がいる。

There are six tanetanefriends: sunny, reliable Haretane-kun; lively, energetic Yattane-kun; thoughtful little Komame-chan, the only girl; laid-back, no-worries Dosshiri-kun; Sodattane-kun who acts like a father to the rest, and clever inventor Minottane-kun.

クリアファイル　Clear File

カレンダー　Calendar

スペシャルサイト「未来のタネをまこう。」
Special Site "Let's plant the future seeds." www.tanetane.jp

新聞広告　Newspaper AD

3匹の大人ブタ　The Three Big Pigs

不動産仲介　Real Estate

CL: 野村不動産アーバンネット　Nomura Real Estate Urban Net Co., Ltd.　CD: 兼坂 章　Akira Kanesaka　AD: 平田 陽　Yo Hirata　D: 金子いずみ　Izumi Kaneko　CW: 東野みゆき　Miyuki Touno / 松原勇馬　Yuma Matsubara　SB: 電通　DENTSU INC.　Japan

Concept

ノムコムの「ネットで住みかえ」を身近に感じてもらうためのキャラクターを考えたときに思いついたのが「3匹の子ブタ」。ひとつの物語のなかで、わらの家→木の家→レンガの家へと引越しをした彼らはまぎれもなく"究極の住みかえキャラ"。というようなことから、物語が生まれてだいぶ時間が経っていたので彼らもすっかりオジさんになっており、「3匹の大人ブタ」とした。

When ideating on characters that would help nomu.com's "Buy and sell your home on the Net" feel more familiar, "The Three Little Pigs" came to mind. The move from a house of straw, to sticks, to bricks in the course of a single story made them the "ultimate house-moving characters". Time passed and the three of them became middle-aged men: "the three big pigs".

Profile

長男（ながお）は、3兄弟のさえない長男坊。中小企業係長で、ちょっとぼんやりさん。次男坊の次男（つぎお）は、小さな製本屋の社長。クールだが怒りっぽいところがある。三男坊の三男（みつお）は、広告代理店勤務。かわいい顔をした毒舌家でもある。

Nagao, the dull oldest of the three brothers, is the president of a small company and a bit absent-minded. Tsugio, the middle brother and president of a bookbindery, is cool but tends to fly off the handle. Mitsuo, the baby who works at an advertising agency, is handsome but wags a venomous tongue.

新聞広告　Newspaper AD

カレンダー　Calendar

ウェブサイト　Website

テンプりん。 Temprin. 総合人材サービス業 Temp Agency

CL, SB: テンプスタッフ Tempstaff Co., Ltd CD: 田尾新治 Shinji Tao AD: 新村なつ絵 Natsue Shinmura I: 平沢けいこ Keiko Hirasawa DF: エージー AZ, INC. Agency: アサツーディ・ケイ ASATSU-DK Japan

Concept
ファッションだって、遊びだって、自分にピッタリのものを選びたい。もちろん仕事だって、自分らしく働きたい……「テンプりん。」はそんな派遣社員の代表として、テンプスタッフの「テンプ」と女の子が大好きな「プリン」を組み合わせて生み出されたキャラクター。おしゃれでスタイリッシュだが、親しみがあって、憎めない。派遣社員が自分に重ね合わせることのできるキャラクターを目指した。

Be it fashion or fun, one wants to select the things that suit them best. So of course in our work we also wants to be able to be ourselves... Such are the temporary staff that Tempurin – a character who combines the "temp" of temp staff and "purin" (pudding), every girl's favorite – represents. Chic and stylish, yet endearing and hard to dislike: the aim was to create a character with which temps could identify.

Profile
テンプりん。は19XX年10月2日生まれ（満24歳）のA型。現在派遣社員として働いている。趣味はお菓子作りと旅行。長所は明朗活発で、とにかく一所懸命お仕事に打ち込むところ。短所はおっちょこちょいなところ。こう見えて、普通自動車免許を持っている。

Tempurin. Born: October 2, 19XX. 24 years old. Blood type: A. Currently work as temp staff. Her hobbies are baking and traveling. Her strong points are her cheerfulness and liveliness, and throwing her heart and soul into her work. Her weak point is her absentmindedness. And contrary to what one might expect, she has a regular driver's license.

交通広告 Traffic AD

交通広告　Traffic AD

交通広告　Traffic AD

サービス　Service

≫ テンプりん。 Temprin.

タンブラー　Tumbler
クリアファイル　Clear File
ティッシュ　Tissue
ブランケット　Blanket

もみじん MOMIJIN　銀行 Bank

CL: もみじ銀行　MOMIJI BANK　　CD, CW: 土井 薫　Kaoru Doi　　AD: 坂本剛志　Takeshi Sakamoto　　D: 中 将哉　Masaya Naka　　CW: 折出奈津子　Natsuko Oride　　I: カミガキヒロフミ　Hirofumi Kamigaki
DF: アルフォックス　ARFOX / IC4　　SB: 電通西日本　DENTSU WEST JAPAN INC.　Japan

Concept
合併間もなかった広島の第二地銀である、もみじ銀行のカードローンのキャラクター。銀行の知名度アップを目的とし、生活者に印象づけるため、もみあげをもみじ型、アフロヘアという銀行らしからぬ風貌で話題を呼ぶことを狙った。単なる怪しいキャラクターで終わらせないために、地元思いの優秀な熱い銀行マンという設定でコピーワークを行い、商品訴求とファン作りにつなげた。

Adopted as the character for card loans at MOMIJI BANK, Hiroshima's second-largest regional bank, soon after its creation. The aim was also to raise the bank's profile by drawing consumer attention to the character's un-bank-like appearance, i.e. his maple leaf shaped sideburns. To ensure MOMIJIN became more than a simple "creature" character, he was positioned as an outstanding, passionate bank employee in tune with local needs, an image used for product promotion and to build a fan base.

Profile
「もみじん」は、もみじ銀行きってのやり手営業マン。29歳のとき、超難関、ハーバードビジネススクールのMBAを取得したという噂。夢は広島発のグローバルベンチャー企業を育てること。今は、街のみんなの夢を実現することに夢中。5月31日生まれの31歳。

MOMIJIN is the MOMIJI BANK's most hardworking salesman. Rumor has it that at the age of 29 he earned an MBA from the tough Harvard Business School. His dream is to start a global venture business based in Hiroshima. At present he keeps busy helping local people make their dreams come true. 31 years old. Born: May 31st.

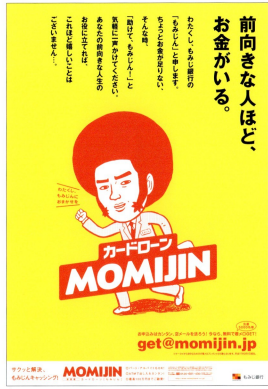

ポスター　Poster

メールオーダー　Mail Order

ATM短冊ポスター
ATM Reed-shaped Poster

ナットくん、レジロ　Natto-kun, Rejiro　　不動産 Real Estate

CL: 三井不動産レジデンシャル　Mitsui Fudosan Residential Co.,Ltd　　CD: 北谷竜一　Ryuichi Kitadani　　AD, D, I: カミガミヒロフミ　Hirofumi Kamigaki　　D: スギヨーコ　Yoko Sugi
DF, SB: IC4 DESIGN　　Japan

Concept

マンションの構造や品質、性能といったハード面を分かりやすく説明するためのキャラクター。ロボットの視点（データ解析、透視機能等）を使って、普段見えにくい箇所や複雑なマンションの構造を紐解いていく。

A character developed to explain the technical aspects of mansions such as structure and quality in easy to understand ways. Using the perspective of a robot (data analysis, x-ray vision, etc), features that are normally difficult to see or tend to be complex, such as a building's structure, are explained.

Profile

三井マンションの品質管理ロボットとして開発されたが、好奇心旺盛で、お散歩が大好き。仕事を忘れて、ついついマンションの探索に出かけてしまい、その性能に納得ばかりしている。

Developed to be a quality-control robot for Mitsui mansions, but is roaring with curiosity and loves to go for walks. He tends to forget his work and heads out to investigate mansions instead, the efficiency of which he finds persuasive.

  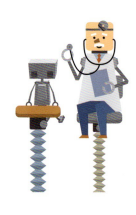 

パンフレット　Pamphlet

HOME'Sくん HOME'S-kun 不動産物件ポータルサイト Real Estate Properties Portal Site

CL, SB: ネクスト　NEXT Co., Ltd.　Japan

Concept
HOME'Sくんは、ネクストとともに歩んできたオリジナルマスコットキャラクター。コンセプトは、不動産ポータルサイト「HOME'S」の各種サービス（賃貸物件検索、売買物件検索、新築分譲マンション物件検索、新築分譲戸建検索、リフォーム業者検索、注文住宅業者検索、HOME'Sカードサービス、HOME'Sオークションなど）を体現すること。多くのユーザーにとって情報通の友人でありたいと願っており、自分らしい住まい、暮らし、まちを発見する手助けを行う。

HOME'S-kun is an original mascot character who came the way of NEXT. The concept is to experience the different services (search engines for rental properties, new condominiums, new homes, renovation contractors, design/build contractors, HOME'S card service, HOME'S auction, etc.) of the real estate portal site HOME'S. The hope was for him to act as a friend with the latest info to a great many users, and to help them discover the homes, lifestyles and communities that suit.

Profile
生年月日：1997年3月12日・性別：男・血液型：O型・好きな食べ物：おむすび・趣味：まちと住まいについて考え、関係することを調べる・性格：とても物知りで好奇心旺盛、フットワークが軽く情報通、打たれ強いけどちょっとドジなところも。夢中になっていることはサッカー。

Born: March 12, 1997. Male. Blood type: O. Favorite food: rice balls. Hobbies: thinking about homes and the community, researching related subjects. Personality: very well-informed, inquisitive, fast on his feet, up on all the latest, can take a punch but also has a klutzy side. Crazy about soccer.

新聞広告　Newspaper AD

交通広告　Traffic AD

メジャー　Tape Measure

グリーンズ GREENS 医療センター Medical Center

CL: 東京女子医科大学附属 八千代医療センター TOKYO WOMEN'S MEDICAL UNIVERSITY YACHIYO MEDICAL CENTER　CD: 竹内真由美 Mayumi Takeuchi　AD, D: 木本禎子 Yoshiko Kimoto
SB: フジテレビジョン 美術制作局 CG・タイトル部　FUJI TELEVISION NETWORK, INC.　Japan

Concept
日本の大学附属病院では画期的ともいえる本格的なキャラクターを制作。2006年12月の開院に向け、広く親しみのある病院づくりを目指す象徴として誕生した。千葉県八千代市のあふれる自然をテーマにデザインされたキャラクターの存在は、そのまま新しい病院の在り方を提案している。葉・花・菜・実・土・水をモチーフにしており、可愛らしさだけでなく、個性豊かな性格設定も施されている。多くの広報シーンで活躍するキャラクターであるが、第一に「八千代医療センターが広く地域に親しまれ、愛されるように」という願いが込められている。

The creation of the GREENS for the opening of the YACHIYO MEDICAL CENTER in December 2006 was a milestone for Japanese university hospitals. The characters, inspired by the verdant city of Yachiyo, represent the determination to offer a more friendly hospital experience. Featuring leaves, flowers, vegetables, fruit, soil and water, the characters have their own distinctive personalities. And because they are employed in a variety of settings, the GREENS have also been designed to soothe and reassure.

Profile
東京女子医科大学附属八千代医療センターのキャラクター、GREENS。八千代の病院近くの森に棲む小人たちで、やんちゃなフタバくん、マメ姉・オニオンくん・おみきさん・ハナー・ナッシッシ・ミズミズくんとジョウロくんの8人で構成。病院を訪れる大人を和ませ、子供たちには友情のパワーを送っている。

The "GREENS" are eight mischievous elves living in the forest near the TOKYO WOMEN'S MEDICAL UNIVERSITY YACHIYO MEDICAL CENTER. Together they help to relax and reassure adults, and make the hospital less intimidating for children.

タオル　Towel

ステッカー　Sticker

ケータイうさぎ Cellular phone rabbit

通信事業 Telecommunications

CL: エヌ・ティ・ティ・ドコモ東北　NTT DoCoMo Tohoku, Inc.　CD: 山路裕一　Yuichi Yamaji　AD: 富樫信光　Nobumitsu Togashi　D: 遠藤歩美　Ayumi Endo / 坂本由紀　Yuki Sakamoto
P: 田上明（スクープ）　Akira Tagami (SCOOP)　I: 遠藤歩美　Ayumi Endo　Photo Cordinator: 菅原美代乃（アーク・イメージギャラリー）　Miyono Sugawara (ARC IMAGE GALLERY)
DF: 畠山 敏デザイン事務所　Satoshi Hatakeyama Design Office　SB: 電通東日本　DENTSU EAST JAPAN INC.　Japan

Concept
携帯電話の主な故障原因である水濡れ、落下、圧力、結露等を紹介し、故障受付時にはメモリのバックアップを行うように案内をするのが目的。注意喚起専用のキャラクターとして、子どもにもわかりやすく、説明的になりすぎないよう、おっちょこちょいでマヌケだけど、なぜか憎めないヤツという設定に。「ケータイを大切に扱ってほしい」というメッセージ性を持たせるため、手描きのラインを活かし、全体的にやさしい雰囲気でまとめている。

Cellular phone rabbit explains the main reasons for mobile phones malfunctioning and tells people to back up their phone's memory when they take it to be repaired. As a character for increasing awareness, he is easy for children to understand, and so as to avoid overexplanation, he is a scatterbrain fool so somehow people find him hard to dislike. Because his message is that we should take care of our mobile phones, hand-drawn lines have been used and overall he has a gentle air.

Profile
おなかにポッケのある新種のうさぎ（オス）で、大切なものをポッケに集める習性がある（ケータイが一番大事）。お菓子が大好きで、特にクッキーには目がない。趣味は読書（ゲーテを我が師と仰ぐ）。おっちょこちょいで失敗が多い困ったさん。

A new breed of rabbit (male) who has the habit of keeping his favorite things (his mobile is his most favorite) in the pocket in his stomach. Cookies are his weakness. His hobby is reading (he regards Goethe as his mentor). A bit of a bungling scatter-brain.

ポスター　Poster

チラシ　Flyer

はしぞう　Hashizou　総合情報サービス（住宅情報タウンズ「借りる」）Information Service (Housing Information: Towns Rental)

CL, SB: リクルート　RECRUIT CO., LTD　I: 岡林みかん　Mikan Okabayashi　Japan

Concept

ターゲットである20代女性の「かわいい」の定義が広いことを考え、ストレートに「かわいい」キャラクターではなく、あえておじさん体型の「キモかわいい」を狙った。キャラクター世代である20代女性は、背景にあるストーリーを通じて、そのキャラクターにいっそう愛着を持つ傾向があるため、生い立ちや性格などを細かく設定。部屋探し中という設定により、はしぞうが常に読者と同じ目線でいることも意識した。また季節ごとにイベントを考え、その中で動きのあるはしぞうを生み出している。

The aim was to be not a typically cute, but rather an oafish cute character with the physique of middle-aged man, considering the broad perception of "cute" among the target market of women in their 20s. As part of the "character generation" these women tend to develop greater affection for a character through a background story, thus details of his childhood and personality were established. By having him in the midst of apartment-hunting, he always has the same perspective as readers. With seasonal events in mind, a Hashizo active role in that environment is under development.

Profile

30畳・風呂なしトイレ共同という謎の物件にて1人暮らし（愛猫・うに助と）。恋人のバス美に風呂を借りる日々。広い風呂のある部屋に引越したいと思っている。趣味はパンツ、帽子収集。風呂。パンツの洗濯。好きな食べ物はゆで卵、梅干、たこ焼きのような丸いもの。

Lives alone (with his cat, Unisuke) in a curious 30-mat room with no bath and a common toilet. He bathes at his girlfriend Pasumi's place every day. He wants to move to a place with a spacious bath. His hobbies are collecting hats and underpants, bathing, and washing his underpants. His favorite foods are hardboiled eggs, umeboshi plums, takoyaki and other round-shaped foods.

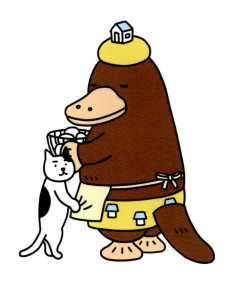

表紙イラスト　Cover Illustration

ジュータロー、マンシロー、マドリ　Jyutaro, Mansiro, Madori　総合情報サービス　Information Service

CL, SB: リクルート　RECRUIT CO., LTD.　I: タラジロウ　Tara Jiro　Japan

Concept

リクルートの住宅情報サイト「住宅情報ナビ」で、ナビゲーション役を務めるキャラクターとして登場。ジュータローは「一戸建て」、マンシローは「マンション」、マドリは「間取り」をモチーフにデザイン。堅苦しい、難しいというイメージのある「家選び」を、より楽しく紹介できるよう、愛らしく親しみやすいキャラクターとした。サイト内では「ナビ使いこなしガイド（http://www.jj-navi.com/edit/howto/index.html）」などで活躍している。

Navigators of the housing info website Housing Info Navi operated by RECRUIT. Designed respectively with house, apartment building and floor plan motifs to be endearing and friendly and thus make house-hunting – which tends to be seen as formal and difficult – an easier, more pleasant process. They also feature in the site's "navigating this site guide".

Profile

ジュータローは一戸建てから生まれた長男坊。頭が三角屋根の形。もちろん一戸建て専門。マンシローは、マンションから生まれたしっかりものの次男坊。マンション専門。マンション好きなだけにいつも語尾に「しょん」がつく。マドリは間取りから生まれた居候。いつも二人にくっついて行く。

Jyutaro is the oldest son of a one-family house, his head the shape of a peaked roof. Mansiro is the sturdy second son of an apartment building – his specialty – who has a habit of adding the suffix "shon" to all sorts of words. Madori (room plan) is a sponger, always tagging along with the other two.

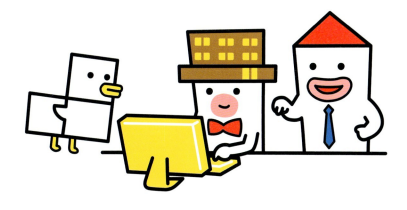

ハットトリックス　**オーエルサン**　Hat-tricks　OL3　総合情報サービス（週刊フリーペーパー「L25」）Information Service (Free paper "L25")

CL: リクルート　RECRUIT CO., LTD　I: あべ たみお　Tamio Abe　SB: バタフライ・ストローク　butterfly・stroke inc.　Japan

Concept
「L25」の読者層であるOLを意識し、「O」「L」「3」の文字を髪型で表現。読者の代弁者として身近に感じてもらうため、年齢や性格を三者三様にプロットし、詳細なキャラクター設定を行った。姉妹誌の「R25」と差別化を図るため、線を細くしたりすることでやさしい女性的なイメージになるようにした。

The characters O, L and 3 are shown in the characters' hairstyles, bearing in mind L25's OL readership. To create characters to which readers could relate, and which they felt spoke on their behalf, the trio were assigned different ages and personalities. To differentiate L25 from its sister magazine R25, fine lines were used for a gentle, feminine effect.

Profile
フリーペーパー「L25」の読者層であるOLをモチーフにしたOL3。恋愛が何より大切で頼りがいのある男性が好きなオーちゃん・自分ならではの趣味を見つけるこだわり屋のエルン・アネゴ肌のミーコさんの3人衆。

OL3 are three characters inspired by the female office worker (OL) readership of the free paper L25: O-chan, for whom love is all, preferably with a man she can depend on; Ellen, obsessive when it comes to her leisure pursuits, and bossy Miko.

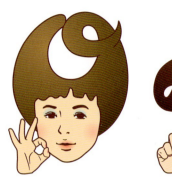

オーちゃん　　エルン　　ミーコさん

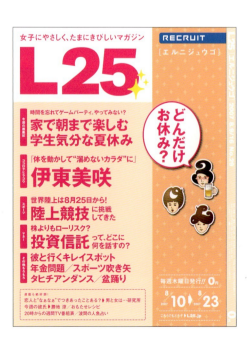

| ハットトリックス　就活篤志、就活もえ　Hat-tricks　Atsushi Shukatsu, Moe Shukatsu | 情報流通 Information Service |

CL: 日経HR NIKKEI HUMAN RESOURCES   I: あべ たみお Tamio Abe   SB: バタフライ・ストローク butterfly・stroke inc.   Japan

Concept
就職情報サイトのイメージキャラクターであることから、就職に燃える学生をコンセプトに制作。頭をメラメラと燃やすことで、就職活動への意欲の高まりを表現している。就職活動にまつわる堅苦しいイメージを払拭するため、まじめなだけではなく、今どきの個性あふれる学生像をバリエーション豊かに表した。また、ターゲットである学生に興味を持ってもらうため、シンプルながらも印象に残りやすく、インパクトのある存在になることを目的とした。

Because these characters are for a career information site, the concept is that of students burning with ambition. Doing away with the rigid formality associated with job-hunting in Japan, the students are shown as not just serious, but individuals with their own distinct personalities, like real students today. To attract interest from the target group, the aim was to create characters that were simple yet made a strong impression.

Profile
就職情報サイト「日経ナビ2008」のキャラクターである、就活篤志と就活もえ。篤志は、大手企業に憧れる格好つけたがりの大学生。髪型がビシッと決まると一日がウマくいくと信じている。もえは篤志の妹で、TPOに合わせてメガネを変える用意周到さを持つ。

Atsushi and Moe Shukatsu were created for the 2008 Nikkei Navi career information sites. Student Atsushi is a bit of a poser with corporate ambitions who believes that perfect hair is the key to success. Moe is his well-organized sister, who changes her glasses to suit the occasion.

ポスター　Poster

ハロー、メロー Hellow, Mellow　　通信事業　Telecommunications

CL: KDDI　　AD, D: 山下浩平（マウンテンマウンテン）　Kohei Yamashita (mountain mountain)　　SB: マウンテンマウンテン　mountain mountain　Japan

Concept
ハローメッセンジャーは、メールを中心としたコミュニティサイトであるため、メインキャラクターを黒ヤギ、白ヤギとした。キャラクターは、マウンテンマウンテンのオリジナルキャラクター「Maule bear and friends」シリーズの仲間である。

Because they function as the "hello messengers" for a primarily email-based community website, the characters were made a black goat and a white goat. They are members of the mountain mountain Maule bear and friends series.

©Yamashita Kohei・mountain mountain

リーフレット　Leaflet

使用例　Example of the use

ふくろう教授　FUKUROU KYOJU　　投信投資顧問業　Investment Management Business

CL, SB: ニッセイアセットマネジメント　Nissay Asset Management Corporation　　CD, AD, D: 秋丸裕一　Hirokazu Akimaru　　D, I: 棚田 清　Kiyoshi Tanada　　DF: イージーユーズ　eZuz Japan k.k　Japan

Concept
ギリシャ神話をはじめ、世界中で「知恵と信頼のシンボル」として慕われている「ふくろう」をモチーフにすることにより、「知恵」＝投資信託に強くなる、「信頼」＝投資信託の運用会社が提供する確かな情報、というふたつの側面をアピールしている。投資信託の実用的教育サイト「ふくろう教授の投資信託ゼミナール」にて投資信託の理解を深めてもらいたい、という思いを伝えるのにも最適なキャラクターとなっている。

As it appears in Greek Myths, owl is adored as a symbol of "wisdom" and "confidence" around the world. The character "FUKUROU KYOJU (Professor Owl)" is intended to appeal the following dual perspectives; owl's "wisdom" helps increase and improve people's knowledge of investment trusts and owl's "confidence" shows that information provided by the asset management company is truly "confident". Professor Owl, appears in the company's educational website "Professor Owl's investment trusts seminar", is an ideal character to express the importance of improvement of individual investor's knowledge standard.

Profile
ふくろう教授は投資信託の魅力や運用方法を世の中のみんなに知ってもらうため、常に世界中を飛び回っている。そんな教授を信頼する教え子も多く、理念に賛同した仲間たちは教授とともに普及活動に励んでいる。教え子や仲間には、福よし、福はな、はな福教授がいる。

Professor Owl is always flying around the glove informing people about the characteristics of investment trusts and asset management. His pal and students, HANAFUKU KYOJU, FUKUHANA, and FUKUYOSHI, work hard together to support Professor Owl's promotional activity.

パソコン君　Mr. Personal Computer　　教育事業　Educational Industry

CL: ベネッセコーポレーション　Benesse Corporation　　AD, D, I, SB: Maniackers Design　Japan

Profile
ベネッセコーポレーションの「進研ゼミ中学講座チャレンジネット」のインターネットサービスの解説についてサポートしてくれるキャラクター。自分自身がパソコンなので、自分で考えて行動し、自分で入力や勉強をする。

His name is Mr. Personal Computer, a character who helps explain Benesse Corporation's ChallengeNet junior high seminar coarse internet service.

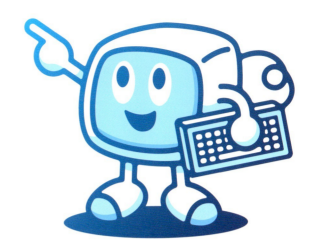

Dr.あおきくん　Dr. Aoki-kun　　医院　Clinic

CL: 柴崎駅前皮膚科　Shibasakiekimae dermatological clinic　　I: 市原 淳　Jun Ichihara　　DF, SB: イエロードッグスタジオ　Yellow dog studio　Japan

Concept
「柴崎駅前皮膚科」の実在する医師をモチーフとし、親しみやすくチャーミングで楽しいキャラクターをデザイン。医院の象徴として安心感・清潔感を重視して制作を行った。

Designed to be a friendly, charming and pleasant character, making the actual doctor of the Shibasakiekimae dermatological clinic the motif. In producing what would be the symbol of the clinic, emphasis was placed on imparting feelings of security and cleanliness.

Profile
「柴崎駅前皮膚科」のオリジナルキャラクター、Dr.あおきくん。お医者さんで、明るくやさしい性格が患者さんたちに大人気。

Dr. Aoki-kun is the original character of the Shibasakiekimae dermatological clinic. The doctor's cheery and gentle personality is very popular with patients.

看板　Sign　　　ウェブサイト　Website　　　診察券　Patient's Registration Card

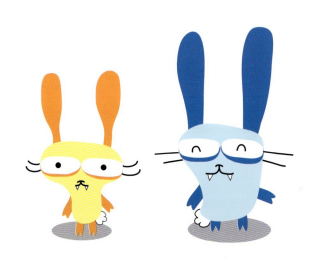

1. クレアティーくん **Cleaty-Kun** 家政婦サービス Home Help Service / CL: クレアティー・サービス Cleaty Service CO., LTD AD: 細島雄一 Yuichi Hosojima Character Design: マッシュルームカフェ mushroom cafe SB: サンクディレクションズ CINQ DIRECTIONS INC. Japan
2. 中林歯科 キャラクター **Character of NAKABAYASHI DENTAL CLINIC** 歯科医院 Dental Clinic / CL: 中林歯科 NAKABAYASHI DENTAL CLINIC AD, D, I, SB: Maniackers Design Japan
3. リフォーム・ワン キャラクター **Character of Reform One** リフォーム事業 Reform Industry / CL: TM Co., Ltd. CD, AD, D, I, SB: Maniackers Design Japan
4. ゴールドボーイズ **GOLD BOYS** DVD・CD・書籍・ゲームのレンタル＆販売店 Rental & Retail Shop of DVD, CD, Book, Game / CL: TSUTAYA Co., Ltd. SB: DEVILROBOTS Japan
5. ダブル子ちゃん **Double-ko-chan** DVD・CD・書籍・ゲームのレンタル＆販売店 Rental & Retail Shop of DVD, CD, Book, Game / CL: TSUTAYA Co., Ltd. SB: LIGHT graphics Inc. Japan
6. **Ogosagi** 通信事業 Telecommunications Company / CL: Swisscom D: Wale Buri I: syl Hiller///tapetentiere DF: Emoticom SB: tapetentiere Switzerland

マ・マー ファミリー MA・MA Family　　食品メーカー（マ・マー）　Food Manufacturer (MA・MA)

CL: 日清製粉グループ　Nisshin Seifun Group Inc.　CD: 川添裕一　Yuichi Kawazoe　AD: 長島 慎　Shin Nagashima　D: 名和田 剛　Go Nawata / 伊藤奈美　Nami Ito　D, I: 岩瀬なおみ　Naomi Iwase
CW: 田中竜太　Ryuta Tanaka / 山内真太郎　Shintaro Yamauchi　DF: アドソルト　adsalt　Agency, SB: 博報堂　HAKUHODO Inc.　Japan

Concept
50年の歴史を持つマ・マーのマークはもともと上半身のみだったが、全身のキャラクターに変更。赤いラインが個性的で印象が強いデザインだったので、このアイデンティティを崩さずに、家族や友達のキャラクターを新たにデザインした。現在、マ・マーを中心に、その家族やパスタに関係する道具や食材などをモチーフにしたキャラクターが合わせて16人いる。

The MA・MA mark, with its 50-year history, was originally just a bust, so the project began with making her a full figure. Because red lines were a distinguishing feature of the original mark, care was taken to preserve this identity and a series of new family and friends designed. A total of 16 characters were created revolving around MA・MA, all related to the ingredients or tools involved in making pasta.

Profile
料理が得意でちょっとオテンバなマ・マー。のんびり屋のパ・パーに、食いしん坊のボ・クー。そんなファミリーの友達には、ト・メトー、ガ・リクー、チ・ズーやナ・ベーがいる。みんなマ・マーが作るスパゲッティが大好きで、いつも食卓は大にぎわい。

The somewhat boisterous MA・MA who loves to cook, the very laid back PA・PA, and their big-eating son BO・KU. The family's friends include Tometoo, Garlicuu, Cheezuu, and Nabeii. They're all crazy about MA・MA's spaghetti and there's always a big turnout for dinner.

キャンペーングッズ(フィギュア)　Campaign Goods (Figure)

キャンペーングッズ　Campaign Goods

マ・マー ファミリー　MA・MA Family

ポスター　Poster

ミス・カフェオーレ Miss Cafe au lait   食品メーカー（カフェオーレ） Food Manufacturer (Cafe au lait)

CL: グリコ乳業 Glico Nyugyo   CD: 若井公一 Koichi Wakai   AD: 若田野枝 Noe Wakata   I: 寄藤文平 Bunpei Yorifuji   Planner: 松本 巌 Takeshi Matsumoto   DF: 文平銀座 Bunpei Ginza
SB: 電通 DENTSU INC. Japan

Concept

発売から28年のグリコ・カフェオーレが今まで培ってきたブランドイメージを保ちながら、まったく新しいカフェオーレ像をつくり上げるため、独特の円錐形パッケージをそのままキャラクターとした。ポイントは圧倒的なゆるさと間の抜けたかわいさ、そして誰もが知っている懐かしさのバランス。瞬きひとつとっても、子どもから大人までがキュンとくるような動きを徹底的に追求している。コンセプトは「白黒つけないカフェオーレ」。3人のどっちつかずな関係の今後の展開も興味をそそる。

To maintain the brand image Glico cafe au lait had fostered in 28 years on the market, and at the same time build a new cafe au lait image, the product's distinctive conical package was made into a character. The point was to balance an overwhelmingly lackadaisical, something-missing-upstairs kind of charm with a nostalgia familiar to all. The subtlest movement, even the blink of an eye, was pursued to the nth degree to grab the hearts of people young and old. The concept of "neither black or white, cafe au lait" is reflected in the noncommittal relationship between the three, piquing interest in the way it will play out.

Profile

フランス生まれの女の子「ミス・カフェオーレ」は小悪魔的な魅力でモテモテ。優柔不断な性格が無意識のうちに男の子を振り回す。そんな彼女に思いを寄せるのが、コーヒーの「ゴービー」とミルクの「ミルーク」。たくましいゴービーは男らしく、文学青年のミルークはやさしさたっぷりに求愛する。

Born in France, Miss Cafe au lait is a petite, diabolically attractive beauty. Her indecisiveness inadvertently has men at her mercy. There are however two boys wooing her: the strong and masculine Gobi (coffee) and tenderhearted bookworm, Miluku (milk).

ポスター Poster

ウェブサイト Website

製造 Manufacture   061

きのこ組 kinokogumi

きのこ総合メーカー　Mushroom Manufacture & Retail

CL: ホクト　Hokuto Corporation　CD: 太田 豊　Yutaka Ota　I: 鈴木幸子　Sachiko Suzuki　CM Director: 中野達人　Tatsuhito Nakano　Production: 東北新社　TOHOKU SHINSHA FILM CORPORATION
SB: 博報堂　HAKUHODO Inc.　Japan

©HOKUTO / H / T

Concept

もともと陽のあたるところは苦手で、日陰でひっそりと仲間同士、肩寄せ合って生きている。決してパワフルに活動するわけではなく、威勢は良いけれど、いろいろデリケート。そんなきのこたちを表すキーワードを「へなちょこ」とした。さらに見た目の特徴からそれぞれの性格付けを行っている。エリンギは太くて男らしく、かさの反り返りがちょっとキザ。マイタケはパーマをかけた、おしゃれを気にする女の子。ブナシメジはちっちゃくて元気いっぱいのおてんばさん。ブナピーは真っ白な純粋無垢で夢見がちな少女といった具合。

Having never fared well in the sun, this gang of mushrooms lives together side-by-side quietly in the shade. Although they are by no means powerful in their activities, they are cheerful, but rather delicate. And so the key word selected to represent these mushrooms was "paltry". Their looks also reflect their personality traits: Eringi is heavy-set and masculine, and a bit ridgy under the cap; Maitake is fashion-minded and wears her hair permed; Bunashimeji is a small but spirited tomboy; and Bunapi, is pure white and innocent and tends to be a dreamer.

Profile

ホクトの商品である4種類のきのこに、社名ロゴの赤いきのこ（ホクトくん・普段は緑色）をプラスした5人がメンバーの「きのこ組」。ホクトくん、エリンギは男の子、他の3人は女の子。やや遅れて登場したブナピーは他の4人よりちょっと年下で、ブナシメジの親戚。みんなはいつも仲良く遊んでいる。

The five-member kinokogumi consists of Hokuto's four varieties of mushrooms plus the company logo red mushroom Hokuto-kun (who's normally green). Hokuto-kun and Eringi are boys and the other three girls. Bunapi, who arrived on the scene a bit later, is the younger cousin of Bunashimeji. They all always play together nicely.

CD

ハンドタオル　Towel

「きのこ組」ぬいぐるみキーホルダー
"kinokogumi" Stuffed Animal Key Holder

ノベルティ（ピクニックセット）　Novelty (Picnic Set)

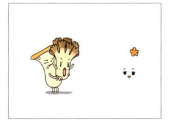

TVCM

TVCM

製造　Manufacture

アジパンダ® Aji Panda® 食品メーカー Food Manufacturer

CL: 味の素 Ajinomoto Co., Inc.　CD: 大倉泰平 Taihei Ohkura　AD: 瀬川浩樹 Hiroki Segawa　D: 相川一明 Kazuaki Aikawa / 青山京子 Kyoko Aoyama　CW: 後藤由里子 Yuriko Goto
DF: コモンデザイン室 COMMON DESIGN INCORPORATION　SB: ビルド・クリエイティブハウス BUILD creativehaus　Japan

Concept
チャーハンなど中華料理の味の決め手となる「味の素®」のキャラクターであるため、中華から連想される中国を代表する動物のパンダをモチーフにした。白黒ではなく、「味の素®」のキーカラーに合わせて赤白パンダにし、体の模様も、台所に似合うようにエプロン柄とした。キャンペーンボトルとして、アジパンダ®の顔がついた「アジパンダ®ボトル」を制作した際は、「味の素®」独特のボトルの形状をパンダの顔の輪郭として活かすことができた。アジパンダ®の部屋、http://www.ajinomoto.co.jp/ajipanda もある。

Because Ajinomoto flavor enhancer is the decisive ingredient in fried rice and other Chinese dishes, a panda, the animal most associated with China, was chosen as the character. It is not black and white, but rather a combination of Ajinomoto's key colors of red and white, with a body pattern reminiscent of a apron. An bottle unique to Ajinomoto with the contours and features of Aji Panda's face was produced for the campaign, as was the Aji Panda's room website <www.ajinomoto.co.jp/ajipanda>.

Profile
特技は、パパパッと「味の素®」を振ること。普段はどこかに隠れているが「チャーハン」と聞くと台所に現れ、チャーハンに「キメのひと味、味の素®」を振って立ち去る。密かに家族の団らんを恋しく思っているので味の素®を振りかけた後、実は後ろ髪をひかれる思い。妹は、しっかり者のアジパンナ。

His talent is sprinkling Ajinomoto flavor enhancer. Usually hiding away in his room, upon hearing the words "fried rice" he appears in the kitchen, sprinkles on the decisive ingredient, and leaves. Inwardly he longs for family life and would love to linger, but doesn't. His younger sister is strong and dependable.

ウェブサイト　Website

レシピブック　Recipe Book

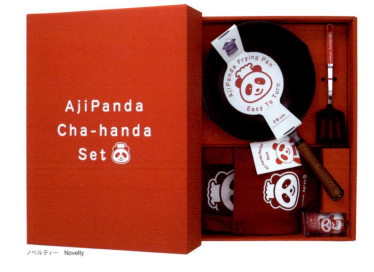

ノベルティー　Novelty

プレート　Plate

タオル　Towel

製造 Manufacture　065

プッカ Pucca　食品メーカー（プッカ）　Food Manufacturer (Pucca)

CL, SB: 明治製菓　Meiji Seika Kaisha, Ltd.　CD: 狩野雄司　Yuji Kano　AD: 高橋秀明　Hideaki Takahashi　Agency: 電通　DENTSU INC.　Japan

Concept
のんびりと、とぼけた感じの脱力キャラ。決して多くを語ったり、押しつけがましい笑顔や媚びた表情は見せない。また、アクティブに前に出てくる暑苦しさもない。しかしマイペースで力の抜けた存在は、忙しく、ストレスの多い現代社会で"癒し"を与える、不思議な魅力をかもしだしている。

A laidback, spacey, lackadaisical character. Short on chat; flashes no pushy smiles or fawning expressions. Neither does he aggressively make his way to the fore. His off the pace, tension-free existence does however have a strange allure and a healing effect on our busy, stress-filled lives.

Profile
プッカ国家の王子さまであるオージ・プッカをはじめ、パパ・プッカ、ママ・プッカ、ヒメ・プッカなど、現在22種類のプッカ星の仲間たちがウェブや携帯サイトで活躍している。

Twenty-two friends from the planet Pucca, starting with the prince of the state of Pucca, Prince Pucca, and including Papa Pucca, Mama Pucca, Princess Pucca, are currently active on the Internet and mobile phone websites.

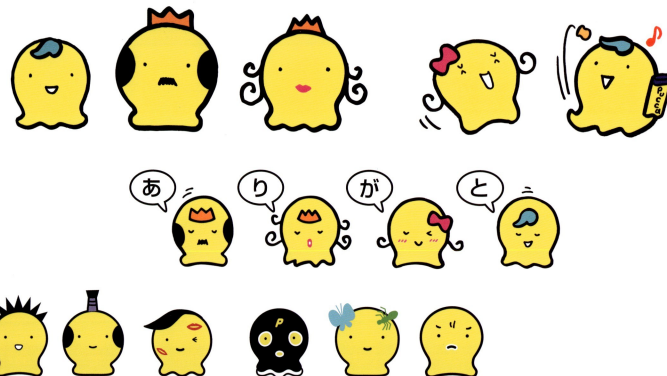

ウェブサイト　Website

こんガらガっち KONGARAGACCHI

食品メーカー（明治サイコロキャラメル） Food Manufacturer (Meiji Saikoro Caramel)

CL, SB: 明治製菓 Meiji Seika Kaisha, Ltd.　　Planning, Production: ユーフラテス EUPHRATES　　CD: 佐藤雅彦 Masahiko Sato　　AD, D: 貝塚智子 Tomoko Kaizuka　　I: うえ田みお Mio Ueta　　Japan

Concept
2つの箱の組み合わせによって新しいキャラクターが生まれる仕組み。ユーザーが自分の手の中で新しい「こんガらガっち」をつくり、楽しめるようになっている。

The device is simple: each combination of two boxes creates a new character. Users enjoy creating new KONGARAGACCHI in the confines of their hands.

Profile
明治サイコロせいぶつ「こんガらガっち」とは、いろんな動物がこんがらがってできた新しい生物のことである。144種類のこんガらガっちがおり、それぞれ固有の特長をもつ。

例）いぐら…記入もれが多い／ありりん…自分の名前が気に入っている

The Meiji dice creature "KONGARAGACCHI" is a new being created from a mix of different animals. There are 144 varieties of KONGARAGACCHI, each with his or her own virtues. Examples: Igura - tends to omit data; Aririn - loves her own

  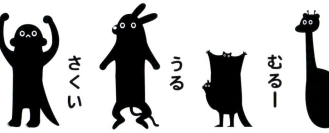    

暴君ハバネロ　Tyrant HABANERO

食品メーカー（暴君ハバネロ）　Food Manufacturer (Tyrant HABANERO)

CL: 東ハト　Tohato Inc.　CD: 北風 勝　Masaru Kitakaze　AD, I: 鈴木克彦　Katsuhiko Suzuki　CW: 斎藤賢司　Kenji Saito / 坪井 卓　Taku Tsuboi　D: 門脇 亮　Ryo Kadowaki　D: 柿崎裕生　Yusei Kakizaki
DF, SB: 博報堂　HAKUHODO Inc.　Japan

Concept
「暴君ハバネロ」は、"とびきり辛いけどとびきりウマい"をコンセプトにした激辛スナック菓子のキャラクター。毒があるのにシリアスになりすぎない過激なキャラクター。

Tyrant Habanero is the character for a fiery hot snack that was based on the concept "outrageously hot, outrageously good". Ghastly he is, but not too seriously radical.

Profile
「暴君ハバネロ」本名はハバネロ・オレンジ三世。ハーバーネロ大学卒。ウマ辛帝国絶対君主。激辛の暴言苦言で人々を混乱させ、横暴で理不尽だがどこか憎めない。暴君に成る前の幼少時代はまだ辛さも可愛かった「暴君ベビネロ」。

Tyrant Habanero's real name is Habanero Orange III. He is a graduate of Habanero University, and the absolute monarch of the Tasty Hot Empire. He takes people aback with his fiery outspokenness, is highhanded and outrageous, but something about him makes him hard to dislike. As a boy he was a mildly hot, sweet little Tyrant Habanero.

    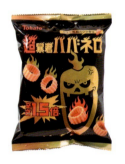 

    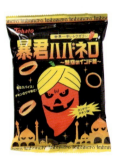

ポスター　Poster

「暴大入試」キャンペーン The Tyrant HABANERO UNIVERSITY "The Desperate Entry Exam"
Web Direction, Flash Authoring: 辻 恭平 Kyohei Tsuji / 中野美緒 Mio Nakano Programing, Flash Authoring: 石野敏之 Toshiyuki Ishino / 石橋由悠 Yoshichika Ishibashi
DF: クロッシング Crossing Inc. / モクバ MOKUBA INC. / ステージ STAGE, INC.

ポスター Poster

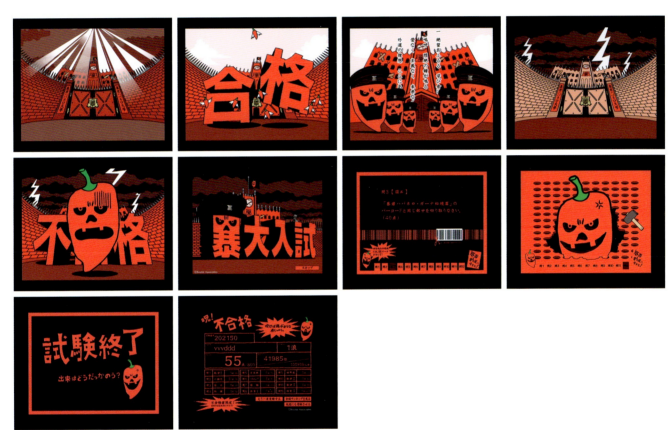
ウェブサイト Website

壁紙 Wall Paper

製造 Manufacture 069

キャラメルコーン君　Caramel Corn-kun　食品メーカー（キャラメルコーン）　Food Manufacturer (Caramel Corn)

CL: 東ハト　Tohato Inc.　CD: 北風 勝　Masaru Kitakaze　AD: 杉山ユキ　Yuki Sugiyama　D: 遠藤祐子　Yuko Endo / 佐藤るつ子　Rutsuko Sato / 鈴木亜希子　Akiko Suzuki / 黒瀬幸水　Yukimi Kurose
CW: 斉藤賢司　Kenji Saito / 井口雄太　Yuta Iguchi　Agency, SB: 博報堂　HAKUHODO Inc. Japan

Concept
33年ぶりのリニューアルに伴い、「パッケージそのものをキャラクターに」という発想をもとに制作。もともとのパッケージの財産である「赤」「ロゴ」「円の中のシズル写真」を生かし、店頭で目立つシンプルなデザインを目指した。

With the product's first revamping in 33 years, a character was produced based on the idea that "the product package itself would become a character". The aim was to develop a simple design that would stand out in the store, retaining the characteristic elements of its original package, such as red color, logo and the circular photo of appetizing snacks inside.

Profile
おるすばんの時、おでかけ、遠足……、いつも傍らにいてくれる友だちのような存在のキャラクター。願いをかなえてくれる「カナエルコーン」やイチゴミルクちゃん、抹茶ミルク君など50種類近くの仲間がいる。

When you stay at home alone, you go to town, or you take a field trip...Caramel Corn-kun is like your friend that will always be with you. There are 50 characters including Kanaeru Corn who grants your wishes, Ichigo Milk-chan (strawberry milk) and Maccha Milk-kun (green tea milk).

ポスター　Poster

クリップ　Clip

ノベルティー　Novelty

クッション　Cushion

製造　Manufacture　071

ポテコとなげわ POTECO & NAGEWA

食品メーカー（ポテコとなげわ）　Food Manufacturer (POTECO & NAGEWA)

CL: 東ハト　Tohato Inc.　CD: 北風 勝　Masaru kitakaze　AD: 鈴木克彦　Katsuhiko Suzuki　D, I: 新保裕章　Hiroaki Shinbo　CW: 福部明浩　Akihiro Fukube / 熊谷正晴　Masaharu Kumagai
Agency, SB: 博報堂　HAKUHODO Inc.　Japan

Concept
今まで別商品だった「ポテコ」と「なげわ」の2商品を関連づけてリニューアルした。形状が似ている両方の商品に関係性を持たせ、認知度の高まりを目指した。"幼い頃、商品を指にはめて遊んだ"という顧客の声からヒントを得て、手をモチーフにしたキャラクターを考案。

A connection was created between two rebranded products: salt-flavored Poteko and consume-flavored Negewa. The aim was maintain a sense of relationship through their similar shapes, and boost recognition. The idea of a character with a hand motif for was gleaned from customers who recalled as kids "wearing the ring-shaped crisps on their fingers"

Profile
「ポテコ」は関東に住む元気な男の子、一方の「なげわ」は関西在住のニヒルないとこのお兄ちゃん。

Poteko is a spirited young boy who lives in the Kanto region. Nagewa is his skeptical older cousin who lives in Kansai.

インナーグッズ＆ノベルティー
Gloves produced for company employees & Novelty

ノベルティー（キャラクターを使った手話の早見表）　Novelty (Quick reference sign language chart using characters.)

チン Chin 食品メーカー（Chin） Food Manufacturer (Chin)

CL: 日清食品 NISSIN FOOD PRODUCTS CO.,LTD. CD: 岩井伸之祐 Shinnosuke Iwai AD, I: 鈴木克彦 Katsuhiko Suzuki CW: 嵐田 光 Hikaru Arashida D: 門脇 亮 Ryo Kadowaki
P: 西田宗之 Muneyuki Nishida DF, SB: 博報堂 HAKUHODO Inc. / モクバ MOKUBA INC. Japan

Concept

お湯のいらない、レンジ調理のボックス型カップ麺商品のキャラクター。「ボックスをチン！カンタン！おいしい！」がキャッチコピー。レンジで作る箱型の新しいヌードルだから、レンジのキャラで名前もChin。

The character for a box-shaped cup-noodle product made without boiling water, in the microwave. Coupled with the catch copy: "Chin (zap) the box! Easy! Delicious!" Being a new type boxed noodle made in the microwave, the character is also a microwave, named Chin.

ポスター Poster

ハットトリックス モビ　Hat-tricks mobi　食品メーカー（モビ）Food Manufacturer (mobi)

CL: 東ハト　Tohato Inc.　I: あべ たみお　Tamio Abe　SB: バタフライ・ストローク　butterfly・stroke inc.　Japan

Concept
新商品のスナック菓子ということから、まずは手に取ってもらえるように、陳列棚で目立つことを最大限に考慮。それぞれの原材料に使われている素材を頭に載せ、そのキャラクターに合わせたヘアスタイルにまとめた。ターゲットである若年層に向け、インパクトと遊び心を表現した。"カブりもの"というシンプルでストレートな手法を取りつつも、応用が効き、なおかつひとクセもふたクセもあるキャラクターへと昇華させた。

Being for a new range of snacks, the main object was to make the characters stand out on the store shelf. Ingredients used in each product in the range were fashioned into hairstyles to suit each character, for a playful but powerful look targeting the younger age group. While using the simple, straightforward technique of "headgear", the characters are versatile and have been given special quirks of their own.

Profile
頭にさまざまなものを載せたパンキッシュなキャラクター、ハットトリックスシリーズのひとつ。東ハトのモバイルスナック「モビ」の原材料として使われている素材を頭に載せた個性的なキャラクターたち。メインキャラクターの5人は"モビ5"というバンドを結成している。

One of a "Hat-Tricks" series of punk-like characters with various things on their heads. These distinctive characters wear ingredients used in the "mobi" pocket-size snacks produced by Tohato. The five main characters form a band called "mobi 5."

改札ステッカー　Wicket Sticker

車内広告　Poster in Train

ADカード　AD Card

074　製造　Manufacture

ナッツボン イメージキャラクター　NUTBON Image Character

食品メーカー（ナッツボン）
Food Manufacturer (NUTBON)

CL: カンロ　KANRO CO., LTD.　CD: 片桐依里（カンロ）Eri Katagiri (KANRO CO., LTD.)　I: 福田 透　Toru Fukuda　DF: マネット　MA・NET　Artist Agency, SB: ヴィジョントラック　visiontrack　Japan

Concept

商品の特性であるピーナッツキャンディの「香ばしくてはじけるようなクランチ感」を意識したデザインに。キャラクターの外観は、キャンディの形そのものからデフォルメし、はじける感じを出すために、飛び跳ねてダンスしているような大きなポーズと表情をつけている。カートゥーンテイストのポップな絵柄とカラーリング、そしてキャラクターとともに新たにデザインしたロゴによって、陽気な笑い声が聞こえてきそうな賑やかな雰囲気を最大限に表現している。

Consciously designed to express the "nutty, bursting crunchiness" characteristic of the product, a peanut-based candy. Outwardly, the character takes the form of the candy itself, slightly deformed, and expresses the candy's explosive crunch by assuming a bouncy dance pose. The character's pop, cartoony design and coloring together with the newly designed logo express to the max a lively atmosphere, from which one can almost hear loud, jovial voices.

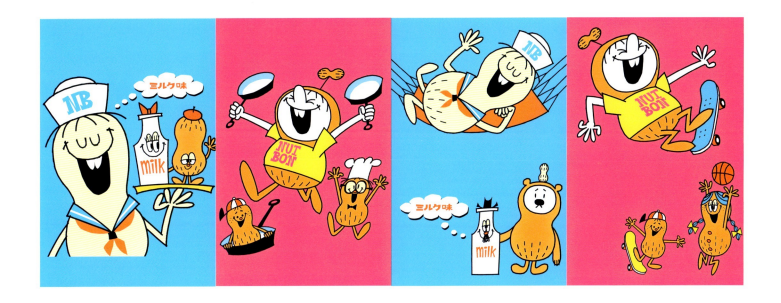

ホームラン坊や Home Run Boy 食品メーカー（ホームランバー） Food Manufacturer (Home Run Bar)

CL: 協同乳業 Kyodo Milk Industry Co., Ltd.   Strategic Planner: 五味田雅彦 Masahiko Gomita   CW: 今江有希 Yuki Imae   AD, D: 堀田聡（ZUGA）Satoshi Hotta (ZUGA)
D: 佐々木統剛（ZUGA）Togo Sasaki (ZUGA） / 高橋マリコ（ZUGA）Mariko Takahashi (ZUGA)   I: 土器修三 Shuzo Doki   SB: 大広ブランドデザイン Daiko Brand Design Inc.   Japan

Concept
ホームランバーの最大の特徴は「当たりつき」。「当たり」はラッキーであると同時に驚きである。そんな「Lucky & Surprise」という当たりのシズルを強化・強調すべく、そのシンボル的存在として「ホームラン坊や」を設定。また、この商品は野球のイメージとの結びつきが強いため、野球少年としてデザインした。

The Home Run Bar's most distinguishing feature is its lottery sticks. Striking a winner is to be lucky and at the same time, a surprise. Home Run Boy's symbolic existence strengthens and emphasizes the sizzle of "getting a hit", i.e. the elements of "luck and surprise". And because the product image is associated strongly with baseball, the character was made a little leaguer.

Profile
野球少年ではあるが、投手なのか野手なのかは不明。最近はパッケージだけでなく、ウェブやイベントにも顔を出しているため認知度はうなぎのぼり?!　とにかく人を楽しませることに生きがいを感じている。愛嬌と意外性が売りのラッキーボーイ!!

A little leaguer, position unknown. Recently appears not only on packaging but also on the Web and at events, thus recognition has skyrocketed!? Nothing inspires him as much as bringing people pleasure. His charm and element of surprise make him the selling lucky boy!!

ノベルティー Novelty

着ぐるみ Character - shaped outfit

エンブレム　Emblem

ウェブサイト　Website

製造　Manufacture　077

マルロー　Marulo

和洋菓子製造販売（丸ぼうろ）　Manufacture and Sales of Japanese and Western Confectionaries (MARUBOLO)

CL: 北島 KITAJIMA　　CD: 植原政信 Masanobu Uehara　　AD, D: 常軒理恵子 Rieko Tsunenoki　　P: 牧野正文 Masahumi Makino　　CW: 左 俊幸 Toshiyuki Hidari
DF: アド・パスカル AD-PASCAL CO., LTD　　SB: 電通九州 DENTSU KYUSHU INC.　　Japan

Concept

老舗である「北島」を若い主婦や子供たちに身近に感じてもらえるよう、主力商品の『丸ぼうろ』をおやつとしてデイリーに食べてもらえるよう、丸ぼうろをモチーフにしたキャラクターを制作。商品の特徴である、"昔なつかしく素朴で美味しく、安心な商品である"というイメージを活かしたキャラクターづくりを心がけた。また、シンプルな素材で作られているお菓子なので、キャラクターも極力シンプルに、子供でも簡単に描けるものにした。

To appeal to young housewives and children, veteran bakers Kitajima devised characters based on the round MARUBOLO cakes that are their most popular product, to encourage daily consumption of the cakes as a snack. Care was taken to create characters that reflected the company's vision of a "simple, tasty and trusted old-fashioned treat." The characters were made as simple as possible, befitting cakes made from simple ingredients, so even children could draw them.

Profile

佐賀県の菓子メーカー「北島」のキャラクター。ポルトガル生まれ・佐賀育ち。カステラやケーキ地面、リーフパイの森などのお菓子でできた世界に暮らし、『花ぼうろ』の女の子や、『ごまぼうろ』のお友達、『こぼうろ』のウサギなど、たくさんの友達と毎日楽しく遊んでいる。

"Born in Portugal, raised in Saga", this charming band of characters created for longstanding Saga confectioners Kitajima enjoy a carefree existence in a delightful world of sponge cake and leafy pie forest.

  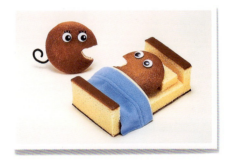

ポストカード　Postcard

携帯ストラップ　Mobile Phone Strap　　POP

新聞広告 Newspaper AD

トッテモちゃん Tottemo*

飲料メーカー (Tottemo*ミルクティー) Beverage Manufacturer (Tottemo* Milk Tea)

CL: ネスレ日本 NESTLE JAPAN LTD.　CD, AD: 細島雄一 Yuichi Hosojima　D: 益子佳奈 Kana Mashiko　P: 北浦敦子 Atsuko Kitaura　CW: 藤井涼子 Ryoko Fujii
Character Design: マッシュルームカフェ mushroom cafe　SB: サンクディレクションズ CINQ DIRECTIONS　Japan

Concept

強力な競合商品が並ぶコンビニエンスストアの店頭では、逆にちょっと力の抜けたシンプルなデザインが良いのでは、との思いでこのデザインに。

Developed upon the idea that set among its hard-hitting competition on the convenience store shelf, a simple design deliberately lacking "strength" would be preferable.

Profile

Tottemo*ミルクティーのパッケージにデザインされていた女の子が、いつの間にかTottemoちゃんと呼ばれるようになった。おっとりとした性格のTottemoちゃんは、まわりの友だちをほのぼのとした気持ちにしてくれ、困っている友だちがいると、しあわせを運ぶ不思議なクローバーで解決してくれる。オフィシャルサイト：www.tottemo.net

The character of a young girl developed for the Tottemo* Milk Tea packaging inadvertently began being called Tottemo* (Little Miss Tottemo*). Official Site: www.tottemo.net

スタンプ　Stamp

CD

DVD

ポスター　Poster

ポスター　Poster

展覧会　Exhibition

製造　Manufacture　081

ハイネケン・ロングネック　Heineken Longneck　飲料メーカー（ハイネケン）　Drink Manufacturer (Heineken)

CL: Heineken　CD, AD, I: Erik Kessels　AD: Karen Heuter　CW: Dave Bell　SB: KesselsKramer　Netherlands

Concept
ハイネケンのモダンな新ボトルを宣伝するために生み出されたキリンのロングネック。あえてブランド名を出さず、アンダーグラウンドな雰囲気を持たせている。クールで、好みにうるさい、こだわりをもつクラバーたちにもすぐに受け入れられ、国内屈指のバーやクラブでも定着しつつある。

Longneck (the giraffe) was brought to life to communicate this new, more modern bottle in an unbranded, more underground way. Longneck was soon adopted by the cool, hard to please clubbing crowd and now has its home in the best bars and clubs in the country.

Profile
ハイネケン・ロングネックは緑色のキリン。これは、オランダで発売されたネックの長いグリーンボトルに入ったハイネケンの新商品の名前でもある。

Heineken Longneck is a green giraffe. It is also the name given to a new green, long-necked bottle of Heineken. Introduced in the Netherlands.

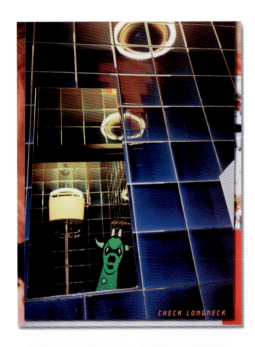

TVCM

ポスター　Poster

ブランドブック
Brand Book

体内怪人 Tainaikaijin

製薬・飲料・食品メーカー（ファイブミニ）　Pharmaceutical, Drink, Food Manufacturer (Fibe Mini)

CL, SB: 大塚製薬　OTSUKA PHARMACEUTICAL CO., LTD.　CD: 古田彰一　Shoichi Furuta　AD: 藤田誠　Makoto Fujita　D: 藤田純平　Junpei Fujita　P: 上田義彦　Yoshihiko Ueda
DF: スパイス　SPICE INC.　Agency: 博報堂　HAKUHODO Inc.　Japan

Concept

このキャラクターたちは、体内で悪さをする毒素。彼らを、子どもの頃に見たヒーローものの怪人をイメージしてキャラクター化。テーマとなる毒素を顕微鏡で覗いたフォルムをモチーフに、症状をユニークに取り入れてデザインした。例えば、「カサカーサ」は体から無数の突起物が出て、肌に悪そうな印象に。また、「ダルダル」は重くて垂れていて、全身がだるいイメージとした。「こんなのが体の中にいたら嫌だな」という気持ち悪さと、広告のアイキャッチとしてのチャーミングさを共存させたことで、今までにないキャラクターデザインが生まれた。

Baddies for the body turned into monsters inspired by the superheroes of childhood. Using the shape of toxins seen through the microscope, symptoms were incorporated into the design in unique ways. For example, Kasakaasa has lots of protuberances from its body, giving the impression of being bad for the skin, while Darudaru is heavy and ponderous, conveying the idea of sluggishness. The coexistence of "yuck factor" and eyecatching advert give rise to a totally new kind of character design.

Profile

食物センイ不足の現代人の体内には、さまざまな不調の原因となる不要物が存在する。それらを広告用のモチーフとして表現したのが「体内怪人」という名前のオリジナルキャラクター。「私の体から出ていってほしいもの」の象徴として、アウトプットドリンク・ファイブミニのキャンペーンの主役(!?)として活躍した。

Modern lifestyles can lead to a lack of fiber and buildup of waste in the body that can cause a variety of illnesses. The "monsters" represent these in advertising, playing the starring role in a campaign for the Fibe Mini laxative drink, as symbols of "the things I want to get out of my system".

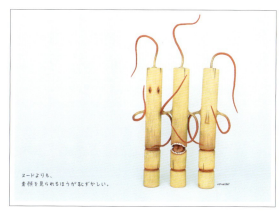

ポスター　Poster

ぼく、ミミミ、マウマウ、ティッキ・ウィッキ、ドードー Boku, Mimimi, Maumau, Ticky Wicki, Dodo

食品メーカー（キティランド）　Food Manufacturer (kittyland)

CL, SB: 江崎グリコ　EZAKI GLICO CO., LTD　CD: 光居 誠　Makoto Mitsui　AD: 関 奈央子　Naoko Seki　I: 大滝まみ　Mami Ohtaki　DF: スプーン　SPOON CO., LTD　Japan

Concept
ビスケットにキャラクターが描かれたキティランドというお菓子は、親子に愛されているロングセラー商品。子供たちに絵本を読んであげるように、お菓子を食べながら、お母さんが子どもにキャラクターたちのお話をしてもらえたら……そんな思いから、楽しいキャラクターが誕生した。

Kittyland biscuits, which feature pictures of characters on their surfaces, have been a long-selling favorite of parents and children. These fun little characters were created with the idea of mothers telling their children stories about the characters while enjoy their snack, much the way they might read them a picture book.

Profile
100年に一度、離れているふたつの島がくっつくと言われているビス島とケット島。このふたつの島には犬の「ぼく」を中心にかわいい仲間がたくさん住んでいる。いたずら好きの「ぼく」は、手長ザルの「ティッキ・ウィッキ」やねずみの「マウマウ」、くまの「ドードー」といつも一緒に遊んでいる。

On the neighboring islands of Bis and Kett, which come together every 100 years, live Boku the dog and his sweet little friends. Mischievous Boku always plays with his pals Ticky Wicki the long-armed monkey, Maumau the field mouse and Dodo the bear.

タオル　Towel

ウェブサイト　Website

ベジタブリート　VEGETABLETES

食品メーカー（「みんバラ」みんなの栄養バランスチェックキャンペーン）
Food Manufacturer ("Minbara" Maintenance of Inner Body Functions Promotion)

CL: カゴメ　KAGOME CO., LTD.　AD: 清水武穂（博報堂アイ・スタジオ）Takeo Shimizu (HAKUHODO i-studio Inc.)　D: 望月重太朗（博報堂アイ・スタジオ）Shigetaro Mochiduki (HAKUHODO i-studio Inc.)
Producer: 足立 学（博報堂アイ・スタジオ）Manabu Adachi (HAKUHODO i-studio Inc.)　Excective Producer: 橋本真人（博報堂）Masato Hashimoto (HAKUHODO Inc.)
Planner: 後藤康之（博報堂アイ・スタジオ）Yasushi Goto (HAKUHODO i-studio Inc.)　Agency: 博報堂　HAKUHODO Inc.　Production: 博報堂アイ・スタジオ　HAKUHODO i-studio Inc.
SB: タロアウト　tarout　Japan

Concept

キャンペーンのキャッチフレーズ「野菜で体内環境正常化」をもとに、ユーザーが頑張って続けられるよう、一緒に頑張ってくれる優秀なアスリートを創り上げた。種であるタネリートからベビリートへ、そしてベジタブリートに成長し、食事バランスや体型による変化を繰り返し、飽きさせないために次から次へと新しいベジタブリートにバトンタッチし、成長を楽しめる。また、ユーザーのためにともに頑張るチームであることを表すタスキをすることで、愛着のわく一体感を与えた。ブログパーツとしても使われた。

Based on the campaign's catch phrase of "regulate your body's internal environment", talented athletes were created to encourage user's to keep up the good work by working with them. By design they grow from TANELETES (sprout) to BABYLETES to full-grown vegetabletes, VEGETABLETES, changing repeatedly in relation to their diets and physiques and switching off with other vegetabletes to maintain their appeal and fun with users. And to show their support for users as a team they carry a baton, a symbol of team spirit. It was used as the blog parts as well.

Profile

ベジタブリートは、体内環境正常化を目指す人とともに一緒にがんばるアスリート。ベジタブリートには、キャロリート、カボリート、ホウレンリート、ブロッコリート、タマネリート、ナスリート、トマリート、ピーリートの8リートがいる。
VEGETABLETES are athletes that works with people to help them regulate their body's internal environment. There are eight vegetabletes: CAROLETE, KABOLETE, HOURENLETE, BROCOLETE, TAMANETE, NASULETE, TOMALETE, and PEELETE.

CAROLETE　キャロリート

KABOLETE　カボリート

HOURENLETE　ホウレンリート

BROCOLETE　ブロッコリート

TAMANELETE　タマネリート

TANELETES　タネリート

BABYLETES　ベビリート

NASULETE　ナスリート

TOMALETE　トマリート

PEELETE　ピーリート

P&G プロキープ キャラクター　Character of P&G Prokeep

日用品メーカー（プロキープ）
Home Products Manufacturer (Prokeep)

CL: P&G　CD: DDB東急エージェンシークリエイティブ　DDB TOKYO AGENCY INC. Creative　D: 山下浩平（マウンテンマウンテン）Kohei Yamashita (mountain mountain)
SB: マウンテンマウンテン　mountain mountain　Japan

Concept

冷凍庫で使用する商品であるということから、ペンギンをキャラクターとして起用。また、ファミリー感を出すため、親ペンギンと子どものペンギンを登場させた。

A penguin was selected as the character because the product is used in the freezer. And to create a sense of family, parent and child penguins appear on the scene as well.

TVCM

つくしちゃん Tsukushi-chan　健康食品メーカー（桜のつくし飴）Health Food Manufacturer (Tsukushi Candy)

CL: 桜 SAKURA, Inc　AD: 寺坂幸男 Yukio Terasaka　I: 広田桂子 Keiko Hirota　Web Designer: 猪熊信次 Shinji Inokuma　SB: ポレポレーション・スタジオ polepoletion. STUDIO　Japan

Concept
商品パッケージや販売用サイトなどに登場させることで、商品に親しみをおぼえるような可愛らしさを表現。鼻は「つくし飴」をイメージしている。また、つくしちゃんを取り巻く世界や仲間たちを設定し、物語を楽しんでもらう単独のウェブサイトも開設。"つくし飴のつくしちゃん""つくしちゃんのつくし飴"と、商品としての認知度が双方向から上がることを狙いとしている。

The character was used on packaging and for online sales to foster familiarity with the product. Tsukushi-chan's nose is shaped like a drop of Tsukushi Candy. An entire imaginary world including other characters and a delightful story was devised on a separate website, the aim being to raise the profile of the product from the dual perspectives of "Tsukushi-chan of Tsukushi Candy" and "Tsukushi Candy from Tsukushi-chan".

Profile
春のつくしから生まれたキャンディー「桜のつくし飴」のキャラクター。サクラサク島に「ハナの救世主」として誕生した、つくしちゃんは、マイペースでちょっぴり頑固な女の子。丸くて黒いお鼻には、ある力が秘められている……。座右の銘は「尽くし尽くされ」。

Character for candy made from the tsukushi (horsetail) plant, known for its hayfever-fighting properties. Tsukushi-chan, who has come from sakura-saku (full-blown cherry blossoms) island to "save noses", is a determined lass who likes to do things at her own pace, with a round black nose harboring special powers...

ポスター　Poster

ポストカード　Postcard

はのちゃん　hano-chan　飲料メーカー（葉の茶）　Drink Manufacturer (Hanocha)

CL, SB: ダイドードリンコ　DyDo DRINCO　Japan

Concept

鮮やかなグリーン、ひと目で葉っぱと分かる形状。可愛らしく、人なつこいイメージでありながらも、人の手を加えること、つまり茶葉は揉まれないと自分らしさを出すことができないことから、ちょっと頼りなげで憎めないという設定に。ユーザーに愛されるキャラクターであることも意識して制作した。

Vivid green and instantly recognizable as a leaf, hano-chan may be cute and friendly looking, but without human input, in other words without being processed, he is unable to be his true self, making him a slightly forlorn character impossible to dislike. Consciously designed to be a character users will grow to love.

Profile

飲料メーカー「ダイドードリンコ」が販売している商品『葉の茶』のキャラクター、はのちゃん。氏を"はの"、名を"ちゃん"という。5月2日生まれで、出身は静岡県。趣味は、読書（お茶に関する本のみ）と散歩。性格は、打たれ強く、立ち直りが早い。

hano-chan, character for Hanocha, a tea drink sold by beverage manufacturer DyDo DRINCO. Born May 2 in Shizuoka, enjoys reading (but only books about tea) and walks. A tough character who can take the punches and get right back up again.

コパンくん　COPAN-kun　食品メーカー（コパン）　Food Manufacturer (COPAN)

CL, SB: 明治製菓　Meiji Seika Kaisha, Ltd.　CD: 狩野雄司　Yuji Kano　AD: 笹沼 修　Osamu Sasanuma　Agency: 電通　DENTSU INC.　Japan

Profile

コパンくんは、イタリア南部の小さな村のパン屋さんの子供。おじいちゃんのパン屋を手伝っている。理由は不明だが、おじいちゃんと2人で暮らしている。

COPAN-kun is the son of a baker in a small village in Southern Italy. He helps at his grandfather's bakery. He lives with his grandfather, reason unknown.

製造　Manufacture

チー坊 Chibo 食品メーカー（チチヤスヨーグルト） Food Manufacturer (CHICHIYASU Yoghurt)

CL: チチヤス CHICHIYASU CO., Ltd. CD: 増村 顕 Ken Masumura AD: イシザキミチヒロ Michihiro Ishizaki CW: 岡山真子 Shinko Okayama D: 矢沢由実 Yumi Yazawa / 杉山紘一 Koichi Sugiyama
DF, SB: ドッポ doppo inc. Japan

Concept

ナツカシイ、から、あたらしい、へ。ヨーグルトの老舗、チチヤスのリブランディング作業の中心に「歴代のチチヤスキャラクターの初代」であった「チー坊」をリバイバルさせた。すべてのコミュニケーションを「チー坊」で展開、特に、プロダクトデザインでは、メイン商品の「オリジナル」「低糖」において、清潔感と鮮度感を出すため白を多用しながら、赤と青で記号性を高め、一方前面に「チー坊」を大きく置き、背面に「後ろ姿のチー坊」をレイアウトすることで、品質感と現代的なかわいらしさを同時に生み出した。

From nostalgic to new. Central to the rebranding of the long-selling yoghurt retailer Chichiyasu, was the revival of their very first character Chibo from successive its generations. Chibo was featured on all communications, particularly on the two main products, original and low-sugar, where on a clean and fresh-feeling white background and with identity-building red and blue accents, he appears large as a frontal view on the face of the package, and a rear view on the back, thereby generating a sense of quality, contemporaneity and charm.

ケロケ郎 Kerokero　　自動車メーカー　Auto Manufacturer

CL: トヨタ自動車　TOYOTA MOTOR CORPORATION　　AD, D, I: 杉山ユキ　Yuki Sugiyama　　D: 上野慎二　Shinji Ueno　　D (Movie): 坂本嘉章　Yoshiaki Sakamoto
CW: 井口雄太　Yuta Iguchi　　Agency, SB: 博報堂　HAKUHODO Inc.　　Japan

Concept
排気ガスの代わりに水を出す環境負荷の少ないFCHV（燃料電池ハイブリッド）バス。バスの車内にてその特性や高機能を大人から子供までに分かりやすく伝えるため、体が水でできたカエルのキャラクター「ケロケ郎」と説明ビデオを制作。クリーンなイメージを効果的に見せるため、水彩画を使用して、透明度をテーマに全体をデザインした。

FCHV (fuel cell hybrid vehicle) is an environmentally friendly bus that puts out water instead of exhaust fumes. Kerokero, the frog character made of water, and the explanatory video, were produced to convey the FCHV's characteristics and advanced functions in an easy-to-understand way to both adults and children on the bus. The character was designed on the theme of transparency using water-color painting technique which enhanced its clean image.

Profile
ケロケ郎は水の妖精。体は水でできているけど、カエルのかたちをしているから「ケロケ郎」という。雲の上からみんなを見守り、ときどき地上にやって来て、人々を幸せにしてくれる。

Kerokero is a water nymph, made of water. He derives his name (kerokero represents croaking of frogs) from his frog-like shape. Seated on a cloud, he keeps watch over us all, and sometimes comes down to Earth to make people happy.

絵本　Picture Book

チラシ　Flyer

ステッカー　Sticker

Movie

製造　Manufacture　089

ユニ＆エコちゃん　Uni & Eco chan　総合家電メーカー　Household Appliance Manufacturer

CL: 三菱電機　Mitsubishi Electric Corporation　　Character Production, SB: アイプラネット　IPLANET Inc.　　Character Production: メイアン　Meian Corporation　　Japan

Concept
ユニ＆エコのシンボルであるロゴマークから生まれた、人でも動物でもない不思議なキャラクター。「人も地球も気持ちよく」という思いがひと目で伝わるように、見る人みんなが癒されるようなデザインを心がけた。カラーはロゴマークと同じくオレンジ＆グリーンとし、ユニ＆エコならではの個性を印象づけるキャラクターを目指した。

Curious creatures, neither human nor animal, developed from the Uni & Eco logomark. Designed to comfort the people who see them and convey at a glance the idea of "comfy for people and Earth". Their colors, like the logomark, are orange and green. The aim was to impress with personalities that could only belong Uni & Eco.

Profile
三菱電機、家電品のものづくりコンセプト「ユニバーサルデザイン」と「エコロジー」のユニ＆エコマークから誕生したユニ＆エコちゃん。人の優しさから生まれたユニ＆エコ（オレンジ）ちゃんとキレイな空気から生まれたユニ＆エコ（みどり）ちゃんは、「人も地球も気持ちよい」製品が大好き。

Uni & Eco emerged from the Uni and Eco marks for the concepts of universal design and ecology upon which Mitsubishi Electric bases the development of its home appliances. Uni & Eco (orange) who was born from human kindness and Uni & Eco (green) who was born from clean air, like products that are "comfy for people and Earth".

交通広告　Traffic AD

リーフレット　Leaflet

パンフレット　Pamphlet

ノベルティー　Novelty

ウェブサイト　Website

そうじろう、なまけたろう Sojiro, Namaketaro

家電メーカー（エアコンXシリーズ）
Household Appliance Manufacturer (Air-conditioning X series)

CL: 松下電器産業　Matsushita Electric Industrial Co., Ltd.　CD: 津山克則　Katsunori Tsuyama / 高須泰行　Hiroyuki Takasu / 山内 登　Noboru Yamauchi　AD: 小森秋雄　Akio Komori / 河崎博之　Hiroyuki Kawasaki　D: 前田弘史　Hiroshi Maeda　P: 小松正幸　Masayuki Komatsu　I: 森垣 潤　Jun Morigaki　CW: 山内 登　Noboru Yamauchi / 山本宏雄　Hiroo Yamamoto　CG Creator: 瀬賀なな惠　Nanae Sega　DF, SB: アデル　Adel Corporation　Japan

Concept
フィルターお掃除ロボット搭載エアコンを象徴するキャラクターとして誕生。エアコンのフィルターを自動で掃除することにより「手間なし」「清潔」「省エネ」を実現できる未来感があり、人にやさしいロボットとして、エアコンをモチーフにデザインされた。

A character created to symbolize the filter-cleaning robot built into air conditioners. Designed as a people-friendly robot with an air-conditioner motif and a futuristic sense of realizing the easy, sanitary, and energy-saving aspects of a self-cleaning air conditioner.

Profile
「そうじろう」は、とってもキレイ好きのお掃除ロボット。フィギュアスケートをしながらお掃除するのが得意。「なまけたろう」は、お掃除が大嫌いなそうじろうの兄。すぐお掃除をさぼるので、住んでいる古いエアコンや部屋がほこりやカビだらけ。

Sojiro is a clean-freak of a cleaning robot. His forte is figure skating and cleaning at the same time. Namaketaro, who despises cleaning, is Sojiro's big brother. When it comes to cleaning he lies down on the job so the old air conditioner and room in which he lives are full of dust and mildew.

絵本　Picture Book

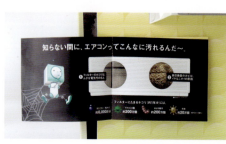

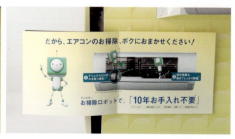

つよインク、つよインク200　Tsuyo Ink, Tsuyo Ink 200

情報関連機器の製造・販売
Business Equipment Manufacture and Sales

CL: エプソン販売　EPSON SALES JAPAN CORPORATION　　CD: 佐々木洋一　Yoichi Sasaki　　AD: 鈴木克彦　Katsuhiko Suzuki　　PR (Tsuyo Ink): 林 丈二　Joji Hayashi
PR (Tsuyo Ink 200): 山本 浩　Hiroshi Yamamoto / 梶原伸博　Nobuhiro Kajiwara　　PR (Goods): 猪又幸成　Yukinari Inomata　　CG Designer: 西田健一　Kenichi Nishida.　DF: 博報堂　HAKUHODO Inc. / 博報堂プロダクツ　HAKUHODO PRODUCTS / スパイス　Spice Inc. / ガレージフィルム　Garage Film Inc. / ワイズ・インテグレーション　Wise Integration　Japan

Concept

カラープリンターのインクの保存性能の革新的な進化をキャラクターで表現。「つよインク」という名前と体のフォルムでインクの強さをアピール。さらに進化した「つよインク200」は頭の形が変わり、エンブレムとマントでパワーアップした。

A character created to express the high-degree of permanence and revolutionary progress of color printer inks. The name Tsuyo (Strong) Ink and form of his body make an appeal for the strength of the inks. The power of even more highly evolved Tsuyo Ink 200 was enhanced up by changing the shape of his head, and through his emblem and cape.

Profile

ピコリットル（1のマイナス32条リットル）という世界最小のミクロの戦士。プリンタの色褪せを防ぐために今日も頑張り続ける。仲間にはイエローの他に、シアン、マゼンタ、ブラック、マットブラック、ライトシアン、ライトマゼンタ、レッド、ブルー、グロスオプティマイザー（透明）などがいる。

Picoliter (a trillionth of a liter) is the world's smalled micro warrior, fighting night and day to prevent printer colors from fading. His comrades include, Yellow, Cyan, Magenta, Black, Matte Black, Lt. Cyan, Lt. Magenta, Red, Blue, and Gloss Optimizer (clear).

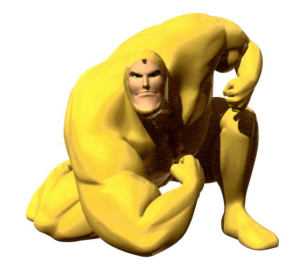

つよインク　Tsuyo Ink

ポスター　Poster

つよインク200　Tsuyo Ink 200

POP　　　　　　　　　　　　　　　　　　　　　　　　　　ノベルティー　Novelty

製造　Manufacture

カンタンランド　Kantan Land　　プリンタメーカー　Printer Manufacturer

CL: レックスマークインターナショナル LEXMARK International k.k.　　CD: 鎌田孝史 Takashi Kamada　　AD: 江口カエ Kae Eguchi　　D: 佐藤 求 Nozomi Sato / 村上陽子 Yoko Murakami / 小笠原信義 Nobuyoshi Ogasawara　　I: 熊井 正 Tadashi Kumai　　CW: 宮坂雅春 Masaharu Miyasaka　　Agency: 島津アドコム Shimadzu Adcom Co., Ltd.　　Web Production: スパイスグラフィックス Spice Graphics　　SB: 浪漫堂 Romando Co., Ltd.　　Japan

Concept

高機能ばかりが注目される日本のプリンタ市場で、プリンタ専業ブランドとして世界シェア1位のLEXMARK（レックスマーク）は、グローバルスタンダードの視点から「もっとみんながカンタンに使えるプリンタ」を提案。「カンタンサイコー。」のスローガンのもと誕生したのがこれらのキャラクター。同社プリンタの特長を端的に表現しつつ、家族で楽しめるペーパークラフト企画でインクの需要を喚起。店頭、WEBなどを最大活用した総合キャンペーン展開が可能なキャラクターを目指した。

In the Japanese printer market, where the focus is very much on hi-tech features, LEXMARK, the world's top-selling printer-only brand, offers printers simple (i.e. kantan) for everyone to use. While providing a brief guide to the company's printers, they boost demand for ink via papercraft ideas for all the family. The aim was to design characters suitable for a comprehensive ad campaign making maximum use of POP material, websites etc.

Profile

カンタンランドには、簡単で楽しいことが大好きなカンタンパンダを中心に、ワンタッチーター、ウツクシマウマ、デジカメレオンなど、レックスマークのプリンタの特長を名前にした楽しい動物キャラクターが大集合。個性豊かな全12種の愉快な仲間たちがカンタンプリンタの魅力を伝えている。

Kantan Land is home to Kantan Panda, who loves anything simple and fun, and his animal friends named for LEXMARK printer features, such as One Toucheetah, Utsukushimauma the "beautiful" zebra, and Digichameleon. In all 12 delightful characters represent the features of Lexmark printers.

チラシ　Flyer

POP

ポスター　Poster

ペーパークラフト　Paper Craft

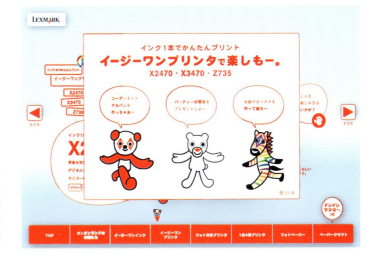
ウェブサイト　Website

製造　Manufacture

ごみゼロ右衛門　Gomizeroemon　総合家電メーカー　Household Appliance Manufacturer

CL: 松下電器産業　Matsushita Electric Industrial Co., Ltd.　CD: 三浦洋一　Yoichi Miura / 光居 誠　Makoto Mitsui　AD: 田島秀憲　Hidenori Tashima / 米田清美　Kiyomi Yoneda　D: 加藤 剛　Go Kato / 河野誉通　Takamichi Kono　I: 橋井康隆　Yasutaka Hashii　SB: 大広　DAIKO ADVERTISING INC　Japan

Concept
商品の魅力をPRするキャラクターとして、皆に親しまれるもの、ひと目で覚えられるもの。そういったデザインの強さに加え、しっかりした意味のあるものを制作しよう、と企画された「ごみゼロ右衛門」。ご覧のとおり、デザインモチーフはごみ袋。その口を結んだところがチョンマゲのようになっていて、このままごみ袋に印刷すれば、ごみを入れた時に、ゴミゼロ右衛門の顔になるように考えられている。日頃のごみ捨ての瞬間に「ごみゼロ右衛門」を思い出し、生ごみ処理について考えてもらいたい、という願いが込められている。

Being a product-promotional character, Gomizeroemon was planned and produced to be endearing to all, have the design strength that makes it memorable at a glance, and be clear in meaning. It is imaged after a trash bag. Printed on trash bags, when users fill and tie the bags, the bags become the character's face. In this way it was hoped people will recall Gomizeroemon whenever they put out their trash, and think more about the kitchen trash disposal.

Profile
日本全国の家庭から生ごみをなくすために生まれたキャラクター。エコの意識が現代より進んでいたといわれる江戸時代からやって来たという説もある。年齢不詳だが、ごみ袋の口を結んだようなチョンマゲスタイルが子供たちにも人気。生ごみ処理機の購入に助成金がある街の駅などに現れては、生ごみ処理機のPR活動を頑張っている。

A character born to campaign for zero kitchen waste from Japanese households nationwide. He comes from the Edo period when it is said that the ecological awareness was greater than it is today. His age is unknown. His topknot, which resembles the tied top of trash bag, is popular with children. He appears at the stations of towns that subsidize the purchase of kitchen waste composting machines, in his effort to promote these machines.

ポスター　Poster

パンフレット　Pamphlet

クリアファイル　Clear File

ゴミ袋　Trash Bag

新聞広告　Newspaper AD

製造　Manufacture　097

ハットトリックス ファーボ　Hat-tricks FAVO　パソコン周辺機器メーカー（FAVO）　Computer Peripherals Manufacturer (FAVO)

CL: ワコム　Wacom Co., Ltd.　CD: 青木克憲　Katsunori Aoki　I: あべ たみお　Tamio Abe　CW: 中崎裕之　Hiroyuki Nakazaki　DF, SB: バタフライ・ストローク　butterfly・stroke inc.　Japan

Concept
商品の機能を分かりやすく説明するため、それぞれのキャラクターが頭に思い"描く"ことを、頭に被せて表現。分かりやすさとともにインパクトを与えることができ、その結果、キャラクターに機能を説明させるという流れにも説得力が出た。分かりやすさ・インパクト・ユーモアという要素を同時に表現できるキャラクターとして、広告のみならずパッケージにも使用した。

To explain the features of the product in an accessible way, the "pictures" conjured up by each character in their minds are actually shown on their heads. This makes for ready understanding of the product and ensures optimum impact, and as a result the characters are able to explain the functions in a persuasive manner. The characters were used on packaging as well as in advertising, due to their ability to simultaneously express simplicity, impact and humor.

Profile
頭にさまざまなものを載せたパンクなキャラクター、ハットトリックスシリーズのひとつ。ペンタブレット家族"富亜暮家"は、ペンタブレット「ファーボ」のキャラクター。フデオパパ・カキコママ・ペンイチジィージ・タブバーバ・アイちゃん・ハジメちゃんの6人で構成。

One of the "Hat-tricks" series of punk characters with various things on their heads. The "FAVO" pen tablet family of mom, dad, two children and grandparents are the characters for the FAVO range of graphic tablets.

POP

雑誌広告　Magazine AD

てくてくエンジェル ポケット　tekuteku angel pocket　ネットワーク・コンテンツ事業　Internet Contents

CL: ハドソン　Hudson soft Co., Ltd　CD, AD, D: 青木克憲　Katsunori Aoki　I: あべ たみお　Tamio Abe　CW: 中崎裕之　Hiroyuki Nakazaki　SB: バタフライ・ストローク　butterfly・stroke inc.　Japan

Concept

女性向け商品であることから、さわやかで軽い印象のものがよいと考え、単色の絵画キャラクターが誕生。まず新聞広告という媒体の特性を踏まえ、絵画キャラクターが映えることを考慮した。その結果、「歩いてキャラクターを育てるゲーム」であること、ゲームに登場するキャラクターと広告用キャラクターを共生させることから、絵画キャラクターは好結果につながることに。"常に携帯する商品=商品そのものが歩くキャラクター"であることが、商品のシズルをすべて表現できることを意識した。

Because the product was aimed mainly at women, characters with a fresh, light impression were thought best, giving rise to single color pictorial figures. These too would stand out in newspaper advertising. The character appearing in the advertising also appears in a "nurture-the-walking-character game", which led to positive results. Thus "walking character = a product always on the move", expressing the appeal of the product.

Profile

育成散歩計「てくてくエンジェル pocket」のキャラクターで、パッケージや広告などに展開。

The characters for the tekuteku angel pocket, a step-counting device designed to encourage walking, and used in the product packaging and advertising.

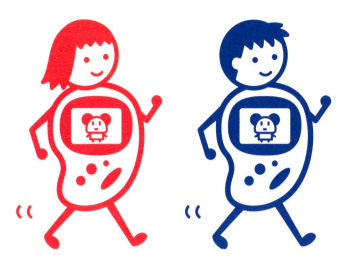

ポスター　Poster

中吊り　Hanging Poster

製造　Manufacture　099

トウシバ犬 Toshiba Ken 電気機器の製造・販売 Electronics Manufacture & Retail

CL, SB: 東芝 Toshiba Corporation　Japan

Concept

2003年に東芝ユーザークラブサイトのキャラクターとして登場したトウシバ犬。東芝製携帯電話の機種名に入っている「T」の文字をベースにシンプルで分かりやすく親しみの持てるデザインに。「T」をそのまま顔にしたのは、東芝携帯の認知度を上げるという狙いもあった。キャラクター設定の意外性や個性溢れる周辺キャラなどにより、見る人を飽きさせない工夫もしている。ファンからの要望に応えてキャラやエピソードを増やすなど、今後もさらなる成長が期待されている。

Toshiba Ken debuted as the Toshiba User Club Site mascot in 2003. Taking the letter T – the initial of all Toshiba cellphone models – as his basic form, he is simple and endearing in design. To enhance recognition of Toshiba cellphones, the T forms his face. The unique character of Toshiba Ken and his buddies was devised to prevent viewers from losing interest, and characters and episodes are expected to increase further in response to requests from fans.

Profile

無口でのんびり屋。しゃべると関西弁。好物は緑茶とプリン。友達にホネ子やチュー吉がいる。ウェブ媒体で紹介された2005年からは、携帯の壁紙やノベルティとなって一躍人気者に。現在はTUCSのキャラクターとして定着しつつあり、動画コンテンツや携帯向けSNS、Second Lifeなど、活動の幅を広げている。

Reticent and carefree. Speaks in Kansai dialect. Likes green tea and pudding. Has buddies such as Honeko and Chukichi. Since his Internet debut in 2005, he has appeared on cellphone cellphone wallpapers, cellphone straps, and so on, leaping in popularity. He is now a regular on TUCS, and also expanding his activities to animation, SNS for cellphones and Second Life.

パネル　Panel

ピノ犬　Pino-ken　　自動車メーカー（日産ピノ）　Auto Manufacturers "NISSAN PINO"

CL, SB: 日産自動車　NISSAN MOTOR CO, LTD.　　D: 日暮明紘　Akihiro Higure　Japan

Concept
日産PINOの世界観を、キャラクターを通して消費者により分かりやすく伝えていくことを狙って、そこに存在するだけで愛着と親しみがわき、和むようなキャラクターに仕上げた。PINOとの関連性が感じられるデザインとするため、サイコロと柴犬をモチーフとした。角が丸くなった立方体に素朴な柴犬のアイコン的な顔や足を融合させ、犬そのものでもなく、幾何学的でもないコロンとしたたたずまいのピノ犬が車のシートの上にちょこんと乗っている、というほんわかしたイメージを作り上げた。

The aim was to convey the worldview of the Nissan PINO in an easy-to-understand way through a character whose mere existence would inspire feelings of affection and friendliness, thus created with soft, calming qualities. To relate the design to the car, the motif is a dice and Shiba-inu dog hybrid. Fusing a rounded cubic form and the naïve, icon-like face and legs of a Shiba-inu, made for an image that is neither dog, nor geometric shape, but rather a pet-rock-like friend sitting in the seat of your car.

Profile
1月22日生まれの男の子。血液型は新型。東京在住。マイペースな性格で、趣味はドライブとお昼寝とインターネット。運転はできないけどドライブが大好きで、ピノの気持ちいいシートの上がお気に入り。好きな食べ物はチョコレート。今は、コーディネートにハマっている。

Male, born on January 22. Blood type: new. Lives in Tokyo. Self-paced, his hobbies are taking drives, naps, and surfing the Internet. He can't drive, but loves going for drives, and Pino's comfy seats are his favorite. He likes chocolate. He's into interior coordination at the moment.

ウェブサイト　Website

すごいあわ　Sugoi awa　　家庭用製品（チャーミー「泡のチカラ」）　Home Products (CHARMY "Awa no Chikara")

CL, SB: ライオン　Lion Corporation　　CD: 柳島康治　Koji Yanagishima　　AD: 近田郁子　Ikuko Konda　　D: 生駒香織　Kaori Ikoma　　I: 南家こうじ　Koji Nanke　　CM Planner: 山中律子　Ritsuko Yamanaka / 鈴木聡　Satoshi Suzuki　　Direction: 藤田淳一　Junichi Fujita　　Animation Production: ナイスデー・トゥーン　NICE-DAY Toon　　DF: ジェ・シー・スパーク　J.C.SPARK inc　　Japan

Concept
台所用洗剤「CHARMY泡のチカラ」の商品特徴は「泡」であり、つぎ足しなしで一気に洗えるのがウリ。「この新商品を最も喜ぶのは誰だろう？」という問いからキャラクター開発が始まり、「いつも洗剤をつけられるスポンジが一番喜ぶはず」というアイデアのもと、豊かな泡を、豊かな髪のようになびかせた「すごいあわ」さんが生まれた。スポンジは2次元アニメ、泡は実際に撮影した3次元の泡の映像を用い、CGで加工している。2次元と3次元の違和感から、より泡に目がいく仕掛けになっている。

The dishwashing liquid CHARMY Awa no Chikara is distinguished by its foam, and its main selling point is the ability to wash up without extra detergent. Her creators figured that the dishwashing sponge would be the happiest with this new product, and Sugoi Awa with her head of foam was born. The sponge was designed using 2D animation and the foam a CG-manipulated 3D image of actual foam. The contrast between two and three dimensions is a device to draw the eye more readily to the bubbles.

Profile
明るく社交的で新しいもの好き。キメ細やかで豊かな泡を頭に載せている。汚れてしまったお皿くんたちを見ると放っておけない姉御肌。体全部を使ってお皿くんたちの汚れを落としていく様は圧巻。決め台詞は「つぎ足しなしで、一気に洗うわよ！」趣味はもちろん食器洗い。愛称は「泡奥さま」。

Cheery, sociable and keen on new things, she's fussy too. With a big head of foam, she can't leave dirty dishes alone. Her stock phrase is "I'll wash'em all at once, no need for top-ups!" Her hobby is of course washing dishes, and her nickname, "Mrs. Bubbles".

POP

製造　Manufacture　　101

キューボと仲間たち　CUBO & FRIENDS

自動車メーカー　Auto Manufacturers

CL: 日産自動車　Nissan Motor Co., Ltd.　Agency: TBWA＼HAKUHODO / 博報堂　HAKUHODO Inc.　SB: タロアウト　tarout　Japan

Concept

CUBEが持つこだわりの外観と居心地のよい内観から、箱庭のような世界を創り上げた。ドライブの楽しさを伝えるために、街や郊外、宇宙などのドライビングスポットCUBOXを用意し、それぞれのCUBOXをホームとするキャラクターを設定。彼らはメインキャラクターであるキューボの運転するCUBEに乗り、そのほかのCUBOXに移動、さまざまな表情を見せる。ユーザーが複数のCUBOXを用意することでより楽しむことができ、キャラクターのたくさんの表情を楽しめることを目的とした。

A box-garden-like world was created from the CUBE's distinctive exterior and comfortable interior. To convey the fun of driving, the CUBOX of driving spots ranging from city to suburbs to outer space were created, each being the home of one of the characters. They board the main character CUBO's CUBE visiting the different CUBOX spots and showing info along the way. The aim in providing multiple CUBOXES was to make acquiring all the info from all the characters more fun.

Profile

日産自動車「キューブ」のスペシャルコンテンツ「Cube Blog」のブログシール、CUBOXのキャラクター。CUBEのドライバーであるキューボは、CUBEとドライブと友達が大好き。愛犬キュービーや元気で活発な女の子ニッキー、おしゃまなリンラちゃん、シャイな野うさぎピナ、物静かで思慮深いシンタローとフレンドリーなアシュー。個性的で愉快な仲間たちを連れ出し「CUBOX」内のスポットを巡る。

The blog seal for the Cube Blog segment of the Nissan CUBE website and the character for the CUBOX. CUBO is a CUBE driver. He loves his CUBE, driving and his friends: Cubie the dog, the high-spirited girl Nikki, precocious Rinra-chan, the shy bunny Pina, quiet and prudent Shintaro, and friendly Ashu. CUBO takes the fun-loving gang to CUBOX spots.

壁紙　Wall Paper

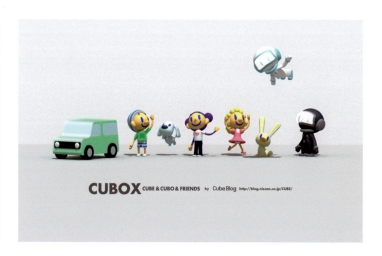

ハコロボ チョコラッタ　Hakorobo Cioccolata　おもちゃメーカー　Toy Manufacturer

CL: セガトイズ SEGA TOYS CO., LTD.　CD, D: 平井カズ Kazu Hirai　Music: Jaermulk Manhattan　DF, SB: フリフリカンパニー Furi Furi Company　Japan

Concept

大きさわずか2cm角のキュートな立方体ロボット「ハコロボ」。ちょこちょこと歩くその素体を使用しオリジナル設定を盛り込むことで、チョコラッタというキャラクターを制作。チョコレートをコンセプトに3色のキャラクターをデザインした。

Sega Toys sells a range of cute little robots measuring only 2cm square. The Cioccolatas were created by taking plain models of these little walking robots and creating three chocolate characters in different colors.

Profile

街の片隅にひっそりとある小さなスイーツショップのパティシエが、素敵な魔法をかけてチョコレートに命を吹き込むことでできあがるチョコラッタたち。パティシエの作るチョコレートは、勇気のでる味や優しくなる味……チョコラッタたちは、周りのみんなを幸せにするためにトコトコと歩いていく。

The Cioccolatas are the creation of the patissier of a little sweet shop tucked away in a corner of town, who employed magic to breathe life into his chocolates. There's a flavor to give courage, a flavor to add kindness... Pottering about on their little legs, the Cioccolatas make the lives of everyone around them a little happier.

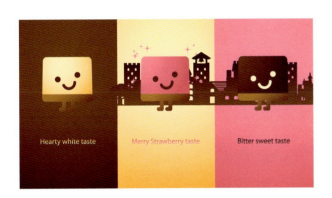

ハコロボ カク家族　Hakorobo Kakukazoku　おもちゃメーカー　Toy Manufacturer

CL: セガトイズ SEGA TOYS CO., LTD.　CD, AD: 青木克憲 Katsunori Aoki　I: あべ たみお Tamio Abe　DF, SB: バタフライ・ストローク butterfly・stroke inc.　Japan

Concept

ハコロボはちょこちょこと歩くメインキャラクターと、マグネットの磁力によりメインキャラを引きつけたり引き離したりするサブキャラクター2体の対の計3体セット。この遊び方の特徴を活かし、家族という世界観を構築することで、ストーリー性という付加価値を与えた。その遊び方も、キャラクター達の関係性もユーザーのクリエイティビティに委ねられるという、能動的に楽しむことのできるおもちゃである。

Hakorobo (box robots) are a set of three characters: the main character with his toddling gait and two sub-characters with magnets inside who attract and release the main character. Taking advantage of this form of play and building a family atmosphere, the value of a story-like nature was added. A toy actively enjoyed that charges the user with determining the method of play and the relationship between characters.

Profile

カク家族は2cm角のちょこちょこ歩くキュートな小型ロボット一家。前歯がかわいい純真無垢なボーイと妹のガールちゃん。そしてペットのドッグ。危険な香りのするパパと優しいママ。陽気なアニとアネ。ガンコなジジとのんきなババ。We are KAKUKAZOKU!!

Hakorobo Kakukazoku is a family of 2 cm cube robots with a characteristic shuffle: Pure-white Boy with his endearing single front tooth, his younger sister Girl, and their pet dog; papa, with his dangerous air and tenderhearted mama; cheery big brother and sister; and bullheaded granpa and happy-go-lucky granma. We are Kakukazoku!!

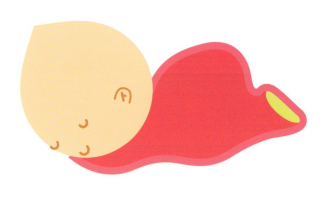

1 | 2

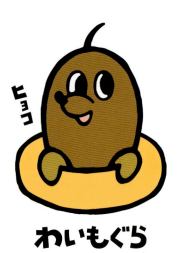

3 | 4

5

1. 3分クッキングお試しプレゼントキャンペーン キャラクター　**Character of 3 Minutes Cooking Present Campign**　食品メーカー　Food Manufacturer / CL: キユーピー　Q.P. Corporation
　　AD: 細島雄一　Yuichi Hosojima　Character Design: マッシュルームカフェ　mushroom cafe　SB: サンクディレクションズ　CINQ DIRECTIONS INC.　Japan
2. キユーピーベビーフード雑誌広告 キャラクター　**Character of Q.P Baby Food Magazine AD**　食品メーカー　Food Manufacturer / CL: キユーピー　Q.P. Corporation
　　AD: 細島雄一　Yuichi Hosojima　Character Design: マッシュルームカフェ　mushroom cafe　SB: サンクディレクションズ　CINQ DIRECTIONS INC.　Japan
3. わいもぐら　**Waimogura**　食品メーカー（カップスナック「わいも！」）　Food Manfacturer (Snack "Waimo!") / CL: 湖池屋　KOIKEYA Co., Ltd.　CD, AD, D, I, SB: Maniackers Design　Japan
4. **Cloud 9 Airplane**　トイレットペーパー製造　Toilet Paper Company / CL: Cloud9　CD, AD, D, I: John Sayles　DF, SB: Sayles Graphic Design　USA
5. **Robochan**　ソフトウェア　Software Company / CL: Robochan LLC　DF, SB: Meomi Design　USA

うまたせ！ UMATASE!   競馬（うまたせ！ キャンペーン） Horse Racing (UMATASE! Campaign)

CL: 特別区競馬組合 TOKYO METROPOLITAN RACING ASSOCIATION　CD: 宇和川泰道 Yasumichi Uwagawa / 長谷川和夫 Kazuo Hasegawa / 栗原敏雄 Toshio Kurihara　AD: 立石義博 Yoshihiro Tateishi / 稲葉光昭 Mitsuaki Inaba　D: 平山 敦 Atsushi Hirayama / 上田崇史 Takashi Ueda / 松田典子 Noriko Matsuda / 野村恭平 Kyohei Nomura　P: 平間 至 Itaru Hirama / 瀬尾 隆 Takashi Seo　I: 鬼塚奉宏 Tomohiro Onizuka　CW: 吉村 泰 Tai Yoshimura / 鈴木 勝 Masaru Suzuki / 米村大介 Daisuke Yonemura / 石松かおり Kaori Ishimatsu / 小林智拡 Tomohiro Kobayashi / 高橋朋之 Tomoyuki Takahashi　DF: 中野直樹広告事務所 NAKANO NAOKI ADVERTISING OFFICE　SB: 電通関西支社「TOKYOROOM」 DENTSU INC. KANSAI tokyoroom　Japan

Concept
べーっとだらしなく出した舌。何か文句を言いたそうな鋭い目つき。決して媚びない、毒のある表情。ただ単純にかわいいだけでなく、人間の心にひそむ本音や愚痴を代弁できるようなキャラクターに設定。素直だし、真面目だし、やる気はあるけど怠け者。それでいてどこか憎めない存在となるよう心がけた。直立している前髪には男としてのこだわりが見え隠れしている。

His tongue sticking out in a lax sort of way, a sharp look in his eyes as if he has something to say. By no means a flatterer, he has a venomous look. Not simply cute, he was fashioned as a character that can be a spokesman of human motives and complaints. He is meek, serious, willing, but lazy. That said, care was taken to make him a character that would be hard to dislike. His spiked forelock reveals his particularity as a man.

Profile
TCKの応援団長であり、宣伝部長でもあり、グルメリポーターでもある「うまたせ！」。実は馬ではなく、ひとりの男である。30歳、独身。好きな食べ物は、TCK場内にある牛すじ串と自分のカラーに似ている理由からプリン。お昼寝が大好きな怠け者だが、「うまたせ！ 徒然ウマ日記」というブログを書いている。

UMATASE! is a TCK (Tokyo City Keiba) cheerleader, a publicity manager and a gourmet reporter. He's not really a horse, but a man: 30 years old and single. His favorite foods are the beef sinew kabobs sold at the TCK racetrack and pudding because its similar to him in color. He's a bit of an idler who love's afternoon naps, but manages to write the blog "UMATASE! Diary of an idle horse".

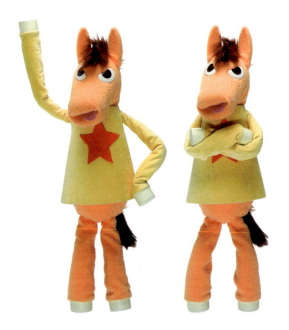

ポスター Poster

ポスター　Poster

ポスター　Poster

≫ うまたせ！ UMATASE!

ポスター　Poster

ストッキング
Stockings

お面付きポスター　Poster with Plastic Mask

お面　Plastic Mask

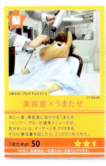

トレーディングカード　Trading Cards

ミニカー　Miniature Car

ボディーウォッシュ　Body Wash

レクリエーション　Recreation

P45くん　Piyongo kun　　総合アミューズメント（プロジェクト45）　Amusement (Project 45)

CL: フィールズ　FIELDS CORPORATION　　CD, AD: 青木克憲　Katsunori Aoki　　I: あべ たみお　Tamio Abe　　SB: バタフライ・ストローク　butterfly・stroke inc.　　Japan

Concept
分かりやすさを打ち出し、プロジェクトタイトルそのものをキャラクターに設定。プロジェクトの遂行をキャラクター自身が表現、一生懸命にカラダを張っている姿をユニークに描いた。

In an attempt to be very easy to understand, the project title itself was made a character. Drawn in a unique way such the character goes out of his way to promote the fact that he is a character promoting the project.

Profile
パチンコファンの人口拡大を目指す「プロジェクト45」のメインキャラクター、P45（ピヨンゴ）くん。

Piyongo kun is the main character for Project 45, a campaign to expand the pachinko-loving population.

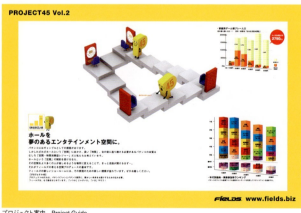

プロジェクト案内　Project Guide

ニコ アンド ラフラフ　Nico & Laugh Rough　ミュージアム Museum

CL: ロボットミュージアム　ROBOT MUSEUM　CD: 仲里カズヒロ　Kazuhiro Nakazato　Coordinator: 庄野裕晃　Hiroaki Shono　SB: ジャイロウォーク　GYROWALK Inc.　Japan

Concept

2006年秋、ロボットと人をつなぐ夢の空間として名古屋にオープンしたロボットミュージアムのキャラクター。どんな世代にもロボットだとひと目で分かるようなデザインを心がけつつ、無表情になりがちなロボットにスマイルを施した。「ロボットはもはや機械ではなく、共存していくパートナーである」という考えのもとこのキャラクターを制作し、人とロボットの明るい未来を、平和で楽しげな表情に託した。

Mascot characters for the ROBOT MUSEUM opened in Nagoya in autumn 2006 as a dream-world linking robots and humans. Care was taken to make them instantly recognizable as robots to people of all ages, and make them smiling (as robots tend to be expressionless). They were produced to embody the idea that "robots are not machines, but partners in living", and imbued with pleasant peaceful expressions to suggest a bright future for man and robot.

Profile

水色のニコは好奇心が旺盛な子供型トモダチロボット。乗り物が大好きで車や電車に乗っくると機嫌が良い。見かけによらずスポーツ好きの負けず嫌い。オレンジ色のラフラフは面倒見のいい世話好きロボット。生き物を育てることが得意で、歌やダンスが大好き。時々古〜いダジャレを言ってしまう。

Nico the light blue Tomodachi (friend) Robot, abounds in curiosity. He loves vehicles and when riding in a car or train is full of glee. Despite his appearance, he likes sports and is very competitive. Laugh Rough is orange, loves taking care of living creatures, likes to sing and dance, and sometimes comes out with very old puns.

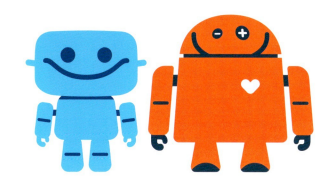

ポストカード　Postcard

缶バッジ　Badge

U-E

イベント事業 Event Industry

CL: Urban Explorers Festival   CD, AD, D, I: Ivo Schmetz / Paul Rickus   DF, SB: 310k   The Netherlands

Concept

フェスティバルは「アーバン・エクスプローラー・フェスティバル」と呼ばれていることから、あらゆるデザインワークを探求するキャラクターを制作。シンプルでありながら強さのある、小さなキャラクターに仕上がった。目の表情によって、感情を表現する。探求／探検というコンセプトやキャラクターには、自分たちがかつて遊んでいた、パックマン、ドンキーコングのような昔のゲームの影響がうかがえる。

Because the event is called the Urban Explorers Festival, we decided to make a character that could be used for exploring all the design works. U-E became a simple but strong little character who expresses his feelings with his eyes. The exploring concept and character were clearly influenced by the classic '80s games we used to play such as Pacman and Donkey Kong.

Profile

U-Eは探求／探検をするミステリアスでダークなキャラクター。男なのか女なのかもわからない。コーラとチョコレートと実験的な音楽、ダンス、アートが好き。

U-E is an exploring character, mysterious and dark. It's not even clear if it's a girl or a boy. (S)he likes cola, chocolate and experimental music, dance, and art.

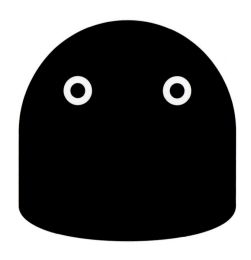

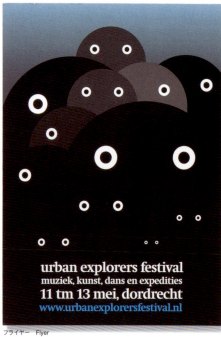

フライヤー　Flyer

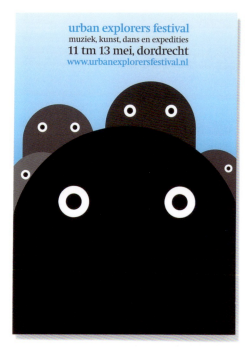

ステッカー　Sticker

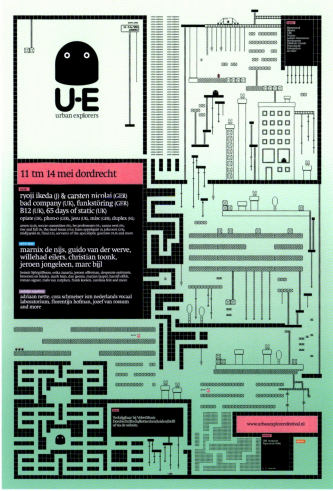

ポスター　Poster

ステッカー　Sticker

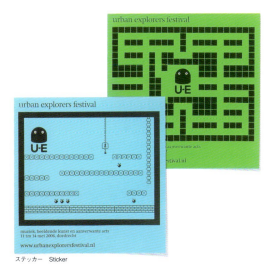

ステッカー　Sticker

チケット　Ticket

レクリエーション　Recreation

パトン＆クーピー　　PATON & COOPEE　　レジャープール施設　Swimming Pool

CL: ヤマハ発動機　プール事業部　YAMAHA MOTOR CO.,LTD　　I: 矢倉可菜　Kana Yagura　　DF, SB: リ・ポート　RE-PORT CO.,LTD　Japan

Concept
兵庫県神戸市六甲アイランドの大型スポーツ・コンプレックス「デカパトス in Rokko Island」のキャラクターとしてデザイン。デカパトスでは、夏シーズン開園のレジャープールのほか、一年を通じてインラインスケートなどのXゲームやフットサルも楽しめる。プール施設には架空の動物「花グマ」を設定し、元気でかわいらしく健康的なイメージで子どもたちのスポーツライフを提案。阪神淡路大震災から10年目の年、震災当時全壊した大型プール跡地北側に開園し、地域住民待望のプール施設復活の意味からも、愛されるキャラクターを目指した。

The mascot characters for the Dekapathos sports center in Kobe. In addition to a leisure pools open in summer, visitors can enjoy X-Games such as inline skating. PATON, the imaginary animal known as the flower-nosed coati, was designed with a charming and healthy image to encourage children to do sports. The park opened ten years after the Kobe earthquake at the former site of a city pool and as the new facility fulfilled the hopes of local residents, we aimed to create a character they would love.

Profile
花グマのパトンちゃんは、正義感の強いがんばり屋。特技は泳ぐことで、夢はプールの安全を守るライフセイバー。日本中のプールを転々として、現在はデカパトスで修行中。クーピー君はカナヅチだけどプールが大好き。だから二人はいつも一緒、大の仲良し。

PATON the flower-nosed coati is tenacious and has a strong sense of justice. Her talent is swimming, and her dream is to be a lifeguard. She goes from pool to pool throughout Japan, and is currently training at Dekapathos. COOPEE can't swim but loves swimming pools. Thus the two are best of friends, and always together.

チラシ　Flyer

ハンドタオル　Towel

モリー、モモリー、アニモリー mory, momory, animory

新聞社、放送事業（世界の巨大恐竜博2006）
Newspaper Company, Broadcasting (The Gigantic Dinasaur Expo 2006)

CL: 日本経済新聞社　NIKKEI Inc. / NHKエンタープライズ　NHK ENTERPRISES Inc.　AD, D: 山下浩平（マウンテンマウンテン）　Kohei Yamashita (mountain mountain)
SB: マウンテンマウンテン　mountain mountain　Japan

Concept
一般公募から選ばれた小学生のイラストをもとにデザイン化。世界に緑を増やすため世界中を旅し、キレ者でクールな兄のアニモリーや、甘えん坊だが優しく兄思いで、歌が得意な妹モモリーなど、兄妹キャラクターを追加設定し、キャラクターの幅をもたせた。http://www.kyoryu.jp/に詳しく紹介されている。

The design was based on a drawing by two elementary school students selected through an open contest. By adding family members, such as his shrewd big brother animory who travels the world campaigning for more green and their somewhat spoilt little sister momory who's sweet to her brothers and loves to sing, the character's range was expanded. They are introduced at www.kyoryu.jp.

Profile
モリーはアメリカ・ワイオミング州モリソン層生まれの恐竜の男の子。人が集まるところが大好き。おっとりして見えるが、卵の殻のサッカーではリーダーを務める。好きな食べ物はシダの葉。世界一の恐竜になることが夢。手に持っている骨は憧れの兄、アニモリーの旅土産で、驚きの使い方があるらしい。

mory is a dinosaur cub born in the Morrison Formation in Wyoming. He loves place where people gather. Although he looks docile, he's actually a leader in eggshell soccer. He dreams of being number one some day. His favorite food is fern fronds. He uses the bone he holds, which was a souvenir from his big brother animory whom he worships, in a very curious way.

©世界の巨大恐竜博2006

ピンバッジ　Pin Badge

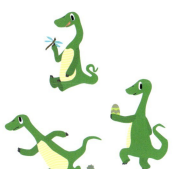 

ルチカちゃん　Ruchika

新聞社（国立ロシア美術館展）　Newspaper Company (The State Russian Museum)

CL, SB: 産経新聞社　THE SANKEI SHIMBUN　D: 丸山朋子　Tomoko Maruyama　Japan

Concept
ロシアを代表する美術館「国立ロシア美術館」所蔵の油彩画を中心とした展覧会であることをPRするため、ロシアの代表的な民芸品・マトリョーシカをベースにし、絵画展であることから絵筆とパレットを持たせた。全体的に"素朴さ"を出すため、頭巾が目立つようシンプルにアイボリー1色に。当初はストラップのみの制作予定だったが、割引引き換え券を配布したところ好評だったため、ステッカー・ミニレターセットを制作した。

Because the character was designed to promote an exhibition revolving around oil paintings from The State Russian Museum, she was based on the popular Russian handicraft, the matryoshka doll, and holds a paintbrush and palette in her hands. Her kerchief was emphasized to give her a feeling of naiveté by keeping the overall coloration a simple ivory. The original plan was to produce only a mobile phone strap, but after favorably noticed on the discount coupons, stickers and mini letter sets were produced as well.

Profile
ロシア・サンクトペテルブルク出身の15歳の女の子。図書館長の父と専業主婦の母との間に生まれる。5歳年下の妹と愛猫をとても可愛がっている。校外学習で訪れたロシア美術館で絵画の魅力に取り憑かれ、将来は画家になることを決意。日々、マイ絵筆とパレットを持って絵画制作に熱中している。

A 15-year-old girl from St. Petersburg, Russia. Her father is a library director, her mother a housewife. She loves her 10-year-old sister and her cat. Ever since she was taken by the beauty of the paintings she saw on a trip to the Russian Museum, she's been bent on becoming a painter and practices every day.

©Tomoko Maruyama

チラシ　Flyer　　ステッカー　Sticker　　　　　　　　　　ミニレター　Mini Letter

レクリエーション　Recreation

せおいクン、ともえチャン　Seoi-kun, Tomoe-chan　　テレビ局　TV Station

CL: フジテレビジョン　Fuji Television Network, Ink.　CD: 川植浩治　Koji Kawaue　AD, D, I: 池田享史　Takafumi Ikeda　I: 黒木南郷　Nango Kuroki　DF, SB: デザインサービス　design service　Japan

Concept
エジプト・カイロで行われた「世界柔道2005」のキャラクター。"柔道→ニッポンのうまさ→おにぎり"という流れで誕生した。ポスターやCF、手ぬぐいなどあらゆるシーンで技を披露し、活躍を収めた。

The characters for the 2005 World Judo Championships held in Cairo, Egypt. They were born of a string of associations: judo→Japanese exquisiteness→onigiri (rice balls). They showed their skills and participated actively in commercials and on posters, Japanese-style hand towels and other novelties.

Profile
天真爛漫なともえチャンは、百戦錬磨のスーパースター。頑張り屋のせおいクンは、日々精進を怠らない努力家。だけど、ともえチャンにはめっぽう弱い。

The unaffected and openhearted Tomoe-chan is a highly accomplished superstar. Doggedly persistent, Seoi-kun devotes himself to constant, rigorous training, but has one weakness: Tomoe-chan.

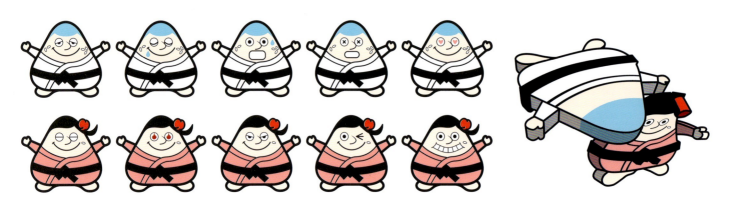

屋外広告　Outdoor AD

ポスター　Poster

TVCM

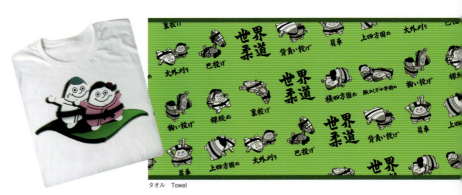

タオル　Towel

116　レクリエーション　Recreation

カンゴルー Kangoroo スポーツ事業 Sports Industry

CL: 大塚ベバレジ　クリスタルガイザーレディスゴルフトーナメント　Otsuka Beverage Co., Ltd.　Crystal Geyser Ladies Golf Tournament　CD, AD: 佐野研二郎　Kenjiro Sano　D, I: 小杉幸一　Koichi Kosugi
D: 岡本和樹　Kazuki Okamoto / 原野賢太郎　Kentaro Harano　SB: 博報堂　HAKUHODO Inc.　Japan

Concept
女子プロゴルフツアー「クリスタルガイザーレディスゴルフトーナメント」のオフィシャルキャラクター「カンゴルー」。カンガルーをモチーフにし、ゴルフ場のグリーンに映えるイエローをベースにして、これからの女子ゴルフがよりカジュアルでポップなスポーツに見えるようデザインした。

Kangoroo is an official character of Crystal Geyser Ladies' Golf Tournament overseen. The yellow color was chosen for this kangaroo character against the green background of the golf courses, reflecting the desire to see women's golf be more pop and casual.

Profile
ゴルフが大好きなカンガルー。水分補給するため、おなかのポケットにクリスタルガイザーを入れている。暑い日には、心配してみんなにそれを配ってくれる優しい心の持ち主。好物はグリーンの草。

A kangaroo, crazy about golf, who carries Crystal Geyser in its pouch for hydration. On hot days, this gentle Kangoroo is worried about players and hands out bottles to all. Green grass is her favorite.

1

2　3

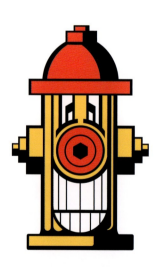

4　5

1. ダルテくん **Darute-kun** スポーツ事業 Sports Industry / CL: 日本フットボールリーグ・アルテ高崎 ARTE TAKASAKI　CD, AD, D, I, SB: Maniackers Design　Japan
2. スターマちゃん **Miss STARMA** スポーツ事業 Sports Industry / CL: ホワイトスター高崎 2007 WHITE STAR Takasaki 2007　CD, AD, D, I, SB: Maniackers Design　Japan
3. 丼丼 **DONDON** 野球チーム Baseball Team / CL: 茨城ゴールデンゴールズ GOLDEN GOLDS　CD: 糸井重里 Shigesato Itoi　AD: 秋山具義 Gugi Akiyama　D: 加藤博明 Hiroaki Katou
　　　　　DF, SB: デイリー・フレッシュ Dairy Fresh　Japan
4. **Fire Fest** イベント Community Event / CL: Des Moines Fire Department　CD, AD, D, I: John Sayles　DF, SB: Sayles Graphic Design　USA
5. **Clock** イベント Community Event / CL: Iowa State Fair　CD, AD, D, I: John Sayles　DF, SB: Sayles Graphic Design　USA

Commerce & Retail
流通・販売

OPENちゃん　OPEN-chan　コンビニエンスストア　Convenience Store

CL: President Chain Store corporation　　CD: 中澤真純　Masumi Nakazawa　　AD: 平田 優　Yu Hirata　　D: 山下紀如　Noriyuki Yamashita / 扇原康成　Yasunari Ogihara / 内山えり奈　Erina Uchiyama
CW: 島森奈津子　Natsuko Shimamori　　DF: プレーリー　Prairie. Inc.　　SB: 電通　DENTSU INC.　Japan

Concept

商品やサービスで消費者の心もOPENにしたい、という思いから「OPENちゃん」に決定。日本のキャラクターの人気が高い台湾で展開、台湾企業のオリジナルキャラクターであることを意識し、これまでにない姿を開発するとともに、「OPEN」というコンセプトをビジュアル的に表現することを目指した。また、台湾の人々は家族を大切にすることから、仲間キャラクターも多数制作。店舗ではオリジナル商品が発売され、WEBでの展開にもファンが多い。

OPEN-chan was born of the desire to get consumers to open their hearts through products and services. An original character for a Taiwanese company for use in Taiwan where Japanese characters are popular, the aim was to develop an image like no other to date, and to visualize the "OPEN" concept. Because the Taiwanese place great value on the family, a number of fellow characters were also created. Original products were sold in stores, and developed a great many fans upon introduction on the Web.

Profile

2005年に登場したキャラクター。人の心をOPENにする修行のため、OPEN星からやってきた宇宙犬、OPENちゃん。スフィンクスのような「OPENヘッド」を持つ。OPENちゃんが嬉しくて「OPEN」な気持ちになるとOPENヘッドが全開になり、逆に、悲しくなるとヘッドがしぼんでしまう。

Debuted in 2005. OPEN-chan is a spacedog from the planet OPEN who came to help people to open their hearts. He has an "OPEN head" much like that of the Sphinx. When he's feeling happy and open-minded his headdress opens fully, but when he's sad it withers.

紙コップ　Paper Cup

≫ OPENちゃん　OPEN-chan

クリアファイル　Clear File

ステッカー　Sticker

ダイアリー　Diary

フィギュア　Figure

流通・販売　Commerce & Retail

ぬいぐるみ　Stuffed Toy

フィギュア　Figure

流通・販売　Commerce & Retail

ワオン WAON

流通業（電子マネー「ワオン」） Commerce (Prepaid Electric Money "WAON")

CL: イオン　AEON Co., Ltd.　　CD: 佐々木 宏（シンガタ）　Hiroshi Sasaki (Shingata Inc.)　　AD: 田中竜介（ドラフト）　Ryusuke Tanaka (DRAFT)　　DF: ドラフト　DRAFT　　SB: 電通　DENTSU INC.　　Japan

Concept
ワオンという名は、色々な音が調和して奏でられる美しい「和音」に由来している。色々な人が、色々なお店で、色々な場面で、色々な思いを込めて、WAONを利用する際に、「いつでも隣にいるペットのような存在となるように」との願いが込められている。

The name WAON derives from the sound of a beautiful "chord"(waon) that harmonizes myriad sounds. WAON was born out of the idea of a pet-like existence that would always be there by the sides of myriad people, in myriad shops and myriad situations, with myriad ideas in mind when they use WAON.

Profile
ワオンの特技はお買い物。「お得」や「便利」を持ち主のために見つけるのが得意。世間ではまだ珍しい存在の「ワオン」という種類の犬で、カッコイイ首輪が「血統書付きのワオン」のしるし。

WAON's talent is shopping: finding bargains and conveniences for his master. The WAON being still a rare breed of dog in the world today, his very chic collar attests to his pedigree.

電子マネー「WAON」
Prepaid Electric Money "WAON"

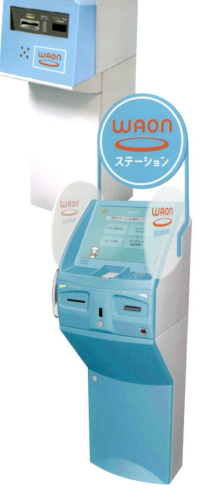

雑誌広告　Magazine AD

流通・販売　Commerce & Retail

タンブラー　Tumbler

TVCM

ピンバッジ　Pin Badge

流通・販売　Commerce & Retail

パルコカード キャラクター　Character of PARCO CARD　商業施設　Commercial Facility

CL: パルコ　PARCO CO., LTD.　CD: 関 一行　Kazuyuki Seki　AD: 秋山具義　Gugi Akiyama　D: 八木ひとみ　Hitomi Yagi / 永楽雅也　Masaya Eiraku　P: 内田将二　Shoji Uchida
DF, SB: デイリー・フレッシュ　Dairy Fresh　Japan

Concept

カードそのものが顔になっていて、様々な季節、用途に合わせて、アイコン的に使用できるよう、汎用性の高いシンプルなデザインとなっている。

With the card itself as its face, the character is simple in design and has great general versatility, so it can be used in different seasons and various applications in an icon-like way.

Profile

ファッションビルPARCOの「PARCO CARD」推進のために生まれたキャラクター。

A character born to promote the PARCO fashion building credit card, PARCO CARD.

ポスター　Poster

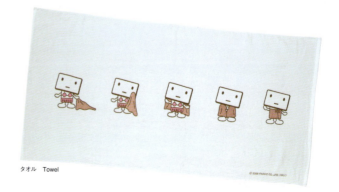
タオル　Towel

ナナコ　nanaco

生活総合産業（電子マネー「nanaco」）(Lifestyle Industries (Prepaid Electric Money "nanaco"))

CL, SB: セブン＆アイ・ホールディングス　Seven & i Holdings Co., Ltd.　Japan

Concept

お買いものをもっと楽しく、便利にする電子マネー「nanaco」。「7」days＝まいにち、いつもの場所で使える身近さ、セブン−イレブンをはじめとする「7つの業態」で使える利便性、など「7」をテーマにキャラクターをデザイン。nanacoの長い首はちょうど数字の「7」に見え、「7」色の模様をもっている。消費者と店舗とを結ぶ鮮やかな架け橋となって、楽しさ、便利さが広がっていくという願いをこめた。

nanaco e-money makes shopping fun and easy. Along with its friendly sound, the name "nanaco" ("seven elements") holds multiple seven-related messages: its coin-like ease of use at Seven & i Holdings, the familiarity of using it at one's regular haunts 7 days a week, and the convenience of the company's seven businesses including SevenEleven. With her thematic seven rainbow colors, nanaco expresses the desire to spread pleasure and convenience by forming a colorful bridge between store and consumer.

Profile

身体に「7」色の模様をもつ、お洒落なキリンの女の子。みんなより少し先がみわたせるため、好奇心があり、新しいものやお買いものが大好き。電子マネー「nanaco」の便利さにいち早く気づいて、一足先に使っている。

nanaco the giraffe, with her long neck shaped like the number 7 and body pattern of seven colors, is a very fashionable little girl. Being able to "see ahead" of others, she tends to fancy things new. She's full of curiosity and loves shopping! She was also quick to realize the convenience of using nanaco.

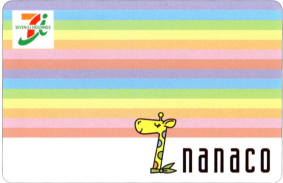

電子マネー「nanaco」　Prepaid Electric Money "nanaco"

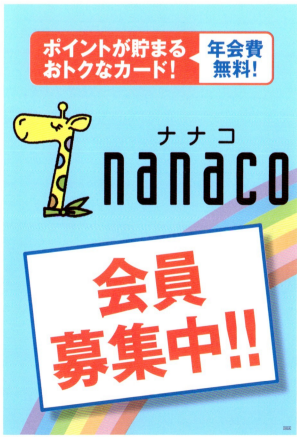

ポスター　Poster

リーフレット　Leaflet

流通・販売　Commerce & Retail

ロクロク星人　The Creatures from Planet 66　ディベロッパー　Developer

CL, SB: 森ビル MORI BUILDING CO., LTD.　CD, AD, D: 村上 隆 Takashi Murakami

©2003 Takashi Murakami / Kaikai Kiki Co., Ltd. All Rights Reserved.

Concept

六本木ヒルズのオープンにあたり、街のキャラクターとして登場したロクロク星人。日本を代表する現代アーティスト、村上 隆氏によって、生まれ変わる六本木のイメージがロクロク星人とともに、カラフルに、生き生きと表現された。実はロクロク星人の胞子から生まれた動物たちのキャラクターがまだたくさんいる設定に。新しいモノやコトを生み出す「クリエイター」ロクロク星人は、六本木ヒルズの体現者であり、その白くて丸いかわいらしいキャラクターは、未来を担う子供たちへの村上氏のメッセージでもある。

The Creatures from Planet 66 appeared as Roppongi Hills' mascot characters upon the opening of the complex, created by Japanese top artist Takashi Murakami to express the colorful and vibrant qualities of Roppongi reborn. According to the concept, there are also a great many animals born from the spores of the Creatures from Planet 66. The cute white round the Creatures from Planet 66, creators of new things, are the personification of Roppongi Hills and Murakami's message to children, the torchbearers of the future.

Profile

宇宙船の赤ちゃんピーちゃんに乗って宇宙から六本木ヒルズにやってきたロクロク星人たちは、シャチョウ、マサムネ、スピカ、ミャンミャン、チェリー、ポヨヨンの6人。彼らは、知の胞子を撒き、生き物たちを進化させたり創造したりして、辿り着いた星を幸せにすることが任務。ブロントサウルスのヨシコとユウコはロクロク星人のピンチに姿を現す仲間。

The Creatures from Planet 66 – ShaCho, MaSaMuNe, SuPiKa, MyanMyan, Cherry, and PoYoYon – came to Roppongi Hills from outer space aboard the baby spaceship Pi-chan. Their task is to scatter spores of wisdom, to evolve living things and create, and to make happy the planet to which they came. Their friends the brontosaurs Yoshiko and Yuko appear whenever the Creatures from Planet 66 find themselves in a pinch.

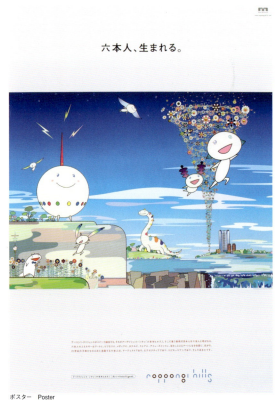

ポスター　Poster

ガイドブック　Guide Book

ポストカード　Postcard

128　流通・販売　Commerce & Retail

エチカちゃん Echika

エキチカ事業、ショッピングセンターの運営・新規開発　In-station Business, Shopping Center Operations

CL, SB: メトロプロパティーズ　Metro Properties Co., Ltd.　　CD: 伊藤浩之　Hiroyuki Ito　　AD: 澤海康弘　Yasuhiro Somi　　D: 小池聡　Satoshi Koike　　Japan

Concept

誰が見てもひと目で「カワイイ」と覚えてもらえて、なおかつ子どもっぽくなり過ぎず、オシャレな大人の街、表参道にふさわしいデザインにこだわった。たとえば、首には高級なファーを巻き、肩にはブランドのバッグをかけるなど、キャラクターとしての愛きょうを残しつつ、どこか洗練された大人の雰囲気を併せ持つ、不思議で魅力的なキャラクターを目指した。

The character had to be regarded as "cute" upon first glance by anyone who sees it, and yet not be too childish, as well as have design qualities befitting the fashionable Omotesando area. By wrapping a classy fur around her neck, for example, or hanging a brand bag from her shoulder, she retains her charm as a character but also reflects the air of a sophisticated adult. The aim was this kind of strange and alluring character.

Profile

キュートでありながら都会的な雰囲気を併せ持つ今どきの女の子「Echika（エチカ）ちゃん」。『不思議の国のアリス』でウサギが主人公のアリスを不思議な穴へと導くように、退屈な日常からワンダーな地下へと誘うエチカちゃんは、「案内人」として「Echika表参道」を楽しくナビゲーションする。

Echika is a cute little city girl of today. Much like Rabbit lured Alice into the hole to Wonderland, Echika invites us from the humdrum of everyday life above into the wonders of the underground and acts as a guide to make navigating Echika Omotesando a fun experience.

メモ　Note Pad　　ステッカー　Sticker

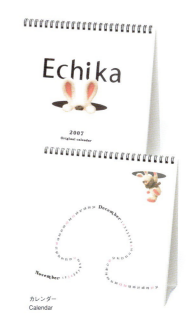
カレンダー　Calendar

絵本　Picture Book

ポスター　Poster

流通・販売　Commerce & Retail

ラゾーナ総理大臣ナゾーラ　NAZOLA Prime Minister of LAZONA

商業施設　Commercial Facility

CL: ラゾーナ川崎プラザ　Lazona kawasaki plaza　　CD: 石川英嗣（石川広告制作室）Hidetsugu Ishikawa　　AD, I, Character Design SB: 西岡範敏（西岡ペンシル）Noritoshi Nishioka　　D: 佐々木 亨　Toru Sasaki / 古川沙苗　Sanae Furukawa / 常門洋一　Yoichi Tsunekado / 伊藤優希　Yuki Itoh　　P: 瀬尾 隆　Takashi Seo　　CW: 小山佳奈　Kana Koyama　　Miniature Produce: 田口雅美　Masami Taguchi　　Stuffed Animal Outfit Production: 山本和弘　Kazuhiro Yamamoto　　DF: たき工房　TAKI CORPORATION　　Japan

Concept

2006年秋、川崎駅西口にオープンした大型商業施設「ラゾーナ川崎プラザ」。その開業告知は、幅広いターゲットや多種多様な店舗をカバーするため、そして他の商業施設との差別化を図るために、「国」という枠組みを採用した。「人生をよくばる国」をコンセプトに、総理大臣ナゾーラと各分野ごとの担当大臣7人で内閣を発足。それぞれ明確に性格づけをしながら、素朴なかわいさと真面目な間抜けさを表現。どこかの内閣とは違い支持率も良好。2007年春には大臣が1人増え、内閣はますますの充実をみせている。

The large-scale shopping mall Lazona Kawasaki opened at Kawasaki Station in autumn 2006. Requiring an opening announcement that would appeal to a broad target market and represent a wide-range of retailers yet set the complex apart from other malls, the framework of a "nation" was used. Based on the concept of "a country hungry for life", a Cabinet was formed of Prime Minister NAZOLA and seven ministers of different fields. While each has a distinctive personality, they all have a simple charm and serious absent-mindedness. Unlike their real-life counterpart, this Cabinet enjoys a high popularity rating. Spring 2007 welcomed another new minister to the lineup.

Profile

「国民すべてのくらしを、楽しく美味しく自分らしくする」をモットーに、ラゾーナの顔としてイベントや広報活動にいそしむ。とぼけたキャラクターで、時々ほかの総理大臣に突っ込まれながらも穏やかに意見をまとめている。その他の大臣も担当の持ち場ごとにライフスタイルの提案を行っている。

Working hard as the face of Lazona at events and promotional activities, with "may every citizen live joyfully, deliciously and in his or her way" as his motto. A bit absentminded, he is sometimes probed by other PMs, but presents his opinions in a genial way. The other ministers also propose lifestyles in conjunction with their posts of charge.

ステッカー　Sticker

蒲田駅 Kamata Station　武蔵小杉駅 Musashi Kosugi Station　品川駅 Shinagawa Station

ポスター　Poster

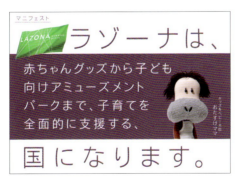

ポスター　Poster

流通・販売　Commerce & Retail　131

吉BOO YOSHIBOO 外食産業 Food Service Industry

CL: 吉野家 YOSHINOYA Co., Ltd.　CD: 中澤真純 Masumi Nakazawa　AD: 平田 優 Yu Hirata　D: 山下紀如 Noriyuki Yamashita　D: 内山えり奈 Erina Uchiyama　CW: 島森奈津子 Natsuko Shimamori
DF: プレーリー Prairie. Inc.　SB: 電通 DENTSU INC.　Japan

Concept
「ぶた丼」という商品を擬人化したものではなく、ぶた丼を応援するために自ら丼に入った、ぶた丼サポーターという設定。主力商品「牛丼」が戻るまでという宿命を背負っていたため、単にかわいいだけではない、哀愁漂う後ろ姿や世界観が作られている。吉ブー得意の「お持ち帰りポーズ」は商品をお持ち帰りできる吉野家ならではのデザイン。「ボクをおもちかえりする?」とささやく吉ブーは、WEBで公開されたマンガやストラップとなって登場した。

Rather than personify the pork bowl, YOSHIBOO jumped into the bowl and worked wholeheartedly as a supporter of the product thereby becoming one of the faces of YOSHINOYA. With his arms and legs sticking out of the bowl, his gallant efforts hiding the situation behind his appearance made him not merely cute, but reflect the sad air and world-view behind him. YOSHIBOO's characterisic "take-away pose" was a design unique to YOSHINOYA's takeout service. His modest "won't you take me home?" appeal appeared in manga etc following its Web debut.

Profile
長い旅に出たGYUちゃん(吉ギュー)の代わりに看板ブタとして大抜擢された吉ブー。「吉ブーWEB店」では店長になることを夢見て働いていたが、GYUちゃんの帰国に伴い、サポーターの役目を終え、今は世界を放浪中。キャンペーン時にはストラップ等のグッズとなり、ファンを集めた。

YOSHINOYA selected YOSHIBOO as their pork bowl supporter in place of YOSHIGYU who was away on a long journey. BOO worked hard in hopes of someday becoming manager of the "YOSHIBOO WEB store", but was made redundant upon GYU's return. He's now bumming around the world. During the campaign he appeared on novelties such as mobile phone straps and drew a number of fans.

ノベルティー　Novelty

フィギュア　Figure

CD-ROM

マウス＆マウスパッド
Mouse & Mouse Pad

ダイアリー
Diary

流通・販売　Commerce & Retail

サクレツ君 Sakuretsu Kun

家電販売 Electrical Household Retailer

CL: さくらや SAKURAYA CO., LTD　　CD: 小沼恭司 Kyoji Onuma　　AD: 碓井宏和 Hirokazu Usui　　D: 上條恵美 Emi Kamijo / 中田浩介 Kosuke Nakada
Character Design: マッシュルームカフェ mushroom cafe　　SB: サンクディレクションズ CINQ DIRECTIONS INC.　　Japan

Concept
大型家電量販店の勢いを感じさせながらも、みんなに愛される、ちょっと変な生き物としてデザインされている。

Designed to be a somewhat zany creature that would reflect the power of the giant home-appliance retailer yet be loved by all.

Profile
安さ爆発さくらや〜♪の「爆発」のキーワードから生まれたキャラクター。いつもお客様のために跳ね回っている。

A character born out of the keyword "explosive" from the jingle: "low price explosion, SAKURAYA". Ever bouncing about for the sake of the customer.

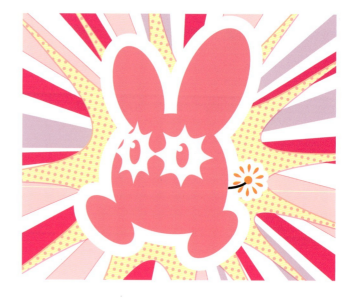

屋外広告　Outdoor AD

134　流通・販売　Commerce & Retail

アルコちゃん、シンちゃん、ゾナちゃん　Alco chan, Shin chan, Zona chan　　百貨店　Department Store

CL: 新宿三越アルコット　SHINJUKU MITSUKOSHI ALCOTT　　AD, D, I, SB: ショーン・ショーノ　sean shono　Japan

Concept
「新宿三越アルコット」がメインターゲットとしている働く女性に、耳よりで素敵な情報をささやき、そして可愛がってもらえるような存在として考案。手のひらに乗るくらいの小さな微笑ましいキャラクター設定にした。

The idea was to come up with charming, pint-sized characters to whisper the latest hot fashion tips in the ears of working women, the main target of SHINJUKU MITSUKOSHI ALCOTT.

Profile
「新宿三越アルコット」のマスコットキャラクター。はるか彼方からやってきた、お姫様のアルコちゃん・王子様のシンちゃん・二人のお友達のゾナちゃん。3人とも地球のスウィーツが大好き。アルコットのお友達として、新しいコトや素敵なコトをキャッチして、みんなの心にたくさんの楽しみを届ける。

Mascots for the SHINJUKU MITSUKOSHI ALCOTT shopping complex, princess Alco chan and prince Shin chan, and their friend Zona chan, are all from a planet far, far away, but lured to Earth by their love of sweets. Acting as the customer's Alcott friends, the trio capture the essence of all that is new, attractive, and full of fun.

ポスター　Poster

ホークスタウンモール キャラクター　Character of Hawks Town mall　　商業施設　Commercial Facility

CL: ホークスタウンモール Hawks Town mall　CD: 山田 彰 Akira Yamada　AD: 酒井理恵子 Rieko Sakai　I: イマイヤスフミ Yasufumi Imai　DF: 西広 Nishiko.Co., Ltd. Artist Agency, SB: ヴィジョントラック visiontrack　Japan

Concept
ホークスタウンは家族で楽しめるショッピングモールということから、キャラクターのテーマは「ファミリー」。犬を含め6体の仲良し家族という設定にした。キャラクターにスポーツ好き、音楽好き、ショッピング好きなどの特性をもたせ、各訴求ポイントをキャラクターの特性に合わせて紹介する役目を担わせた。見た目でキャラクターの個性を出しながらも、統一感のあるシルエットにすることで、モール内、ポスター、POPなどでキャラクターをピクト・サインとしても扱えるように制作した。

Because Hawks Town is a shopping mall that's fun for the entire family, the theme of the characters is family. They comprise a happy family of six, including the dog. The characters were given different traits – sports-fanatic, music-lover, shopping-freak, etc – and the different features of the mall they promote are consistent with their personalities. They were produced however with a consistent style, that allows them to be used as pictographic signs within the mall, in posters, POP, etc.

リーフレット　Leaflet

ポスター　Poster

流通・販売　Commerce & Retail　135

からあげクン Karaage-kun　コンビニエンスストア Convenience Store

CL: ローソン　LAWSON　　CD: 山田英二　Eiji Yamada　　AD, I: 池田享史　Takafumi Ikeda　　D: 近藤ちはる　Chiharu Kondo　　CW: 中山明子　Akiko Nakayama　　DF: ウルトラグラフィックス　Ultra Graphics
SB: 電通　DENTSU INC.　Japan

Concept
大手コンビニエンスストアで知られる、ローソン開業時からの人気定番商品である「からあげクン」の18年ぶりのリニューアルに伴い、キャラクターも見直しを図った。メインターゲットは、部活帰りにおなかを空かせた中高生。"300円を握りしめ、ラーメンとからあげクンのあいだでココロはゆれる……"そこで、ひと目でわかるキャラクターとして鶏くんを抜擢。4羽の個性で味の違いを表現した。

In conjunction with the first revamping in 18 years of top convenience store chain Lawson's popular product, Karaage-kun, the characters also underwent review. The main target market was junior and senior high school students hungry after participating in extracurricular activities … "with 300 yen in hand, debating between ramen or Karaage-kun." Just then, understandable at a glance, they single out Tori (chicken)-kun. The four birds express the products' four distinctly different seasonings.

Profile
からあげクンは、中高生のアイドル。
Karaage-kun is a junior and senior high school student idol.

スリッパ　Slippers　　　クーポン　Coupon

のぼり　Flag

ポン・デ・ライオンと仲間たち　PON DE LION & His Sweet Friends　ドーナツショップ　Donut Shop

CL, SB: ダスキン ミスタードーナツ事業本部　Mister Donut Business Group, Duskin CO., LTD　CD: 田中義一（電通 関西支社）Yoshikazu Tanaka (DENTSU INC. KANSAI)
CW, Planning: 小出みなみ（電通 関西支社）Minami Koide (DENTSU INC. KANSAI) / 堀内弘誓（電通 関西支社）Hirochika Horiuchi (DENTSU INC. KANSAI) /
佐藤朝子（電通 関西支社）Asako Sato (DENTSU INC. KANSAI)　Producer: 宮林和男（東映シーエム 大阪支社）Kazuo Miyabayashi (Toei Commercial Film co., ltd. Osaka)
Production: 東映シーエム 大阪支社　Toei Commercial Film co.,ltd. Osaka　Agency: 電通 関西支社　DENTSU INC. KANSAI　Japan

Concept
ポン・デ・リング独特の形状が活きるデザインを考え、ライオンのたてがみというアイデアを採用。ミスタードーナツの人気NO1商品として「百獣の王」をイメージ。そのほかの各キャラクターはドーナツの味や形状からイメージしてドーナツのバラエティー感を訴求するため、それぞれに個性のある性格を与え、バランスを考えながら仲間たちを構成した。

In developing an original design for PON DE LION, we decided to make use of the most distinguishing feature of a lion, his mane, and image him after Mister Donuts' most popular item as the "king of the forest". To create a sense of variety, the other characters were each given idiosyncratic personalities built on the distinctive flavors and shapes of the chain's line of donuts, and considering the overall balance, positioned as a community of friends.

Profile
自分を百獣の王だと思い込んでいるポン・デ・ライオン、遊ぶのも昼寝するのも一緒、大の仲良しフレンチウーラー。いたずらが大好きなハニーシッポ、体は大きいけど本当はまだまだ子どもの男の子エンゼルダゾウ。見た目も個性も6人6色、元気いっぱいの6人兄弟D-ピピコなど12キャラクター。

Twelve characters including PON DE LION, who's convinced he's the king of his own forest; his best friend French Wooler who loves to nap and play; the prank-loving Honey Shippo; Angel da zo, already elephantine although still a boy; and highly individualistic sextuplets D-pipiko.

TVCM

カレンちゃん　Miss Caren　自動車販売修理業（Let's DUO! Enjoy VW! webサイト）Automobile Sales and Service (Let's DUO! Enjoy VW! web site)

CL: トヨタカローラ（フォルクスワーゲンDUO高松）TOYOTA CAROLLA (Volkswagen DUO Takamatsu)　CD: 八木泰介 Taisuke Yagi　AD: 綾田真紀子 Makiko Ayada　D: 猪熊信次 Shinji Inokuma
I: 広田桂子 Keiko Hirota　CM Director: フクモト ケンジ Kenji Fukumoto　DF: ポレポレーション・スタジオ polepoletion STUDIO　SB: 電通西日本 高松支社 DENTSU WEST JAPAN INC. TAKAMATSU　Japan

Concept
OL層を中心に、多くの人たちに愛されているフォルクスワーゲンブランド。そのブランドイメージを大切にしつつも、地域に根付いたコミュニケーション展開をさらに充実させ、親しまれ、愛されるディーラーとしてのイメージを確立させるために、外国の絵本のような洒落たかわいさと、子どもっぽすぎない楽しい雰囲気を持たせ、色遣いや手描き感を大切に開発した。

The Volkswagen brand is popular with a great many people, particularly young working women. Honoring the value of that brand image, and building on established local communications to create a friendly, likable image for dealers, a character was developed in different colors with a hand-drawn quality to be fashionable and charming like something out of a foreign picture-book, yet not too childish while maintaining a sense of playfulness.

Profile
パパはドイツ人、ママは日本人。陽気で活発、好奇心いっぱい。どこに行ってもすぐにお友達ができちゃうカレンちゃんは、いつでも街の人気者。歌って踊ることと、愛犬のデュオが大好きな女の子。

Her dad is German, her mom Japanese. She's cheerful, vivacious and full of curiosity. Wherever she goes she instantly makes friends and is always very popular. She likes singing and dancing and loves her dog Duo.

ウェブサイト　Website

笑うだるま WARAU DARUMA 飲食店 Restaurant

CL: ウィン・フードシステム WIN FOOD SYSTEM　　CD, CW: 米村大介 Daisuke Yonemura　　AD, D, I: 立石義博 Yoshihiro Tateishi　　D: 富永マサキ Masaki Tominaga　　DF: ファーストブランド Firstbrand, Inc.
SB: 電通関西支社「TOKYOROOM」 DENTSU INC. KANSAI tokyoroom　Japan

Concept
店舗のテーマカラーでもある黒と白を基調にしてシンプルにデザイン。「黒字になりますように」との願いも込められている。また、クールでニヒルな感じを表現するため、微妙な笑顔の表現を口元だけで調整した。

A simple design was created using the chain's corporate colors of black and white, encompassing the company's wish to be "in the black." To give the character a cool, slightly rebellious feel, expressions are created only with its mouth.

Profile
居酒屋「笑うだるま」のキャラクター。人間が笑うときに必ず現れるという黒いだるま、"笑うだるま"。大笑いするとき、苦笑いするとき、含み笑い、泣き笑い……いろんな笑顔のときに、いろんな表情をして現れる。おいしい食事のある風景にも、笑うだるまはよく見られる。

Character created for an advertising campaign for the WARAU DARUMA (laughing dharma) chain of izakaya (Japanese pubs). The black laughing daruma is said to appear whenever a human being smiles or laughs and is also often spotted where people are enjoying good food.

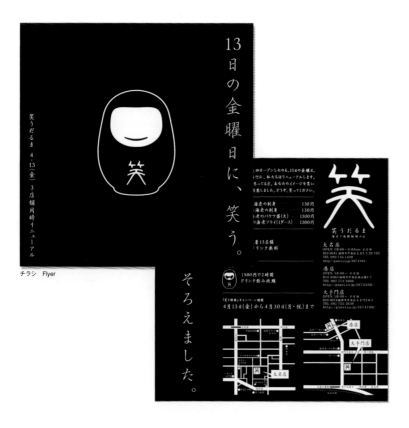

チラシ　Flyer

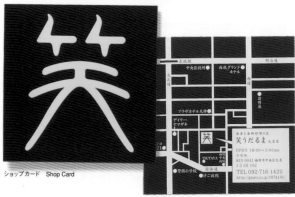

ショップカード　Shop Card

ポスター　Poster

ぷりお PURIO　海鮮類販売 Seafood Sales

CL: ウィン・フードシステム　WIN FOOD SYSTEM　CD, CW: 米村大介　Daisuke Yonemura　AD, D: 立石義博　Yoshihiro Tateishi　I: 羽矢トモコ　Tomoko Haya　DF: アートプロセス　ART PROCESS
SB: 電通関西支社「TOKYOROOM」DENTSU INC. KANSAI tokyoroom　Japan

Concept
"エビ"とひと目で分かりながら、今までに見たこともない海老のキャラクター。表情に敢えて毒を持たせるため、目に個性を持たせた。キャラクターだけでひとり歩きできるような、インパクトの強いキャラクターを目指した。

While obviously a shrimp, this is a shrimp character like no other. PURIO has deliberately been designed with distinctive eyes for a wicked look. The aim was to create a character strong enough to stand alone.

Profile
「誰よりもぷりぷりでいたい。誰よりもプリティでいたい。」海老業界に現れた風雲児、ぷりお。斜めに構えた風貌で、日本人の風習や性格を斬ったりするが、どことなく憎めない存在。大の目立ちたがり屋で、将来は世界進出を目論んでいる。

Striking a defiant pose, buccaneering shrimp adventurer PURIO pulls no punches when it comes to the customs and character of the Japanese, but somehow it's impossible not to like him. A huge show-off, he's already plotting his move onto the world stage.

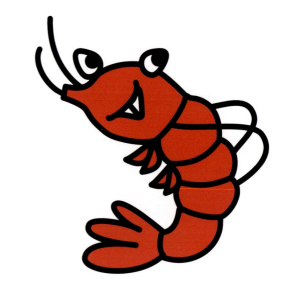

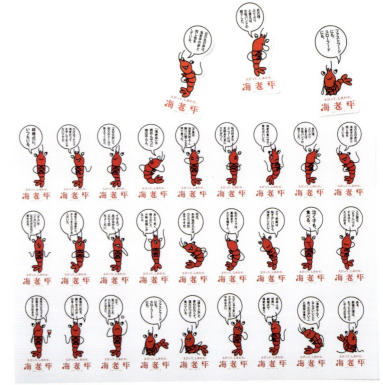

ステッカー　Sticker

ポスター　Poster

流通・販売　Commerce & Retail

ポスター　Poster

1. **Grumpy** バー＆レストラン **Bar & Restaurant** / CL: Grumpy's Bar　DF, SB: Meomi Design　USA
2. **機長さん＆キャビンアテンダントさん　Mr. Captain & Miss Flight Attendant**
   輸入玩具販売　Import Toys Retail / CL: アクタラスカンパニー　actrus company inc.　AD, D, I, SB: Maniackers Design　Japan
3. **Lucy & Matt** 子供服販売 **Children's Clothing** / CL: Look Mum　CD, AD, D, I: John Sayles　DF, SB: Sayles Graphic Design　USA
4. **Spencer** ペットショップ **Pet Store** / CL: Bone-A-Patreat　CD, AD, D, I: John Sayles　DF, SB: Sayles Graphic Design　USA
5. **B-Flat** ミュージックショップ **Music Store** / CL: B-Flat Music　CD, AD, D, I: John Sayles　DF, SB: Sayles Graphic　USA

Public Institution & Organization

公共機関・団体

イズノスケ IZUNOSUKE 地方自治体（伊豆ワカガエル大作戦） Local Government (Operation Izu Rejuvenated)

CL: 静岡県 Shizuoka Pref.　CD: 佐藤雅彦 Masahiko Sato　AD, I, Character Design: 西岡範敏 Noritoshi Nishioka　D: 折重 愛 Ai Orishige　D: 高桑佳奈 Kana Takakuwa　D: 竹山雄平 Yuhei Takeyama
CW: 藤曲厚司 Koji Fujimagari　DF: たき工房 Taki CORPORATION　SB: 西岡ペンシル Nishioka Pencil Co.,Ltd　Japan

Concept

1999年当時の伊豆は、日本を代表する観光地でありながら、構造不況や地震等のために観光客が減少傾向にあった。その現状を見つめ直し、新たな気持ちで新しい伊豆の魅力づくりを実現すべく、心をひとつにして地域を盛り上げ、新しく生まれ変わった伊豆に来てもらおうと1999年12月31日から2001年1月1日にかけて静岡県がキャンペーンを実施。この地域活性プロジェクトにあたり、「伊豆ワカガエル大作戦」というスローガンと「イズノスケ」というマスコットキャラクターが生まれた。

Back in 1999, Izu was one of Japan's model tourist resorts but due to structural recession and the threat of earthquakes tourism began to decline. After reevaluating the situation, and uniting to raise local spirit and generate new attractions for a new Izu, Shizuoka Prefecture held a campaign from December 31 1999 through January 1 2001 to get people to come and experience Izu reborn. In conjunction with this regional reinvigoration project the slogan "Operation Izu rejuvenated" and the mascot character Izunozuke were born.

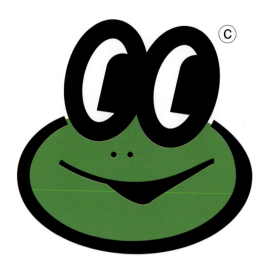

カレンダー　Calendar

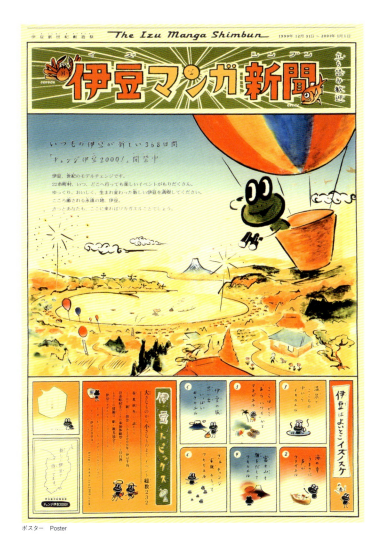

ポスター　Poster

お面　Plastic Mask
万華鏡　Kaleidoscope
弁当　Packed Lunch
ピンバッジ　Pin Badge
根付け　Miniature Carving
伊豆限定ビール　Beer (Limited Edition of Izu)

公共機関・団体　Public Institution & Organization　145

≫イズノスケ IZUNOSUKE

音頭うちわ・手ぬぐい・振りつけパンフレット
Fan, Towel, Pamphlet of Choreography

ポスター　Poster　　　　　　　　　　　CD　　　　　　　　　　　TVCM

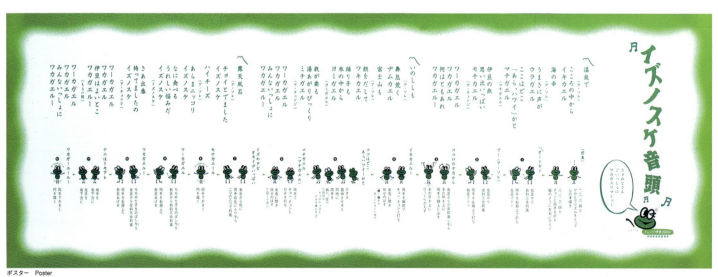

ポスター　Poster

146　公共機関・団体　Public Institution & Organization

フジちゃん fuji-chan NPO法人 NPO

CL: 富士山を世界遺産にする国民会議 National Council on Mt. Fuji World Heritage CD, AD, D, I: 田中 元 Gen Tanaka D: 小島義広 Yoshihiro Kojima CW: 倉成英俊 Hidetoshi Kuranari
Agency, SB: 電通 DENTSU INC. Japan

Concept

「富士山を世界遺産にする国民会議」は、日本のランドマークである富士山を世界遺産のなかの文化遺産として5年後に登録することを目指すNPO法人。国内外で広くPR活動を行うにあたり制作されたシンボルマークは、富士山の一部が欠けているデザインに。"富士山にはまだ何かが足りない"というコンセプトのもと、富士山に対する多くの人々の気持ちを大事にし、"あなたの1ピースが富士山をつくる"というメッセージが込められている。多彩な表情を設定し、プロジェクトをやわらかく伝える結果にもつながった。

The National Council on Mt. Fuji World Heritage is a nonprofit organization striving to make the Japanese landmark Mt. Fuji a World Cultural Heritage site in five years' time. The symbol mark created in conjunction with nationwide and international PR activities shows Mt. Fuji in a puzzle-like design with one piece missing. Based on the concept of "there's still something missing from Mt. Fuji" and respecting the feelings a great many people hold for the mountain, the character contains the message of "the piece you hold builds Mt. Fuji". A variety of expressions were created, conveying the project in a gentle way.

Profile

世界遺産を夢見るフジちゃんは、白い雲を自由にあやつり、日本のみんなに応援を呼びかけている。

Fuji-chan cherishes the dream of becoming a world heritage site. Waving white clouds, she calls to everyone in Japan for their support.

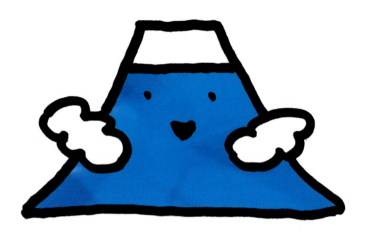

封筒 Envelope

名刺 Business Card

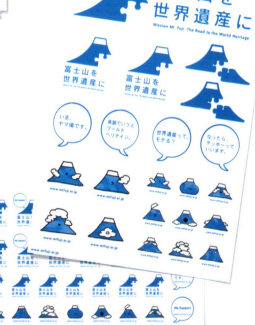

ステッカー Sticker

缶バッジ Badge

ピンバッジ Pin Badge

公共機関・団体 Public Institution & Organization

ワケルくん　Wakeru-kun　　地方自治体（仙台市100万人のごみ減量大作戦）　Local Government (Million People Garbage Reduction Campaign)

CL: 仙台市　環境局リサイクル推進課　Sendai City　　CD: 榎戸勝信（電通東日本）　Katsunobu Enokido (DENTSU EAST JAPAN INC.)　　AD, D, I: 中路聖子　Seiko Nakaji　　CW: 森本聡　Satoshi Morimoto
Planner: 村澤圭一（電通東日本）　Keiichi Murasawa (DENTSU EAST JAPAN INC.)　　Producer: 佐伯真一（dmp）　Shinichi Saeki (dmp)　　Account Excective: 伊東高志（電通東日本）　Takashi Ito (DENTSU EAST JAPAN INC.)
SB: ディー・エム・ピー　dmp Co., Ltd　Japan

Concept
2002年に仙台市の「ごみの分別を促進させ、ごみ減量を図る」という広告目標のもとにプランニングがスタート。キャラクターのデザインコンセプトは、親しみ易さ、わかり易さ、インパクトの強さの3つが柱となっている。以上の3つに基づいて生み出されたビジュアルに、ウィットのあるコピーを付加することによりキャラクターが完成した。現在ではワケルファミリーという複数のキャラクターを展開。キャラクターごとに「紙の分別」、「リサイクル」、「3Rでごみ減量」などのメッセージを添えて、キャンペーン展開に幅をもたせている。

Planning began in 2002 when the city of Sendai declared its aim to "promote the separation and reduce the amount of trash". The design concept for the character had three main stays: familiarity, easily understood and impact. A visual based on these criteria coupled with a witty tag line formed the final character. The program has since been developed to include a family of characters, each with a message such as "separate paper", "recycle", "reduce trash using the 3Rs", giving breadth to the campaign.

Profile
祖父の祖国、ドイツ・シュツットガルトで生まれる。現在27歳。幼少の頃をドイツで過ごした経験から、リサイクルの大切さを自然に体得した。仙台に来たのは社会に出てから。気になる髪型は、中学校から変わっていないらしい。きっちりワケてるね、と言われると、ネグセなんだ、とジョークを言い、頭をかく。

Born in his grandfather's hometown of Stuttgart, Germany. 27 years old. Having grown up in Germany, he realizes the importance of recycling. Moved to Sendai as a young man. His rather odd hairstyle hasn't changed since junior high. Comment on how perfectly it's parted, and he makes light of it.

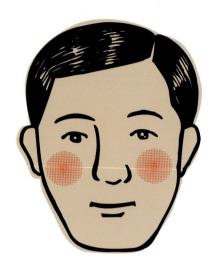

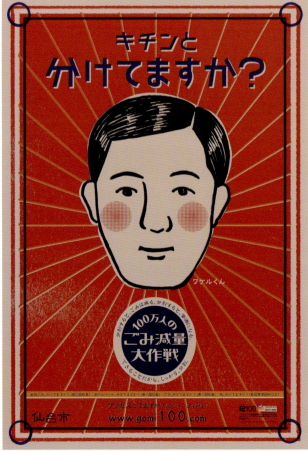

ポスター　Poster

柱巻き広告　Wrapped Column AD

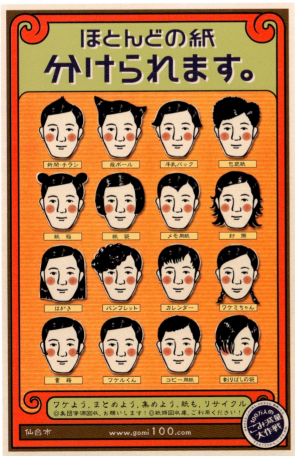

新聞広告　Newspaper AD

» ワケルくん　Wakeru-kun

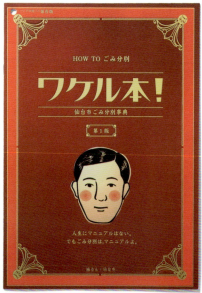

ゴミ分別マニュアル　Manual of Classify the Garbage

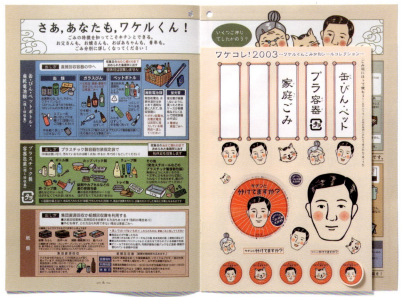

ステッカー　Sticker

コースター　Coaster

トランプ　Cards

のぼり　Flag

ますますくん Masumasu-kun 郵便局 Post Office

CL: 日本郵政公社 Japan Post　CD: 藤田雅弘(博報堂) Masahiro Fujita (HAKUHODO Inc.)　AD: 鈴木克彦(博報堂) Katsuhiko Suzuki (HAKUHODO Inc.)　CW: 田中量司(博報堂) Ryoji Tanaka (HAKUHODO Inc.) / 窪田健美(ツインズ) Takemi Kubota (TWINS CO., LTD.)　D: 館林宏樹(ツインズ) Hiroki Tatebayashi (TWINS CO., LTD.) / 堀川剛志(ツインズ) Takeshi Horikawa (TWINS CO., LTD.) / 土肥純一朗(ツインズ) Junichiro Dohi (TWINS CO., LTD.) / 野尻真紀(ツインズ) Maki Nojiri (TWINS CO., LTD.)　PR (Goods): 猪又幸成(ワイズ・インテグレーション) Yukinari Inomata (Wise Integration)　Agency, SB: 博報堂 HAKUHODO Inc.　DF: ツインズ TWINS CO., LTD. / ワイズ・インテグレーション Wise Integration　Japan

Concept

「ますますくん」は、郵便局の投資信託を身近な存在にするために制作されたキャラクター。多くの人の興味を惹き付けることや認知度の向上を目指し、わかりやすいトーン&マナーを採用した。また、ポスターやパンフレットなどではキャラクターによる内容説明のほか、キーカラーとサブカラーにやわらかな中間色を用いることで、親しみやすさやシリーズ感を出すことにつなげた。

Masumasu-kun is a character produced to help make the postal investment trust a more familiar entity. A readily understood tone and manner were used to attract the interest of a great many people. For applications such as posters and pamphlets in addition to having the character explain the content, gentle neutral colors were used for the main and sub-colors creating a feeling of friendliness and a sense of series.

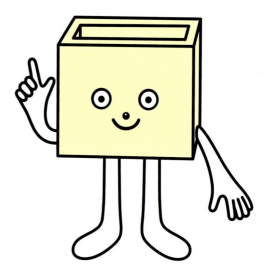

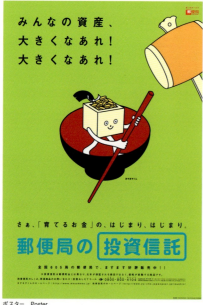

ポスター　Poster

小物入れ　Accessory Case　　栽培セット　Potted Plant　　POP　　　　　　　　　　　　　　POP

リーフレット　Leaflet

資産運用シミュレーションシート　Asset Management Simulation Sheet

ウェブサイト　Website

≫ますますくん　Masumasu-kun

カレンダー　Calendar

携帯用クリーナー
Mobile Phone Cleaner

ブックカバー　Book Cover

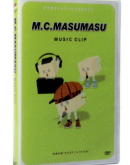

DVD

クリアファイル　Clear File

カンガエルー Kangaeru 業界団体 Trade Organization

CL, D (My Smart Regi Bag): 日本百貨店協会 Japan Department Stores Association   CD, AD, Character Design: 長島 慎 Shin Nagashima   D, I: 岩瀬なおみ Naomi Iwase
D (My Smart Regi Bag): ソトコト SOTOKOTO   CW: 石下佳奈子 Kanako Ishioroshi   DF: アドソルト adsalt   SB: 博報堂 HAKUHODO Inc.   Japan

Concept
適正包装を推奨することから、おなかに袋があるカンガルーをキャラクターに。地球環境を「考える」ことから、「カンガエルー」とネーミングした。さまざまなツールに展開した際のコストも考慮し、あえてグリーン地に黄色1色のシンプルなデザインを採用。

A kangaroo character with a pouch was created to encourage sensible packaging and named Kangaeru from the idea of thinking (kangaeru) about the environment. Bearing in mind the cost of deploying various promotional tools, a deliberately simple design of yellow on.

Profile
「日本百貨店協会」のオリジナルキャラクター。地球のためにできることを考える、カンガエルーくん。ちょっとトボけているけれど、適正包装をはじめ地球の環境問題について考えてやまないマジメな性格。趣味はデパートでのショッピング。

Created for the Japan Department Stores Association, Kangaeru is a character who cares about the planet. He may be a little silly, but he is very serious about things like sensible packaging and addressing environmental issues. His hobby is shopping in department stores.

ポスター　Poster

リーフレット Leaflet

Myスマートレジ袋 My Smart Regi Bag

公共機関・団体　Public Institution & Organization

アルプちゃん　Alp-chan　地方自治体（松本市市制施行100周年記年事業）　Local Government (Matsumoto 100th Anniversary Project)

CL, SB: 松本市市制施行100周年記念事業実行委員会　Matsumoto 100th anniversary Project Executive Committee　Japan

Concept
緑豊かな松本をイメージして、さわやかで親しまれるデザインを目指した。松本平から望める印象的な北アルプスをイメージした帽子をかぶることで岳都松本を表し、松本市が花いっぱい運動発祥地である由縁から、頭に花かざりをつけている。スズキメソードゆかりの地で、毎年サイトウ記念コンサートが開催される楽都松本をイメージして、バイオリンを持っている。また、服の緑は緑豊かな松本を表し、市のアピールのため、胸には松本市の市域の形を入れている。

An upbeat, accessible design inspired by Matsumoto's natural surroundings. Her hat is based on the city's impressive mountain views, the flower in her hair a reference to its reputation as Japan's flower-filled home of outdoor leisure. The violin alludes to the city's status as home of the Suzuki Method and venue of the annual Hideo Saito Memorial Concert. Her green garb pays homage to the city's lovely natural environment, and the shape on her chest is that of its administrative area.

Profile
アルプちゃんは長野県松本市の北アルプスに住む妖精。市制施行100周年で賑わう松本が楽しそうで、北アルプス市街へ降りてきた。松本が大好きなアルプちゃんは市制100周年の広報に任命され、100周年のアピールをがんばっている。好きな食べものは松本名物で、特にりんごが大好物。

Alp-chan is a fairy from the Northern Japan Alps of Matsumoto in Nagano Prefecture, come to join in the fun at the city's centennial celebrations. Assigned to PR for the centenary, she is going all out to promote the occasion. Her favorite foods are Matsumoto specialties, especially apples.

ポスター　Poster

缶バッジ　Badge

ステッカー　Sticker

ハンドタオル　Towel

ひこにゃん　Hiko-nyan

地方自治体（国宝・彦根城築城400年祭）　Local Government (National Tresure-Hikone Castle 400th Anniversary)

CL, SB: 国宝・彦根城築城400年祭実行委員会　National Treasure-Hikone Castle 400th Anniversary Executive Committee　Japan

Concept

国宝・彦根城築城400年祭の開催にあたり、シンボルマーク、ロゴ、キャラクターを制定することとなり、審査の結果、10社あまりの製作会社の作品の中から、シンボルマーク、ロゴともに現在のひこにゃんの図柄を選定。同デザインは、お寺の門前で、彦根藩二代藩主である井伊直孝公を手招きして雷雨から救ったと伝えられる「招き猫」と、井伊軍団のシンボルともいえる「赤備え（戦国時代の軍編成の一種で、あらゆる武具を朱塗りにした部隊編成のこと）」のかぶとを合体させて生まれたもの。

In conjunction with the celebration of Hikone Castle's 400th anniversary, the designs for a symbol mark, logo and character were selected by jury from those submitted by more than ten production companies. Hiko-nyan is an amalgamation of the maneki-neko (beckoning cat) said to have saved the second generation lord of the Hikone clan Ii Naotaka by calling him over to a temple gate during a thunder storm and the red lacquered helmet worn by and symbol of the Ii army.

Profile

年齢・性別不明。お魚、お肉が好物で、なかでもカニと箸で切れるお肉が大好き。散歩が趣味で、彦根城の周辺を散歩するのが好き。特技はひこにゃんじゃんけん、鈴叩き、正座。仕事は国宝・彦根城築城400年祭をPRすること。

Age and sex unknown. Likes meat and fish, crabmeat and juicy steaks being his favorites. His hobby is walking, and he likes strolling around Hikone Castle. His special skills are scissors-paper-rock a la Nyan, bell-tapping and formal sitting. His job is to promote Hikone Castle's 400th anniversary.

チラシ　Flyer

ステッカー　Sticker

リーフレット　Leaflet

nono, gogo, soso 教育プログラム Educational Project

CL: Innovatie Netwerk   CD, AD, D, I: Ivo Schmetz / Paul Rickus   DF, SB: 310k   Netherlands

Concept

nono、gogo、sosoは、子どもたちに食べ物や栄養等について教える教育プログラムのキャラクター。このプログラムはオランダの学校で2007年9月にスタートするもので、プロジェクトが楽しいものになるよう、3つのキャラクターを制作した。これらのキャラクターはプロジェクトに使われる教科書やツール類のいたるところに登場し、色々な場面でコメントする。子どもたちが学ぶ内容にあわせて、ストーリー仕立てとなっている。

This project will be launched at schools in Holland in September 2007 to teach children about food and nutrition. To make the project fun, we created three characters. They appear in all the books and project-related items, making comments as well as characterizing a story that goes along with the subjects the kids learn.

Profile

nonoは悪い面を表すキャラクターで、gogoは良い面を表している。sosoは疑っているキャラクターで、自分がどうすればいいのか、いつも分からないでいる。

nono represents the bad side. gogo represents the good side, and soso represents the doubting side, never sure of what to do.

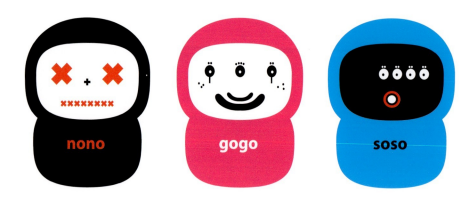

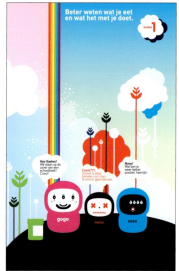

パンフレット Pamphlet

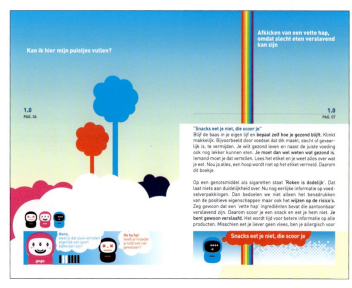

パンフレット　Pamphlet

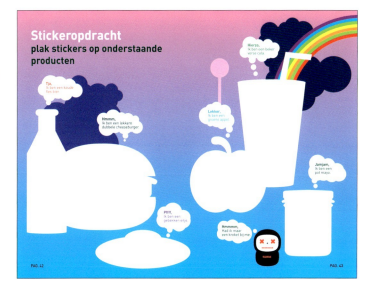
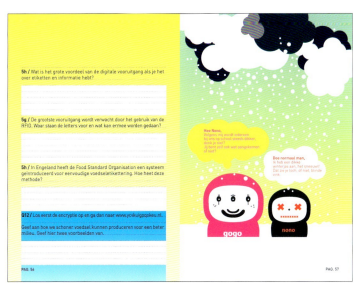
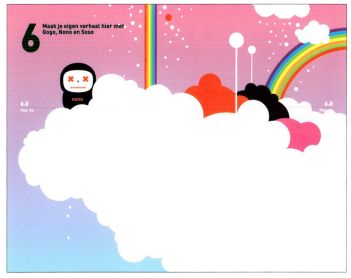

公共機関・団体　Public Institution & Organization　159

Suicaのペンギン Suica's Penguine   交通（ICカード「Suica」） Transportation (IC Card "Suica")

CL: 東日本旅客鉄道 East Japan Railway Company　Executive CD: 大島征夫 Masao Oshima　CD: 山本高史 Takashi Yamamoto　Creative Producer: 松川ゆい Yui Matsukawa
AD: 田中友朋 Yuho Tanaka / 渡邊裕文 Hirofumi Watanabe / 小島洋介 Yosuke Kojima　D: 三河洋子 Yoko Mikawa / 大堀悦子 Etsuko Ohori　I: さかざきちはる Chiharu Sakazaki
CW: 上田浩和 Hirokazu Ueda　DF: ジェー・シー・スパーク J.C.SPARK　SB: 電通 DENTSU INC.　Japan

Concept

ペンギンはJR東日本のICカード「Suica」のキャラクター。ICカードという一見"難しい"ものを"簡単で便利な"ものとして親近感をもって受け入れてもらうためにペンギンを起用した。南極や北極で生活するペンギンはSuica（西瓜）を見たことがないが、SuicaのようなICカードを使ったことがない利用客の代表として登場させることで、Suicaの機能を分かりやすく簡単に伝えていこうと考えた。

Penguin is the character for East Japan Railway's IC card, Suica. He was employed to help change the seemingly "difficult" impression of the IC card to "easy and convenient" by creating a sense of familiarity thereby making it more readily accepted. It was thought that Penguin, who living in the north and south pole has never seen a Suica (watermelon), would represent all rail riders who have never used an IC card like Suica and convey its functions in a simple, easy-to-understand way.

Profile

子どもからおじいちゃん、おばあちゃんまで幅広いSuicaの客層に受け入れてもらえるようなキャラクターということで、ペンギンのプロフィールは特に設定されていない。ただ、魚肉ソーセージが好物であることは確かなよう。

Because the character is designed to appeal to the wide range of Suica customers from kids to grannies, Penguin has no fixed profile. But one thing is clear: he loves fishmeat sausages.

ポスター　Poster

ポスター　Poster

PASMOのロボット　Robot of PASMO　　交通 Transportaion

CL: パスモ　PASMO Co.,ltd.　CD: 嶋田 清（電通）　Kiyoshi Shimada (DENTSU INC.)　AD: 小塚重信（電通）　Shigenobu Kozuka (DENTSU INC.)
D: 渡辺章人（たき工房）　Akihito Watanabe (TAKI corporation)　I: 安達 翼（電通）　Tsubasa Adachi(DENTSU INC.)　DF, SB: 電通　DENTSU INC.　DF: たき工房　TAKI corporation　Japan

Profile

首都圏をキビキビ移動するのが大好きなロボットで、普段はおなかのポケットにしまっているPASMOを使って移動するが、急いでいるときは自ら電車やバスに変身することができる。ロボットといっても決して無機質ではなく、「人に優しい」「便利」であるというイメージを持たせている。「PASMO」の先進性、また電車もバスも乗れるという拡張性を表象するキャラクターとして、様々なシーンに対応した柔軟な姿で数多くの告知媒体に登場している。

A robot who loves to zip around the metropolitan Tokyo area, he generally carries his PASMO rail pass in his stomach pocket, but can turn himself into a train or rail pass when he's in a great hurry. A robot he is, but there is nothing inorganic about him: he projects a people-friendly, convenient image. Symbolizing the spirit of innovation reflected in the PASMO card and its extendibility from train to bus, the character has a flexible form applicable to myriad scenes and has appeared in a great many notification media.

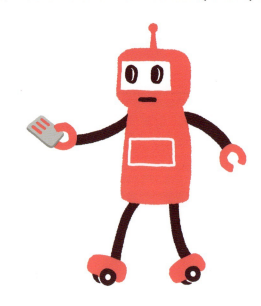

新聞広告　Newspaper AD

交通広告　Traffic AD

TVCM

ぴたポン！ PITAPON!

地方公営企業（ICカードシステム及びICカード「OSAKA PiTaPa」） Municipal Enterprise (IC Card System and IC Card "OSAKA PiTaPa")

CL, SB: 大阪市交通局　Osaka Municipal Transportation Bureau　Character Design: アランジアロンゾ　ARANZI ARONZO

Concept
大阪市交通局のICカードシステム及びOSAKA PiTaPaの利便性を、幅広い世代のお客様にわかりやすく説明するキャラクターとして誕生した。

Born as a character to explain the convenience of Osaka Municipal Transportation Bureau's IC card system and OSAKA PiTaPa in easy-to-understand way to a wide range of users.

Profile
ぴたポン！はちょっぴりあわてんぼうで感激屋さんの大阪弁を喋るたぬきの男の子。いつも元気にOSAKA PiTaPaで地下鉄やバスに乗ってあちこち走り回っている。また、いつも頭に葉っぱをのせている。

PITAPON! is an emotional, somewhat hurried little raccoon dog who speaks in Osaka dialect. He's always rushing about here and there, full of vim, on the subways or buses with his OSAKA PiTaPa card. He also always has a leaf on his head.

©大阪市交通局

リーフレット　Leaflet

メモ　Note Pad

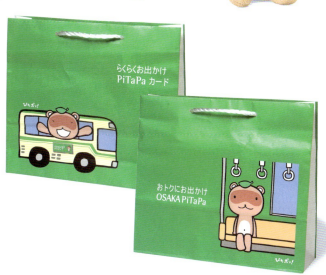

公共機関・団体　Public Institution & Organization

ゆめはんなマスコットキャラクター　Character of Yumehanna　鉄道・地域連携事業 Railroad

CL: 近畿日本鉄道　Kintetsu Corporation / 関西経済連合会　Kansai Economic Federation　CD: 野村裕一　Yuichi Nomura / 磯田礼子　Reiko Isoda　AD: 立花幹也　Mikiya Tachibana　D, I: 福田利之　Toshiyuki Fukuda
P（Carriage）: 清水 薫　Kaoru Shimizu　DF, SB: イエロードッグスタジオ　YELLOW DOG STUDIO　Japan

Concept

近鉄けいはんな線と大阪市地下鉄との相互乗り入れによりつながった「けいはんな学研都市」「東大阪ものづくりゾーン」「大阪ビジネスゾーン」「大阪ベイエリア」の各エリアをイメージしたマスコット・キャラクターたち。地域と地域が手をつなぎ、大阪と奈良との経済・学術・文化面での交流を促進し、暮らしの動脈として地域の発展に寄与する沿線の社会的役割を表現している。

Mascot characters imaged after features of the different areas – such as Kansai Science City, the Higashi-Osaka Monozukuri Zone, the Osaka Business Zone, and the Osaka Bay area – linked as a result of the extension of the Kintetsu Keihanna Line into the Osaka Municipal Subway line.

Profile

「OBP TWIN21」「海遊館」「大阪城」「奈良先端科学技術大学院大学」「花園ラグビー場」「工業技術」「住宅地」など、各地域の特徴をシンボリックに表したメインのキャラクター15体。

Fifteen main characters who symbolically express features of the different areas the Kintetsu Keihanna railway line connects, including OBP TWIN21, the Kaiyukan aquarium, Osaka Castle, Nara Institute of Science and Technology, Hanazono Rugby Stadium, and industrial and residential districts.

公共機関・団体　Public Institution & Organization

記念乗車券　Commemorative Ticket

ハンカチ　Handkerchief
ペットボトルホルダー　Plastic Bottle Holder

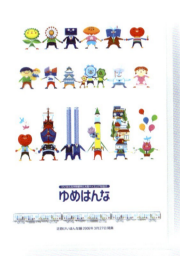
クリアファイル　Clear File

プリペイドカード　Prepaid Card
ノート　Notebook

公共機関・団体　Public Institution & Organization

とれねこ　Train cat　　交通 Transportation

CL: 富山ライトレール　Toyama Light Rail co., ltd.　　CD: 宮沢 功　Isao Miyazawa　　AD: 島津勝弘　Katsuhiro Shimazu　　D: 竹内健人　Takehito Takeuchi　　D, I: 目細 梓　Azusa Meboso
P: 室澤敏晴　Toshiharu Murosawa　　Design Cooperation: 富山北部高等学校情報デザイン科　Toyama Hokubu High Shool Information Design Course
DF, SB: 島津環境グラフィックス　Shimazu Enviromental Graphics　Japan

Concept
開業にあたり、沿線に富山北部高校があることから情報デザイン科の生徒が発案。ポートラムが7色あることからキャラクターも7色で構成し、背中から飛び出しているしっぽで電車のパンタグラフを表現した。

Proposed by students in the information design course of a high school in northern Toyama situated along the new railway line. The seven characters and colors correspond to the seven colored lines of the Portram system. The tails springing up out of their backs represent train pantographs.

Profile
富山ライトレールのキャラクターである7匹のネコたち。富山湾のリーダーのここくん・富山湾でとれた魚が大好物のもぐくん・マドンナ的存在のはなちゃん・ちょっぴり引っ込み思案なゆうくん・環境問題に興味をもっているえこくん・ひとり旅と船旅が好きなるーくんは、電車の旅が大好き。

Toyama Light Rail's seven cat characters – the Toyama Bay leader Koko-kun; Mogu-kun, who likes fresh fish from Toyama Bay; Hana-chan, with her Madonna-like aura; the tad withdrawn Yu-kun; Eco-kun, who's interested in environmental issues; and Ru-kun, who likes traveling alone and boat trips – all love traveling by train.

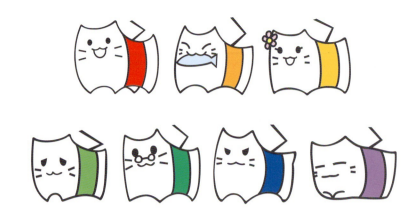

タオル Towel

ネクタイ Tie

スピーフィ Main Mascot Character of TSUKUBA EXPRESS   鉄道 Railroad

CL, SB: 首都圏新都市鉄道 SYUTOKEN SINTOSHI TETSUDO CO.   CD: 青田 司 Tsutomu Aota   AD: 三浦宏幸 Hiroyuki Miura   I: ハマダルコラ Hamada Rucola   Japan

Concept
つくばエクスプレスの車両イメージである「先進性」「スピード感」に加え、「親しみやすさ」を感じさせるキャラクターとして開発。グリーンの目は、沿線の緑との共生を表現し、アルミ合金製のボディは未来的なイメージを表す。ネーミングは一般公募で募集し、審査の結果「スピーフィ」に決定、2005年2月に発表した。

In addition to personifying the advanced nature and sense of speed of a TSUKUBA EXPRESS carriage, the character was developed to be endearing. His green eyes express his symbiotic relationship with the greenery along the railway line, and his aluminum alloy body a futuristic image. The name Speefy was selected by jury from a public call for submissions, and announced in Fabruary 2005.

Profile
2004年12月1日に誕生した、つくばエクスプレスのキャラクター。ボディはアルミ合金製で時速130キロで走るパワーがある。スピードを上げて走る時は、サンバイザーを下ろして顔を覆う。性格は底抜けに明るい。

The character for the TSUKUBA EXPRESS, born December 1, 2004. His body is made of aluminum alloy and he has the power to travel 130 kph. When he travels at high speeds he lowers his sun visor to conceal his face. His personality is exceedingly cheerful.

ステッカー　Sticker

キュウたん、グゥたん、ガァたん Kyu-tan, Gu-tan, Ga-tan   交通 Transportation

CL, SB: 東日本旅客鉄道   East Japan Railway Company   Japan

Concept
岩手県は「カッパ」、青森県は「土偶（どぐう）」、秋田県は「なまはげ」など北東北それぞれの地域を連想させるモチーフをもとに、かわいらしさや親しみやすさを効果的に印象づけられるようなキャラクターを目指した。

Based on motifs commonly associated with the each of the Tohoku regions – the water sprite for Iwate, the dogu clay figure for Aomori, and the demonic folk figure Namahage for Akita – the aim was to give the characters sweet, endearing qualities and to make them effectively impression-making.

Profile
JR北東北デスティネーションのキャラクター。キャラクター名はアンケートによる一般応募により決定。「土偶」の愛称「グゥたん」を基本に、「カッパ」については応募の中で「きゅうり」に関連した名称が多くあげられていたことから「キュウたん」、「なまはげ」については「悪い子はいねがぁ」の台詞から連想した「ガァたん」とした。

The characters for three Japan Railway North Tohoku destinations. Their names were determined through a questionnaire-based open contest: Gu-tan was the local nickname for dogu; Kyu-tan for the water sprite from the great many responses referencing *kyuri* (cucumbers); and Ga-tan from the rhythmic incantation "Any bad boys here gaa?" for the demonic figure.

クリアファイル　Clear File

コマーさる君　koma saru kun　民放テレビ・ラジオの事業者団体　Association of Commercial Broadcasters

CL, SB: 日本民間放送連盟　The National Association of Commercial Broadcasters in Japan　CD: 木下一郎　Ichiro Kinoshita　AD: 棚橋芳雄　Yoshio Tanahashi
D: 黒木一人　Kazuhito Kuroki / 砂川留美　Rumi Sunagawa / 島田修司　Shuji Shimada　P: 加藤教生　Kyousei Katoh　DF: バウ広告事務所　BAU advertising office　Japan

Concept
テレビCMの有用性や楽しさを視聴者に再認識してもらうため、平成17(2005)年度から民放テレビ全社で取り組んでいる「CMのCMキャンペーン」のキャラクター。テレビCMのように誰にでも愛されるキャラクターにしたい！　という思いで、「さる」をモチーフとした。テレビCMを宣伝するキャラクターであるため、テレビをかたどったほか、しっぽの先をコンセントのプラグにしたり、おへそをコンセントのソケットにしたり、おしりをハート型にしたりと、細かいところに工夫を施した。表情や動きを作るときも、かわいらしく、憎めないキャラクターになるよう意識してデザイン。声は、俳優の阿部サダヲさんが担当している。

Like in TV advertising itself, the desire was to create a character that would be loved by all, hence the monkey (saru). And because he represents TV advertising he shares features with a TV: a screen-shaped head, a plug at the tip of his tail, a socket for a bellybutton, and a heart-shaped bum. His expressions and movements were consciously designed to be charming to help make him a character who's hard to dislike. Actor Sadao Abe does his voice.

Profile
「コマーシャル」のことをコマーシャルする、ために生まれた「コマーさる君」。テレビCMが生まれたのと同じ8月28日生まれで、人なつっこく、いたずら好き。だけどちょっとシャイだったりもする愛らしいキャラクター。

koma saru kun was developed to advertise TV advertising. His birthday is August 28, the day TV advertising was born. He's amiable and a bit of a prankster, but also a tad shy, making him a charming character.

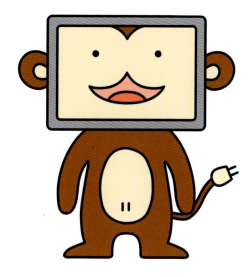

ポスター　Poster

ポスター　Poster

TVCM

トドック Todok   生活協同組合 Cooperative

CL, SB: 生活協同組合コープさっぽろ Coop Sapporo   CD: 松浦秀樹（電通 北海道）Hideki Matsuura (DENTSU HOKKAIDO INC.)   AD: 長内泰代（イザ）Yasuyo Osanai (IZA)   I: 増田久美子 Kumiko Masuda
DF: イザ IZA   Japan

Concept
「トドック」は、「コープの安心が、おうちに届く」をキャッチフレーズにカタログで選んだ商品が宅配されるコープ宅配システムのキャラクターで、2006年10月に生まれた。「届く」ことを明快にアピールすべくストレートなネーミングを採用。北海道で人気のシロクマをモチーフに、親しみやすく、かわいらしく、安心感のあるキャラクターとした。宅配スタッフの目印である赤いエプロンを身につけ、青い宅配ボックスを持っている。また「CO・OP」のCとPを耳に、2つのOを目に見立てている。

Todok is a character created in October 2006 for the Coop's home delivery service where customers select Coop products from a catalogue that are then delivered to their homes, with the catch-phrase "The Coop's assurance delivered to your door." The name Todok comes from the Japanese word for "deliver". A friendly, cute and trustworthy character has been created as a white bear, which is popular in Hokkaido. Wearing the red apron that is the hallmark of the delivery staff, Todok holds a blue delivery box. The letters C and P that are his ears and the two Os of his eyes form the word Coop.

Profile
北海道生まれのトドックは温厚でしっかり者のシロクマさん。好きな言葉は「あんしん」、特技は「安全運転」。チャームポイントはCとPの形になっている耳。北海道で暮らすたくさんの人々にコープの「安心のおいしさ」をお届けしたいといつも思っている。

The white bear Todok is a native of Hokkaido with a mild, steady nature. His favorite word is "assurance" and his special skill is "safe driving." His "best features" are his ears in the shape of the letters C and P. He always wishes to deliver safe food of Coop to a lot of Hokkaido residents.

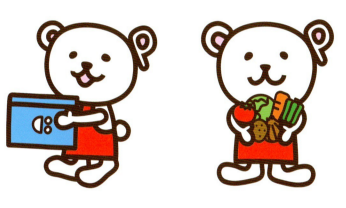

新聞広告 Newspaper AD

弁当箱 Lunch Box

鉛筆 Pencil

TVCM

公共機関・団体 Public Institution & Organization   169

こんせんくん　Konsen-kun　　生活協同組合　Cooperative

CL: パルシステム生活協同組合連合会　pal system　　CD: 南波英希　Hideki Nanba　　AD: 望月昭秀　Akihide Mochizuki　　DF: NILSON design studio　　SB: ゼネラル・プレス　General Press　Japan

Concept

もともとは「こんせん72」牛乳という商品のパッケージに使用されていたイラストで、1986年から約20年間にわたり組合員や職員に広く親しまれていた。パルシステムブランドの認知度を高めるため、このイラストをブランドキャラクターに制定。さらに好感度を高めるため、かわいらしく好ましいデザインとした。

The illustrations used on the original packaging of the milk product Konsen 72 in 1986 had become familiar to union members and employees over approximately 20 years. To increase the recognition level of the pal system brand, the illustrations contain a memorable brand character, and further, to increase likeability, he was designed to be cute and cuddly.

Profile

こんせんくんは1歳の男の子。こんせん地方の牧場に暮らす。優しくてのんびりした性格。好きな飲み物は、こんせん72牛乳で、こんせん地方の自然が大好き。都会の人はもっとこんせん地方に来ればいい、と思っている。牧場や畑で働いている人たちが好きで、いつも「えらいな～」と思っている。

Konsen-kun is a one-year-old boy who lives on a farm in the country. His favorite drink is Konsen 72 milk and he loves the nature of the Konsen countryside. He wishes that more people from the city would visit Konsen. He respects farmars.

ポスター　Poster

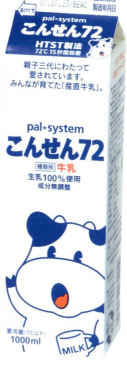

新聞広告　Newspaper AD

配達トラック　Delivery Truck

ごはんぢゃワン　GOHAN-DYAWAN　協同組合 Cooperative

CL, SB: 全国農業協同組合中央会　Central Union of Agricultural Co-operatives　Japan

Concept
お茶碗とかわいい子犬をモチーフに開発された「ごはんぢゃワン」は、JAグループのお米消費推進キャラクター。「ごはんをより美味しく、より楽しく、もっといっぱい食べてもらえるように……」という思いが込められている。

GOHAN-DYAWAN, a character combining the images of a rice bowl and a cute little puppy, was developed for the JA Group to promote rice consumption. It contains the hopes that people will eat more rice, find it tastier and have more fun doing so.

Profile
ちゃわん犬。人間でいう小学校3年生。性格はふんわり、ホッカホカ。好奇心旺盛で食いしん坊。特技は美味しいものをすぐに嗅ぎ分けること。好きな言葉は「いただきます！」「おかわり！」「ごちそうさま！」将来の夢は、ごはん博士になること。

A rice-bowl pup. By human standards he'd be a third-grader. His personality is gentle and warm. He's full of curiosity and a BIG eater. He has a special talent for sniffing out delicious food. His favorite sayings are "Bon appetit!", "Seconds please!" and "That was delicious!" His dream is to become a rice expert.

ペットボトルホルダー Plastic Bottle Holder
まな板 Chopping Board
弁当箱 Lunch Box
茶碗 Rice Bowl

公共機関・団体 Public Institution & Organization

博多うまれ キャラクター Character of Hakata Umare   協同組合 Cooperative

CL: JA全農ふくれん JA Zen-Noh Fukuren　CD: 植原政信 Masanobu Uehara　AD: 常軒理恵子 Rieko Tsunenoki　D: 野村亜紀 Aki Nomura　CW: 水島理恵 Rie Mizushima
I: サンリオ SANRIO CO., LTD.　DF: アド・パスカル AD-PASCAL CO., LTD　SB: 電通九州 DENTSU KYUSHU INC.　Japan

Concept
「福岡県産の野菜・果物 博多うまれ」のブランド全体をPRするためのキャラクター。太陽のめぐみをたくさん受けて育った「福岡県産の野菜・果物 博多うまれ」を分かりやすく表現するために、太陽のキャラクターをサンリオと共同開発。野菜・果物の被りものを身につけて変身し、各農産物のPR活動を行う。また、TVCMにも使用しているオリジナルソングは、若い主婦や子供に親しまれている。

The character was created to promote the "Fukuoka fruit and vegetables from Hakata" brand as a whole. To convey the idea of fruit and vegetables grown under the sunny skies of Fukuoka, a sun character was developed in conjunction with SANRIO. By switching headgear he transforms himself into different fruit and vegetables for various promotions. The original tune penned for TV commercials is also a familiar favorite of young housewives and children.

Profile
「JA全農ふくれん」のオリジナルキャラクター。福岡県生まれ。野菜と果物が大好きで、毎日、明るく元気に福岡県の農産物を育てている。

Character designed exclusively for JA Zen-Noh Fukuren, the Fukuoka branch of the national federation of agricultural cooperatives. Born in Fukuoka and raised in Hakata, he loves fruit and vegetables, and spends his days enthusiastically cultivating Fukuoka produce.

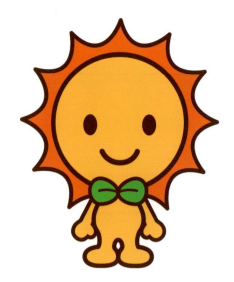

TVCM

もりアフロ　Mori Aflo　　産業団体 Industrial Organization

CL, SB: 石油連盟　Petroleum Association of Japan　CD: 小川恭伸　Yasunobu Ogawa　AD, D: 片岡 学　Manabu Kataoka　I: くまさき なお　Nao Kumasaki　Account Manager: 吉川精一　Seiichi Yoshikawa
DF: コオガ企画　Kooga Kikaku / マルワン　MAL1 Ltd.　Agency: 日本経済広告社　Japan

Concept
デザインコンセプトは、「環境へのやさしさ」。たわわな緑のアフロヘアーは、豊かな自然、豊かな森の象徴であり、また、植物生まれの燃料をブレンドした環境にやさしいバイオガソリンをイメージしている。「もりアフロ」は、バイオガソリンのイメージキャラクターとして、またスポークスマンとして、今後もCO2の削減や地球温暖化防止に貢献していく。

The design concept is environmental friendliness. Their lush, green afros are symbolic of the fertility of nature and the fertility of the forest, and reflect the eco-friendly bio-gasoline, which is blended with a plant-based fuel. The twin "Mori Aflo" bio-gasoline characters in their role as spokespersons are intended to contribute to reduction of CO2 in the atmosphere and prevention of global warming.

Profile
「もりアフロA」と「もりアフロB」の2体で一対を成している豊かな森の守り神。バイオガソリンのイメージキャラクターであるため、バイオガソリンを扱っているサービスステーションで見かけることができる。

The guardian angels of the fertility of the forest (mori), Mori Aflo A and Mori Aflo B. As the characters that represent bio-gasoline, they can be spotted at service stations where bio-gasoline is available.

ポスター　Poster

ステッカー　Sticker

アカンずきん　AKAN-ZUKIN　　地方自治体 Local Government

CL: 大阪市環境局　Osaka City Environment Bureau　CD, AD, Naming: 岩槻浩世　Hiroyo Iwatsuki　AD: 北野朋子　Tomoko Kitano　D, I: 鈴木章人　Akihito Suzuki
Tool Design: 水口ます美　Masumi Mizuguchi　Agency: メディアート　Mediart CO., LTD.　DF, SB: 鈴木章人デザイン事務所　Akihito Suzuki Design Office　Japan

Concept
市民の協力なしには遂行できないマナー・モラルに関わるキャンペーンにもかかわらず、実際のところ、「やわらかくマナーアップを訴えるだけでは期待するような結果は得ることができないだろう」という懸念のもと、迷惑たばこの被害者の代表である子供に着眼し、親を巻きこんで「やめて」と呼びかけることを考えた。そこで単に呼びかけを行うよりも、"やめて→ダメ→アカン"という大阪独特の言葉を用い、赤ずきんと掛け合わせることに。そして、可愛く、気の強い赤い頭巾の女の子「アカンずきん」とネーミングした。

Knowing that a citywide manners/morals campaign cannot be accomplished without the cooperation of citizens, yet concerned that a soft appeal to improve manners might not be effective in this case, the idea was to have a child represent the victims of annoying smoking call out to people to "STOP!" From there associations with the words "Stop→ Don't!→Akan (Osaka dialect for "don't")" were combined with the image of red riding hood. Hence the name of this cute but strong little red riding hood.

Profile
アカンずきんは、大阪市路上喫煙防止キャンペーンのキャラクター。大阪の人々を迷惑たばこから守るため、「歩きたばこはアカンずきん!」「迷惑たばこはアカンずきん!」と呼びかけながら、仲間といっしょに大阪市内をパトロール。2007年4月からは大阪市の「路上喫煙防止に関する条例」を告知する任務も担っている。

AKAN-ZUKIN is the character for Osaka's No Smoking on the Street campaign. She patrols the streets of Osaka with her friends shouting, "walking and smoking is akanzukin (NG riding hood)!" "Troubling others is akazukin!" She also performed the task of announcing Osaka's bylaws regarding smoking on the street, which went into effect in April 2007.

ポスター　Poster

とっぴー、きっぴー、トッキッキ　　Toppy, Kippy, Tokkikki

トキめき新潟国体（第64回国民体育大会）・トキめき新潟大会（第9回全国障害者スポーツ大会）の開催準備
Preparation of the 2009 National Sports Festival and the National Sports Festival for the Disabled in Niigata

CL, SB: トキめき新潟国体・トキめき新潟大会実行委員会　Executive Committee of the 2009 National Sports Festival and the National Sports Festival for the Disabled in Niigata
CD, AD, D: 大溪和身　Kazumi Ootani　　DF: 新潟デザインセンター　NIIGATA DESIGN CENTER　Japan

Concept

2009年開催のトキめき新潟国体（第64回国民体育大会）・トキめき新潟大会（第9回全国障害者スポーツ大会）の「トキめき」の言葉から「新潟県の鳥」である「朱鷺」をイメージ。特に子供に親しみを持ってもらえるよう、シンプルかつ温かみのある印象を持つ丸形を活かしてデザインした。また、「トキめき」と「みんなの熱い想い」をひとつにすることを、朱鷺の特徴でもある顔の赤色をハート形にすることで表現。

The nicknames for the Tokimeki Niigata National Sports Festival & Tokimeki Niigata Sports Festival for the Disabled were imaged after Niigata's prefectural bird, the toki (Japanese crested ibis). To be endearing to a wide age range, and especially children, the design, while simple, makes maximum use of the soft and warm impression inherent in rounded forms. As well, making heart-shaped the red face characteristic of the toki, expresses the desire to make one the tokimeki (feelings of excitement and anticipation) and enthusiastic spirit (heart) of all.

Profile

2つの大会のマスコットキャラクター。男の子のとっぴー・女の子のきっぴーの2人で、ペアでトッキッキという。チャレンジ精神があり、運動神経抜群のとっぴーは、スポーツが大好き。好奇心旺盛でおしゃべりが好きなきっぴーは、友達をたくさん作るのが夢。

The mascot characters for the two events: Toppy, the boy and Kippy, the girl. As a pair they are called Tokkikki. Toppie is very athletic, adventuresome, and loves to watch sports. Kippie is full of curiosity, loves to talk, and has a dream of making lots of friends.

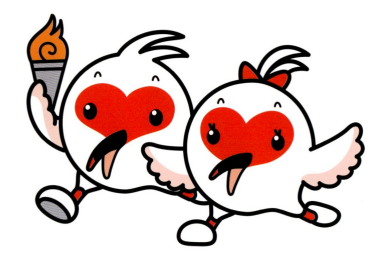

ステッカー　Sticker

ステッカー　Sticker
缶バッジ　Badge
自動車用ステッカー　Sticker for Automobile

チーバくん　Chiba-kun

地方自治体（ゆめ半島千葉国体）　Local Government (2010 National Sports Festival in Chiba-The Peninsula Where Dreams Become Reality)

CL, SB: ゆめ半島千葉国体実行委員会（千葉県国体・全国障害者スポーツ大会局）　National Sports Festival and National Sports Festival for Disabled Bureau　I: 坂崎千春　Chiharu Sakazaki　Japan

Concept

チーバくんは、2010年に千葉県で開催される「ゆめ半島千葉国体（第65回国民体育大会）」および「ゆめ半島千葉大会（第10回全国障害者スポーツ大会）」で使用されるマスコットキャラクター。横から見た姿が千葉県の形をしている。

Chiiba-kun is the mascot character for the "Peninsula Where Dreams Become Reality" 65th National Sports Festival & 10th National Sports Festival for the Disabled to be held in Chiba in 2010. In profile, his body resembles the shape of Chiba Prefecture.

Profile

千葉県に住む不思議な生き物。好奇心旺盛で色々なことに挑戦するのが大好き。未知のものに立ち向かうときほど勇気と情熱が湧き、体が赤く輝く。食いしん坊でいたずら好きな面もある。

A magical creature who lives in Chiba Prefecture. He's a full of curiosity and loves to take on all sorts of challenges. His courage and enthusiasm well up in the face of the unknown and his body glows red. He's a big eater and a bit of a prankster.

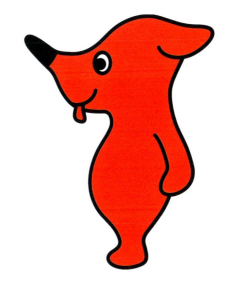

チラシ　Flyer

ステッカー　Sticker

公共機関・団体　Public Institution & Organization

1

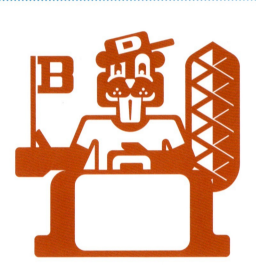

2 3

4 5

1. エコてつ君　Ecotetsu-kun　社団法人　Corporation / CL, SB: 日本民営鉄道協会　THE ASSOCIATION OF JAPANESE PRIVATE RAILWAYS　CD: 岡部正泰　Masayasu Okabe / 新妻真帆　Maho Niizuma　AD, D, I: 黒沼かおり　Kaori Kuronuma　DF: 岡部事務所　Okabe Jimusyo　Japan

2. Adrienne　女性支援団体　Support Group for Girls / CL: You Grow Girl　CD, AD, D, I: John Sayles　DF, SB: Sayles Graphic Design　USA

3. Beaverdale　商業連合　Business Coalition / CL: Beaverdale Business Coalition　CD, AD, D, I: John Sayles　DF, SB: Sayles Graphic Design　USA

4. ウインドブラザーズ　Wind Brothers　地方自治体　Local Government / CL: 群馬県　GUNMA Pref.　CD, AD, D, I, SB: Maniackers Design　I: choco*choco　Japan

5. キャプテンわん　CAPTAIN-WAN　公益法人　Charitable Corporation / CL, SB: 横浜市体育協会　Yokohama Sports Association　D: ゆず香　YUZUKA　Japan

Media & Creative
クリエイティブ

日テレちん Nittele-chin テレビ局 TV Station

CL, SB: 日本テレビ放送網　NIPPON TELEVISION NETWORK CORPORATION　CD, CW: 黒須美彦　Yoshihiko Kurosu　AD, D: 布村順一　Junichi Nunomura / 高梨 貴　Takashi Takanashi　Japan

Concept
「ちん！と鳴る呼び鈴を持つ、身近で親しみやすい奴」をテーマに、子供がおもちゃを寄せ集めて作ったような、あどけないかわいさを表現した。呼び鈴を乗せた木の箱に、目・鼻・口の磁石パーツをくっつけただけの寄せ集めキャラである。ちなみに、顔の外形＆鼻、白目＆黒目のデザインは「日テレ」ロゴマークの「日」のデザインからもってきている。

The character was based on the theme of "a friendly, familiar chap with a bell that rings with a 'chin'," created in the way a child might assemble a toy, and expressing a naïve charm. A wooden block with a bell on top to which magnetic eyes, nose and mouth were stuck on. The shape of the face and nose and design of the white and black eyes derives from the character "ni(chi)" in the Nittele logo type.

Profile
ノイジーで愉快な性格。番組をはじめとするさまざまなコンテンツのナビゲーター役として誕生。季節に合わせて呼び鈴を変えたりしてサービス精神旺盛だが、あまりに強く呼び鈴を鳴らしすぎて顔が崩れてしまったり、おっちょこちょいな面もある。日テレ君、日テレちゃん、日テレ殿、日テレ兄、日テレっち、いろいろ呼び方はあるけれど、いちばん親しみを感じる「日テレちん」と呼んでほしいと思っている。

A noisy but pleasant personality. Born to guide viewers through programs and various other contents. His bell changes with the seasons, and although he has a roaring service-oriented spirit, his face tends to say if his bell is rung too much. While he's been called everything from Nittele-kun to Nittele-chan, Nittele-dono, and Nittele-ani, we'd prefer he be called Nittele-chin.

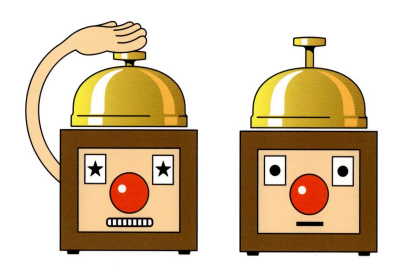

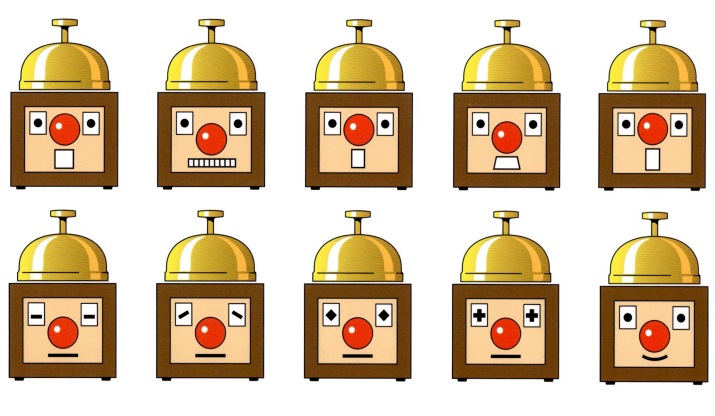

看板 Sign

ポスター　Poster

フィギュア　Figure

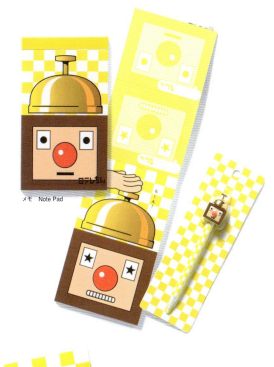

メモ　Note Pad

ネックストラップ　Neck Strap

ステッカー　Sticker

ウキキ Ukiki テレビ局 TV Station

CL, SB: 読売テレビ放送 Yomiuri Telecasting corp　CD, AD: 三條場 章 Akira Sanjoba　CD: かすがいのぞみ Nozomi Kasugai　I: 料所大輔 Daisuke Ryosho　Japan

Profile

恥ずかしがり屋で無口なウキキは気持ちを体で伝えられる体操が大好き。ウキウキしたりわくわくしたりすると、自然と体が動き出してしまう。みんなと一緒に体操をして、仲良くなりたいと思ってるウキキは照れ屋だけど人懐っこいおさるさん。

Ukiki the monkey is always cheerful and fun but also shy and quiet and loves exercising where she can express the way she is feeling with her body. Ukiki wants to do her exercises with you and make friends.

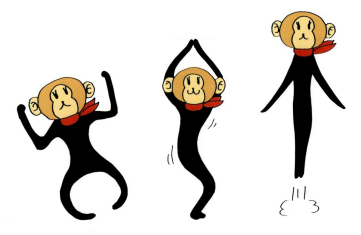
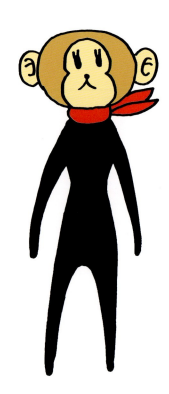

交通広告　Traffic AD

クリアファイル　Clear File　　ステッカー　Sticker

封筒　Envelope

便せん　Writing Paper　　ノート　Notebook

交通広告　Traffic AD

クリエイティブ　Media & Creative　183

テレビ埼玉 キャラクター　Character of Television Saitama

テレビ局　TV Station

CL: テレビ埼玉　Television Saitama Co., Ltd.　CD, CW: 山田慶太　Keita Yamada　AD, I: 渡邊裕文　Hirofumi Watanabe　D: 吉田順一　Junichi Yoshida　CW: 石田百合子　Yuriko Ishida
DF: ジェ・シー・スパーク　J.C.SPARK. inc　SB: ビルド・クリエイティブハウス　BUILD creativehaus Inc. / 電通　DENTSU INC.　Japan

Concept

テレビ埼玉（テレ玉）のキャラクター。埼玉の「玉」の字から玉子をイメージし、キャラクター化。カラの割れた部分を口にした。

Developed to coincide with the name change from Television Saitama to its pet Teletama, with an egg to be the motif. The egg was an association that stemmed from the character "tama" being common to both Saitama and tamago (egg). Personifying the egg, a crack in its shell forms the character's mouth.

Profile

気はやさしいけど、ちょっと皮肉屋さんなところが玉にキズ。口グセは、「まだまだ半熟者ですが……。」

Mascot character for Television Saitama. Good-tempered, but flawed by his cynical cracks. His favorite saying is "I'm still only soft-boiled…"

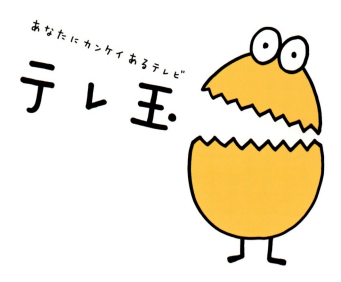

雑誌広告　Magazine AD

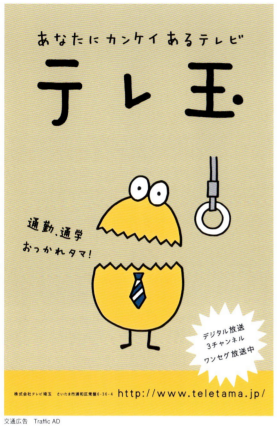
交通広告　Traffic AD

封筒　Envelope
クリアファイル　Clear File

TVCM

OH!くん OH! KUN   テレビ局 TV Station

CL: 岡山放送 OHK   CD, I: 石田康成 Yasunari Ishida   I: 石田孝文 Takafumi Ishida   Production: 電通西日本 DENTSU WEST JAPAN INC. / 石田図工室 ISHIDA ZUKOUSHITSU, LLC
SB: 電通西日本 岡山支社 DENTSU WEST JAPAN INC. OKAYAMA   Japan

Concept
岡山放送（OHK）にちなんでOH!くん。セリフは「OH!」のみ。放送する内容が多岐にわたるテレビ局には、視聴者とコミュニケーションできる汎用性の高いキャラがふさわしいと考え、色々な感情を含む「OH!」をキーワードに、テレビの幅広いイメージを伝えることを目指した。また、「OH!」は老若男女の区別なく人々が口にしやすいという利点もあり、その都度OHKを連想させることも狙った。定番の動物「ネコ」にオレンジのまわし、というアクセントをつけ、見た目にも「OH!」の気分を盛り込んだ。

Associated with Okayama Broadcasting Co.,Ltd (OHK). His only line is "OH!" A generally versatile character able to communicate with viewers based on the keyword of "OH!" and its myriad emotions was thought best suited to the broad image of television. "OH!" also had the advantage of being an expression often used by both men and women, young and old, so we aimed to have it associated with OHK whenever used. Dressing an average cat in an orange loincloth added an element of "OH!" to his appearance.

Profile
驚き、感動、涙、怒り。色々な「OH!」を届けるため2002年5月1日にデビュー。ネコ系の生き物。生息地は岡山・香川で、瀬戸内の小魚が好物。視聴者と真剣に向き合えるよう、常に「まわし」を着用（一度も洗濯したことはない）。おおらか、おおざっぱ、好奇心旺盛で、周囲の大人を困惑させることも……。

Debuted 1 May 2002 to bring viewers all sorts of OH!s (emotions). A feline of the Okayama-Kagawa region who likes small fish from the Inland Sea. In his eagerness to take on viewers, he constantly wears a sumo loincloth (which has never been washed). Broad-minded, casual, inquisitive, he tends to bewilder adults.

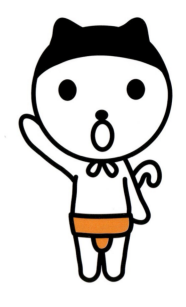

根付け
Miniature Carving

御守り　Charm

CD

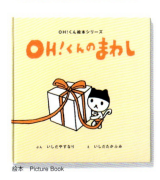

絵本　Picture Book

DVD

たこるくん Takoru-kun   テレビ局 TV Station

CL, SB: テレビ大阪 Television Osaka INC   CD, AD: 福本満美子 Mamiko Fukumoto   D, I, DF: サカモト タカフミ Takafumi Sakamoto   Japan

Concept
黄色をベースのカラーとし、スミ・赤・茶のシンプルなデザインで展開。デザインはサカモト タカフミ氏が担当。打ち出すメッセージや制作するアイテムごとにブレストを重ね、世界観に合ったオリジナルデザインを意識している。"たこるくん" という名前は、大阪の人が大好きな「たこやき」からつけた。

Developed with a yellowish-beige base color plus black, red and brown and a simple design, directed by Takafumi Sakamoto. Each message and each item developed began with brainstorming, with original design befitting his worldview at the fore. The name Takoru-kun derives from Osaka people's favorate, Takoyaki.

Profile
テレビ大阪のたこるくんは、大阪・ミナミのたこやき屋台でオヤジがうっかりタコを入れ忘れたはずみで誕生。のんびり屋、マイペースな性格であるが、行動的な一面も。屋台を飛び出し旅に出た途中、賢く頭脳派のタコベエに兵庫県明石で出会ってからは、いつも行動をともにしている。

Television Osaka's Takoru-kun was born one day when the takoyaki-man forgot to put tako (octopus) in his octopus balls. He's low-key and works at his own pace, but has an active side too. Upon leaving the takoyaki stand on a journey, he met the brainy octopus Takobee and they've been together since.

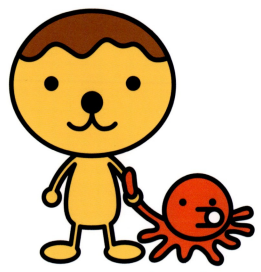

©Television Osaka / Takafumi Sakamoto

クリアファイル Clear File

ステッカー Sticker

ポストカード Postcard

手ぬぐい Towel

ステッカー　Sticker

ステッカー　Sticker

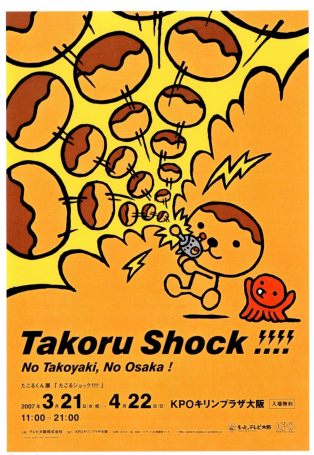
ポスター　Poster

図録　Illustrated Book

ステッカー　Sticker

ポストカード　Postcard

コースター　Coaster

バンダナ　Handkerchief

もんすけ Monsuke テレビ局 TV Station

CL, Character Design, SB: 北海道放送 Hokkaido Broadcasting Co.,Ltd   CD: 松永芳朗 Yoshiro Matsunaga   AD: 遠山寛人 Hiroto Toyama / 大島慶太郎 Keitaro Oshima   D: 岩本奈々 Nana Iwamoto / 児玉美也子 Miyako Kodama   I: 小笠原 大 Dai Ogasawara / 仙庭宣之 Nobuyuki Semba   Web Director: 山崎智子 Tomoko Yamazaki / 有賀一成 Issei Ariga   Animator: 広島祐介 Yusuke Hiroshima / 中川仁史 Hitoshi Nakagawa   DF: マルハマ MARUHAMA   Japan

Concept
10年前にHBC社員のアイデアから誕生したキャラクター「もんすけ」だが、誕生10年をきっかけにデザインをリニューアルして再出発。HBCのチャンネル1に合わせて「もんすけ1BAN計画」をスタートした。北海道のキャラクターの中で人気1BANになれるよう、TV番組宣伝やラジオのイベントなどに出演し、ホームページの日記ブログに公開しながら、地道に頑張っている。

Monsuke was born ten years ago as graffiti at the hand of an HBC employee. At his 10th anniversary, he underwent updating and reintroduction first in conjunction with HBC channel 1 as the Monzuke 1BAN (#1) Project. To make one of Hokkaido's #1 character, he appears in TV program advertising, on radio, and at events. He also posts a diary blog on his website, and plowing ahead.

Profile
年齢8歳。緑の森の一番地に住んでいる。好奇心旺盛で色々なことにチャレンジするが、失敗も多い2枚目半の脱力系キャラ。好きなものはバナナ、嫌いなものは蜘蛛。「もん」というのが口ぐせ。

Eight years old. Lives at One Green Forest. Full of curiosity, he loves trying his hand at all sorts of things, quite often unsuccessfully. He has the looks of a beau and the personality of a comic, but is basically a listless sort. He likes bananas, hates spiders, and has a habit of saying "mon".

メモ　Note Pad

ステッカー　Sticker

フライヤー　Flyer

CD

TVCM

ビープくん Mr. Beep テレビ局 TV Station

CL, SB: 山口朝日放送 Yamaguchi Asahi Broadcasting Co, Ltd.　CD: 三田欣弘 Yoshihiro Mita　AD, D, I: 多田寿一 Toshikazu Tada　D: 佐藤広宣 Hironobu Sato / 河内澄栄 Sumie Kouchi
DF: ハーツ HEARTS Co, Ltd.　Japan

Concept
キャラクターと同時に新ロゴも制作。ロゴのコンセプトは「地域を見わたす目を持ち、目のつけどころがちょっと違う、yab」。このキャラクター「ビープくん」は、その目を所有し、ロゴとシンクロして展開していくことを念頭に置いて制作された。「Y」と「A」がモチーフになっている。

The character was produced together with a new logo. The concept behind the logo was "yab: eyes that survey the area, and alight on the slightly different." The character Mr. Beep has such eyes. He was designed to work in sync with the logo. The letters Y and A form the base motif.

Profile
うれしいことがあったり、何か思いついたりすると頭のツノから電波が出る。マイペースで人懐っこく、さみしがり屋。yabの視聴者が元気の素。

Whenever something delightful happens or an idea comes to mind, Beep's horns emits radio waves. He's affectionate, but tends to suffer from lonesomeness. yab viewers are his source of vitality.

封筒　Envelope

ポストカード　Postcard

192　クリエイティブ　Media & Creative

ティッシュ　Tissue 
ステッカー　Sticker 
色鉛筆　Colored Pencil 
ネックストラップ　Neck Strap 
タオル　Towel

クリエイティブ　Media & Creative

デジタルは10チャンネル　On Digital Channel 10！　テレビ局　TV Station

CL, SB: テレビ愛知　AICHI TELEVISION BROADCASTING CO., LTD.　CD: 大矢明人　Akihito Oya　AD: 三沢あさみ　Asami Misawa　I: 多田真奈美　Manami Tada
DF: デザインオフィス・シック　DESIGN OFFICE CHIC　Japan

Concept
地上デジタル放送は難解なイメージがあるため、視聴者に親しみを持たせ、効果的な広報展開のできる形を目指した。新チャンネル数「10」をモチーフに、印象的な色とかわいさでインパクトを与えるロゴは、数字そのものに娯楽性を持ったところに楽しさがある。「1」の色は創造的なパワーや変化に適応する力を、「0」の色は0の持つ限りない可能性＝デジタルの始まりと未来を表現。また、のびたり縮んだり、自由に形態を変え動く様は、新しい時代を先導する柔軟さを表現している。

Because digital terrestrial broadcasting has the image of being difficult, the aim was to create a form viewers would find endearing and could be developed effectively in advertising. Taking the number of new channels, "10", as its motif, bold colors and charm give the logo impact, and the entertaining nature of the numbers themselves add an element of fun. The color of the "1" expresses the power of creativity and change, and the "0", the infinite potential of digital's start and future. Their ability to stretch and contract and move and change freely in form, reflect the flexibility needed to lead in the new age.

Profile
2003年12月に地上デジタル放送が開始して10ヵ月後に誕生。テレビ、新聞・雑誌広告、タクシーステッカー、社用封筒、手提げ紙袋、名刺などに表記される。キャラクターというよりもロゴ的な扱いで、呼称は、あくまで「デジタルは10チャンネル」とする。

Born ten months after digital terrestrial broadcasting began in December 2003. Used in television, newspaper and magazine adverting, taxi stickers, company envelopes, shopping bags, business cards, etc. used more in the manner of a logomark than a character.

クリアファイル　Clear File

TVCM

ウルフィ Wolfy   テレビ局 TV Station

CL, SB: メ〜テレ（名古屋テレビ放送）Meitele   CD: 岡 康道 Yasumichi Oka   DF: TUGBOAT   Japan

Concept
ウルフィは、メ〜テレのキャッチコピー「羊の皮をかぶったテレビ。」の内なる野性を表したキャラクター。名前は公募で、1万6000件の中から選ばれたもの。「羊の皮をかぶった狼」をイメージしたウルフ（オオカミ）に「ィ」をつけた語感のよさがネーミング決定の理由となった。

Wolfy is a character to express a wild nature as part of Nagoya TV's catch copy "Wolf in sheep's clothing television." The name was submitted by a member of the public and chosen from 16,000 suggestions because of the nuance produced by adding "y" to "wolf" thereby imaging a wolf in sheep's clothing.

Profile
ウルフィは、デジタル放送が始まった2003年生まれ。背中にファスナーがついた、羊の皮をかぶった狼。歩いたり、大きな口を開けたり、跳んだりするが、年齢も家族も棲家も、その実態は謎。だが、皆にかわいがってもらい、少々ファスナーを下ろしにくくなっている。アナログ放送終了の2011年には……！？

Wolfy, a wolf covered in a sheepskin with a zipper in the back was created in 2003, the year digital broadcasting began. He walks, opens his large mouth and jumps around, but nobody has any idea of his age, his family or where he lives.

ポスター　Poster

うちわ　Fan

ライター　Lighter

クリアファイル　Clear File　　ポストカード　Postcard

タンブラー　Tumbler

クリエイティブ　Media & Creative

てれビー Tele Bee テレビ局 TV Station

CL, SB: テレビ西日本 Television Nishi-Nippon Corporation Japan

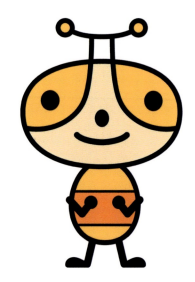

Concept
どこへでも様々なメッセージや情報を届ける働き者で、受敬のあるハチ(Bee)をモチーフとした。頭についているアンテナと顔の造形は、漢字の「西」を表現している。さらに大きな楕円の顔は、テレビをはじめとするモニターをイメージし、21世紀における多様なビジョンを映し出していく「テレビ西日本」そのものの姿を表している。

The charming, hard-working bee, willing to deliver messages and information anywhere, forms the basis of the character. His antennas and facial features form the Chinese character for "nishi (west)", and the large oval that defines his face follows the contours of TV monitors. The character embodies Television Nishinippon itself, a station projecting all sorts of visions of the 21 century.

Profile
てれビーは、はちのす団地に住む5歳のみつばちの男の子。明るく元気、好奇心旺盛で、ちょっぴりいたずらっ子。同じ団地に住むうわさ好きの女の子ビーズちゃんがお友達。

Tele Bee is a five-year-old honeybee boy who lives in a beehive housing complex. He's cheerful, vivacious, inquisitive, and a bit of mischief-maker. Beez-chan, a girl bee who and lives in the same complex and loves to gossip, is his friend.

ウェブサイト　Website

ベスト犬 ハチポ BEST KEN HACHIPO   テレビ局 TV Station

CL, SB: 長野放送 NAGANO BROADCASTING SYSTEM CO.,Ltd   DF: スタッフ コミュニケイション STAFF COMMUNICATIONS INC   Japan

Concept
キャラクターのデザインテーマは、NBSのデジタルチャンネル「8」、誰からも愛される「かわいらしさ」、デジタル時代にふさわしい「先進性」。ということで、特に「かわいらしさ」を最優先した。愛されないキャラクターは存在する意味がない。視聴者にとって最も身近な存在となるキャラクターとの触れあいを通して、視聴者に「NBSの気持ち」を敏感に感じ取ってもらうことを狙った。

The design themes for the character were the NBS digital channel "8," a "cuteness" loved by everyone and a "progressiveness" that is appropriate for the digital age. "Cuteness" was a priority as there was no point in the existence of a character that nobody liked. The aim was for viewers to realize NBS's sentiments through contact with the character that would be the closest presence to viewers.

Profile
名前はハチポ。種類はベスト犬。血液型はB型。性格はのんびり屋できれい好き。趣味は編み物で、特技は人をあったかい気持ちにすること。そして夢は、誰でも似合う「ベスト」になること。

Name: HACHIPO. Breed: Vest dog. Blood type: B. His personality traits are laid-back and clean-freak. His hobby is knitting; his special skill is making people feel good. And his dream is to knit the perfect vest that will suit anyone.

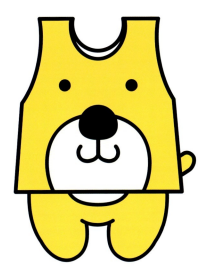

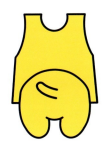

ハンドタオル Towel

クリアファイル Clear File

ポスター Poster

クリエイティブ Media & Creative

プラッピー　PLUPPY　テレビ局　TV Station

CL: 鹿児島放送　Kagoshima Broadcasting Corporation　CD, AD: 山田龍美　Tatsumi Yamada　D: 山本千夏　Chinatsu Yamamoto　I: 讃井久敬　Hisanori Sanui　CG Director: 田上公雅　Kiminori Tanoue　CG Animation: 山田裕也　Yuya Yamada / 高木一成　Kazunari Takaki / 小林由八　Yuya Kobayashi　Stuffed Animal Outfit Production: 帖佐明秀（造形工房 伝）　Akihide Chosa (Zoukeikoubou Den)　CG Production: ハッピープロジェクト　Happy Project, Inc.　DF, SB: アド・パスカル　AD-PASCAL Inc.　Japan

Concept

鹿児島放送（KKB）のキャッチフレーズとして使われている「＋（プラス）KKB」のプラス記号をモチーフにして生まれたキャラクター。カラーリングもKKBのロゴマークに使用しているシャイニングオレンジとオーシャンブルーを基本色としている。衣装は、季節や番組に合わせてそのときどきでコーディネート。ネーミングは、「プラス」と「ハッピー」を合わせたもの。

A character created out of the plus sign from Kagoshima Broadcasting Corp's (KKB) current slogan "+KKB". His coloration of shining orange and ocean blue also stems from KKB's logomark. His outfits change to reflect the seasons or coordinate with specific programs. His name is an amalgamation of the words "plus" and "happy".

Profile

大きな帽子とパッチリおめめがトレードマーク。気ままな性格で、ひょうひょうとしている。見た目のせいか、何を考えているか分からないとよく言われるけど、基本的にはプラス思考。旅と音楽とサツマイモが大好き。

His trademarks are his big hat and his big round eyes. He's aloof and does as he pleases. Perhaps due to his looks, people often tell him they don't know what he's thinking. He basically thinks positive. He likes traveling, music and sweet potatoes.

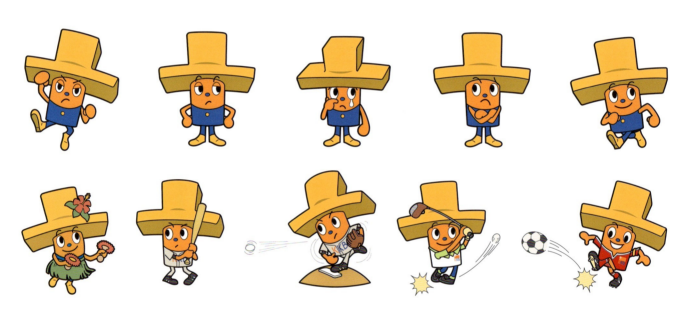

クリアファイル　Clear File　ステッカー　Sticker　ペーパークラフト　Paper Craft

りんご丸　Ringomaru　テレビ局　TV Station

CL, SB: 長野朝日放送　Asahi Broadcasting Nagano Co., Ltd.　CD: 酒井 克　Masaru Sakai　AD: 久保光貴　Mitsutaka Kubo　D: 田上公雅　Kiminori Tanoue
DF: ハッピープロジェクト　Happy Project. Inc.　Japan

Concept
長野朝日放送が2006年4月に開局15周年を迎え、同年10月にデジタル放送を開始する節目の年に、会社ロゴとキャラクター、キャッチフレーズを一新することになった。すべてに共通するのは信州の特産であるリンゴをモチーフにしたこと。リンゴのもつ親しみやすさ、愛らしい形をロゴやキャラクターにもたせた。ロゴは大文字のABNから小文字のabnに。キャラクターもリンゴの形をしつつ、ブタのように好奇心旺盛でコロコロしている感じを表現した。イラストとCGでは表情が微妙に違い、媒体で使い分けている。

To mark its 15th anniversary in April 2006, and the start of digital broadcasting in October the same year, Asahi Broadcasting Nagano decided to update its corporate logo, catchphrase and character. Apples, a local specialty, were chosen for their familiarity and lovable shape. The logo was changed from ABN in upper case to abn in lower case script, while the apple-shaped character rolls around full of porcine curiosity. Its expression was altered slightly for different media.

Profile
「ワクワクする夢に挑戦するabn」のシンボルとして、やんちゃでいつもおもしろいことを探して動き回っている。いつもはリンゴの木の枝にぶら下がっていて、行動する時は降りてくる。顔はブタのようで、リンゴの形をしている。他には両親の「パパりんご」「ママりんご」、友だちの「バグリ」「おさる」がいる。

As a symbol of the "abn determination to make exciting dreams reality" the character has a mischievous streak and is always searching for interesting things. This apple with the face of a pig that hangs from the branch of an apple tree also has a "Mama" and "Papa" apple, plus friends.

ステッカー　Sticker

ゴエティー　Goety　テレビ局　TV Station

CL, SB: 岩手朝日テレビ　Iwate Asahi TV Co., Ltd.　D: 阿部卓也　Takuya Abe　Japan

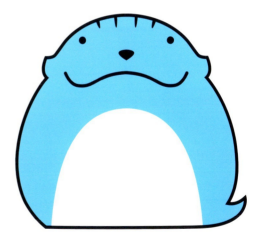

Concept
岩手朝日テレビの開局10周年と地上デジタル放送開始のPRのために開発したキャラクター。IAT＋デジタル5チャンネルの意味を込めて「ゴエティー」と命名。キャラクターの使命は具体的内容の伝達以前に、受け手と送り手をつなぐきっかけやふれあいを作ることにあると考え、そのための「顔」「親しみ」を最重視することとし、デザインには細心の注意を払った。登場シーンがバラエティに富むテレビの特性を考慮し、使用文脈を限定しない普遍性を目指した。

A PR character that was developed for the tenth anniversary of Iwate Asahi TV and the start of terrestrial digital broadcasting. His name is an amalgamation of "five (go)" for channel 5 and IAT. The mission of the character was to be a conduit between the TV company and viewers before transmission of actual content, and scrupulous attention was paid to his design with regard to his face and friendliness. Considering the kind of variety characteristic of television, the aim was a universality that would not be restricted by the context of his use.

Profile
のんびりとした風貌が多くの人をほっとさせ、和ませる。出身地は不明だが、生まれたのはヒマラヤ山脈あたりらしい。おもしろい場所、刺激的な場所を求めて旅をしているうちに岩手へ。IATの「ほっとできる」「おもしろくて時代に敏感」な持ち味が大好物。

His laid-back personality makes people feel safe and calm. His origins are unknown, but may be the Himalayan mountains. He arrived in Iwate on a journey seeking interesting and exciting places. He loves Iwate Asahi TV's (IAT) relaxing atmosphere and the sensitivity with which it portrays the times.

名刺　Business Card

ティッシュ　Tissue

クリエイティブ　Media & Creative

ADエディ　AD Eddie　テレビ局　TV Station

CL: 読売テレビ　Yomiuri Telecasting Corporation　AD: 尾前江美（読売テレビ）　Emi Omae (Yomiuri Telecasting Corporation)
D, I: 仲里カズヒロ（スタジオ・プール・ドット・コム）　Kazuhiro Nakazato (studio-pool.com)　Coordinator: 栗田真一（アイディー／アサヒ精版印刷）　Shinichi Kurita (Idea / asahi seihan printing co., ltd.)
SB: アイディー／アサヒ精版印刷 (Idea / asahi seihan printing co., ltd.)

Concept
AD（アシスタント・ディレクター）という設定で修行中の若者をイメージ。場の空気を和ませる表情と体型で出演者の子供たちとも仲良しというコンセプト。

Being an assistant director, he has a young, still-in-training image. The concept is that his expression and appearance calm the atmosphere of the studio and he get on well with the children appearing on the show.

Profile
忙しくスタジオ内をかけまわるAD（アシスタント・ディレクター）。ちょっとおっちょこちょいな仕草で出演者や番組スタッフに人気も上々！

An AD (assistant director) rushing busily around the TV studio. His slightly scatterbrained body language and expressions make him increasingly popular with the program guests and staff.

着ぐるみ　Character-shaped Outfit

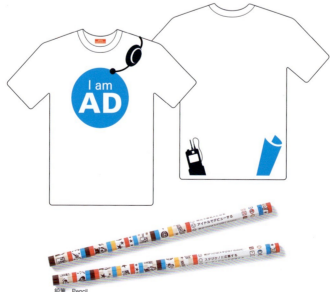
鉛筆　Pencil

そらぽ SORAPO　テレビ局　TV Station

CL, SB: 大分朝日放送　Oita Asahi Broadcasting Co., Ltd　D: 遠矢亜紀子　Akiko Toya　Japan

Concept
大分県を放送エリアとするテレビ局のキャラクターとして、子どもだけでなく地元の不特定多数の人に受け入れられることと、会社のカラー（海のブルー）、地域の活性化（前向きさ）のイメージから誕生。テレビ局のシンボルとしての役割（番組やイベント）だけではなく、故郷の大切さ、環境問題、心のあり方など、様々な問題を「そらぽ」自体がテレビ局を通して発信していけるよう、独立したストーリー展開も可能なフォルムにしている。

Designed to appeal not only to children but all sorts of local people, reflect the company color (sea blue) and reinvigorate the region (in a forward-thinking way). SORAPO has been given a form that has the potential to develop independent stories that generate affection for one's hometown, and awareness of environmental, ethical and other issues through the TV station, in addition to the role as a symbol of the station.

Profile
美しい未来の地球を知っている「そらぽ」は、太陽系から555光年ほど遠く離れたA24星雲からやってきて、自分の故郷にそっくりな大分に住むことにした。そして、大好きな大分を明るくしていくことが、「そらぽ」の夢。「がんばるぽ！」「OABをみてぽ！」と語尾に「ぽ」をつけるのが特徴。

Aware of the lovely future ahead on planet Earth, SORAPO came from the nebula A24, 555 light years away. He settled in Oita because it reminded him of his hometown. His dream is to make the Oita he adores a brighter place. He has a habit of adding the suffix "po" to statements, as in "Go, go, po!" and "Watch OAB, po!"

ろくちゃん rokuchan　放送局　Broadcasting Station

CL, SB: 信越放送　Shin-etsu Broadcasting Co., Ltd.　Japan

Concept
SBCデジタル放送用の6チャンネルから名前は「ろくちゃん」。ふくろうがモチーフだが鋭さは前面に出さず、デフォルメして全体的に丸をイメージさせ、バランスを取った。世代を超えて受け入れられる親しみやすさと認知度を意識。色遣いは環境色ながらビビッドに。ふくろうの特徴であるよく見える目は大きくし、羽毛のふわふわ感を損なわないデザインに。知的でありながら、優しさ、温かさのある癒しのオーラをまとうキャラクターを目指した。番組宣伝、広告も含め、展開の容易さも考慮した。

The name rokuchan came from the six (roku) channels of SBC digital broadcasting. The character is an owl, composed of amorphous shapes, and conscious of a friendliness that can transcend generations, and high recognition. The colors are vivid although environmental. The owl's eyes with their special ability to see things are large and the soft and the fluffy feeling of the feathers is not lost. The aim was to produce a character that, although intellectual, was gentle and had an aura of healing.

Profile
2006年秋、SBCが引っ越した長野市の複合エリア「TOiGO」に舞い降りたろくちゃんは、陽気で優しく、人懐っこいのにきみしがり屋。特技は木の葉のサーフィン、サッカー、ダンス、立ったまま眠ること。みんなを癒してくれるろくちゃんは、大好きな子どもたちと遊びたいと、今日もSBCで活躍中。

rokuchan who flew down to the TOiGO complex in Nagano City, where SBC had relocated in the autumn of 2006, loves the company of people. His special skills are surfing on a leaf, soccer, dancing and sleeping standing up.

新聞広告　Newspaper AD　　　ウェブサイト　Website

ぶんちゃん Bun-chan　新聞社 Newspaper Company

CL: 北海道新聞社　The Hokkaido Shimbun Press　CD: 藤本政恭　Masayasu Fujimoto / 斉藤栄太郎　Eitaro Saito　AD: 菊池啓一　Keiichi Kikuchi　D: 大西貴美恵　Kimie Ohnishi
I: 土車大八　Daihachi Tsuchiguruma　SB: 北海道博報堂　HOKKAIDO HAKUHODO　Japan

Concept
2006年北海道新聞社は、北海道で暮らす人々に役立つ情報や楽しいサービスを提供するため、道新ぶんぶんクラブを発足。そのクラブの顔として、また、新聞社と読者をつなぐパイプ役として、世代を問わず好かれること、新聞社のキャラクターだとひと目で分かることを強く意識したデザインに。

The Hokkaido Newspaper created the Doshin Bunbun Club in 2006 to provide information and fun services to people living in Hokkaido. As the face of the club and also as a conduit for connecting the newspaper company to the readership, Bun-chan was created based on a strong awareness of appeal to all age groups and being instantly recognizable as the character of a newspaper company.

Profile
人なつっこく、やんちゃで好奇心旺盛な「ぶんちゃん」。その正体は謎。トレードマークは、肌身離さずかぶっている北海道新聞で作った「かぶと」。

The friendly, impish and full of curiosity Bun-chan. His true nature is shrouded in mystery. His trademark is his helmet made from the Hokkaido Newspaper, which he never takes off.

©Doshin / HH

ポスター　Poster

おにぎりボックス　Rice Ball Box

どーもくん Domo テレビ局 TV Station

CL: NHK   DF, SB: ドワーフ dwarf inc. Japan

Concept

NHKのイメージキャラであるどーもくん。丸や四角や三角を落書きのように描いているうちに形となったこのキャラクターのコンセプトは「理屈が見えないもの」。放送局のキャラクターらしく頭にアンテナが生えていたり、手がリモコンになっていたりするのではなく、理屈ではないところで視聴者が気になるキャラクターとなることを狙った。

Domo is the image character of NHK. The result of graffiti-like scribbling of circles, squares and triangles, the concept behind this character is embodiment of something unaccountable and mysterious. The aim was not the image of a character befitting a TV-station with an antenna on his head or a remote control for a hand, but rather one viewers would learn to love for no rhyme or reason.

Profile

タマゴから生まれたへんてこ動物。もっさいボディとピュアなハートの持ち主。テレビが大好き。空想に耽りがちなぼんやりさんで、結果、良からぬことになる場合も多い。機嫌を損ねると強烈なおならをする。好きな食べ物は肉じゃがで、りんごが嫌い。（DNAに刻まれた深いナゾがあるらしい。）

A strange creature hatched from an egg. Stout in body, pure in heart. Loves TV. His tendency to daydream and space out often cause trouble. Lets out explosive farts when upset. Favorite food is Japanese-style stewed meat and potatoes. Hates apples (a mystery written into his DNA).

©NHK・TYO

缶バッジ
Badge

セロテープ
Cellophane Tape

ニョコ   Nyoko   出版 Publication

CL, SB: NHK出版 NHK BOOK   CD: 寺島卓男 Takuo Terashima   AD, I: 片瀬奈々 Nana Katase   DF: キャップ・アソシエイツ Cap Associates   Japan

Concept
ニョコのモチーフは「芽生え」。NHKテキストを使って新しい何かを始める人をイメージしている。学んでいく過程で、知識や能力の芽が「にょこにょこ」伸びていくことを表現。上手にできたときは頭に花が咲いたり、逆に失敗したときはしょんぼりと萎れてしまったりと、受講者の喜怒哀楽を共有するキャラクター。

Nyoko has a seedling motif. It is used on NHK textbooks, imaging a person starting something new. It expresses the seedlings of knowledge and capability shooting up in the process of learning. When he does well the flower on his head blossoms, and when he fails it wilts dejectedly, and thus shares the same joys and frustrations as the students in the course.

Profile
動物でも植物でもない謎の生き物。小学校低学年程度の知識、能力を持っている。ちょっと面倒くさがり屋だが、好奇心は旺盛で、とっても素直な性格。

A curious character, neither plant nor animal. It has the knowledge and capabilities of child in the lower elementary school years. A bit on the lazy side, but full of curiosity and gentle in nature.

ミミディ   Mimidy   出版（電子版テキスト「dテキスト」） Publication (Degital Textbook "d text")

CL, SB: NHK出版 NHK BOOK   CD, AD: 鈴木 哲 Tetsu Suzuki   D: 川口創史 Soushi Kawaguchi   I: 波田佳子 Yoshiko Hada   DF: スガタデザイン研究所 Sugata design labo Inc.   Japan

Concept
コンピュータで利用できる電子版テキスト、通称dテキストのキャラクター「ミミディ」は、耳が「d」の形をしている。Dテキストの「d」、デジタルの「d」を象徴的に表現している。親しみやすさとやや未来的な風貌で、dテキストの楽しさや先進性を表している。

Mimidy is the character for the digital textbooks, also known as "d texts", for use on personal computers. His ears (mimi) are shaped like the letter "d" symbolizing the initial "d" of d texts and digital. He is friendly and slightly futuristic in appearance, expressing the fun and advanced nature of d texts.

Profile
性別、年齢は不明。天才的プログラマー。いつもパソコンを持ち歩いて様々な分野で情報通。

Age and sex unknown. A programming genius. Always walks around with a computer in hand, and is well of information on all sorts of subjects.

©キャップ・アソシエイツ、酒井祐子、NHK出版、NHK 2006

マルコX etc　MarukoX etc
テレビ局〈NHK教育TV 小学3年理科「ふしぎだいすき」〉 TV Station (Educational Science Program "Fushigi Daisuki")

CL: NHK　CD: 愛があれば大丈夫 AI GA AREBA DAIJOBU　AD, D: 山下浩平（マウンテンマウンテン）Kohei Yamashita (mountain mountain)　SB: マウンテンマウンテン mountain mountain

Concept
小学校3年生向けの理科番組「ふしぎだいすき」のキャラクター。「時間を縮めて見せてくれる、ハイウェイスターZ」「目に見えないところまで拡大して見せてくれる、まめⅢ世SS」、「ほかのものと比較しながら、知らないことを教えてくれる、ふしぎ兄さんK」など、番組内容に応じてそれぞれのキャラクターがその特性を発揮し、子どもたちに生物や植物の世界を紹介する役割を果たす。それぞれのキャラクターの特性が分かるフォルムにデザインされている。

Characters for the science program "Fushigi Daisuki (I love mystery)" geared towards third-graders. Characters – Highway Star Z who shortens time, Mame III SS who magnifies things invisible to the naked eye, and Big Brother Fushigi K who teaches new things by making comparisons – display their characteristics as suits the content of the program and teach children the wonders of the animal and plant kingdoms. Their forms reflect their special talents.

Profile
何にでも疑問をもつ主人公「マルコX」をはじめ、携帯片手に最新情報を教えてくれる「ダイスケさんG」、ファイバーを伸ばして中を見せてくれる「スケルアイB」、拡大して見せてくれる「メカボーQ」、スローで見せてくれる「ビッグボーンP」など、ふしぎのなかまたちには8つのキャラクターがいる。

A gang of eight curious characters including their ever skeptical leader MarukoX, Daisuke-san G who with mobile phone in hand keeps us abreast of news, Sukeru-eye B who stretches fiber optics and shows us what's inside, Mekabo Q who enlarges things, and Bigbone P who slows us things in slow motion.

© NHK

Baby's, Sennin's, Cat, Dog, Rabbit　出版〈マニアブックシリーズ〉Publication (MANIA Books Series)

CL: エムディエヌコーポレーション MdN Corporation　CD, AD, D, I, SB: Maniackers Design　Japan

Concept
それぞれの仙人たち（Sennin's）の杖を"F""P""I"をモチーフにデザイン。

The design takes the first initials of the different wizards (sennins) "F", "P" and "I" as its motif.

Profile
出版社のMdNコーポレーションが発行する書籍「FONT MANIA」「PATTERN MANIA」「ICON MANIA」のカバー、中面ページに登場するキャラクター。キャラクター名は、Baby's、Sennin's、Cat、Dog、Rabbit。Baby'sは、生まれたときからさまざまなデザインのテクニックを教えてくれるスーパー赤ちゃん。

Characters that appear on the covers and inside pages of the books FONT MANIA, PATTERN MANIA and ICON MANIA published by MdN Corporation. Their names are Baby's, Sennin's, Cat, Dog, and Rabbit. Baby's is a superbaby who has been teaching all sorts of design techniques since the day he was born.

本のムシくん Hon-no-Mushi-kun　出版 Publication

CL: 光文社　Kobunsha Co., Ltd.　AD, D: 杉山ユキ　Yuki Sugiyama　CW: 中村恭子　Kyoko Nakamura / 井口雄大　Yuta Iguchi　Agency, SB: 博報堂　HAKUHODO Inc.

Concept

知恵の「森」を意識して、緑色をキーカラーに、あたたかみのある版画のテクスチャを用いてキャラクターをデザインした。本好きをアイコン化するために、いつもたくさんの本を持っている。

The character was designed with a warm, woodcut-like texture, and green made the key color, referencing the "forest" of wisdom. Iconizing the booklover, the bookworm is always with book in hand.

Profile

知恵の森に住んでいて、好奇心旺盛な「本のムシくん」。本を読みすぎて、ムシになった。

An inquisitive bookworm who lives in the forest of wisdom. Became a worm as a result of reading too much.

ブックカバー　Book Cover

タンブラー　Tumbler

トスポ　Tospo　テレビ局　TV Station

CL: 読売テレビ　Yomiuri Telecasting Corporation　AD: 伊藤大樹（読売テレビ）　Daiju Ito (Yomiuri Telecasting Corporation)
D, I: 仲里カズヒロ（スタジオ・プール・ドット・コム）　Kazuhiro Nakazato (studio-pool.com)　Cordinator: 栗田真一（アイディー／アサヒ精版印刷）　Shinichi Kurita (Idea / asahi seihan printing co., ltd.)
SB: アサヒ精版印刷　asahi seihan printing co., ltd.　Japan

Concept
従来のポスト型のキャラクター『トスポ』のリニューアル。更にかわいく、少しノスタルジックな「ゆるキャラ」の雰囲気や表情を意識して創作。世界観やデザインも合わせてお洒落なイメージで展開。

The upgrading of the traditional post box character Tospo. Consciously designed in atmosphere and expression to be an even more endearing, slightly nostalgic, lackadaisical character. Together his world and the design were smartened up in the development.

Profile
ダウンタウンDX（デラックス）のマスコットのトスポはにぎやかで楽しそうな場所が大好き。おしゃべりしている人たちを見てニコニコキョロキョロ。

The mascot for the TV talk show Downtown DX (Deluxe), Tospo likes lively, fun-looking places. He stares, all smiles whenever he sets his eyes on people chatting away.

手ぬぐい　Towel

ポストカード　Postcard

スタジオ　Studio

ポケットくんとポケットちゃん　pocket-kun & pocket-chan　出版 Publication

CL: ポプラ社　POPLAR PUBLISHING CO., LTD.　CD, AD: 大野耕平　Kohei Ohno　CD, CW: 井口雄大　Yuta Iguchi　D, SB: buffalo-D　P: 廣瀬達郎　Tatsuro Hirose
Image Processing: 宮本准　Hitoshi Miyamoto　SB: 博報堂　HAKUHODO Inc.　Japan

Concept
ひとりひとりのポケットくんとポケットちゃんは、誰かのポケットの分身。広告塔というよりは、本とふれあう新たなきっかけになれるようにという願いを込めて制作。ジーンズやニット、フェルト、コットンなど、ポケット文庫が入ることができそうなさまざまな洋服や鞄の素材、手触り感やあたたかみを大切にしながら形に。子供から大人まで幅広いポケット文庫の読者層に親しんでもらえるよう、懐の大きいデザインを意識した。

Every pocket-chan & pocket-kun is the offspring of somebody's pocket. The characters were created less as advertising vehicles than as new means to get people to encounter books. Their forms stressed a handmade quality and the sense of the texture of materials such as denim, knit, felt, and cotton used to make clothes and bags that a pocketsize book could conceivably slip into. To appeal to pocket book readers young and old, they were imbued with a sense of generosity.

Profile
"誰のポケットにもきっと夢の入る隙間はある"そんな思いから生まれたのがポケットくんとポケットちゃん。そのほか感動屋さんなジーンズのポケット「ジーンジーン」や個性派なカラージーンズのポケット「カラジ」をはじめ、現在総勢9名のユニークな仲間たち。

A gang of nine unique characters including pocket-kun & pocket-chan, who were born of the idea that "in every pocket there's a space for a dream"; Jean-Jean, an impressionable jeans pocket; and Karaji, the very individualistic color jeans pocket.

ポスター　Poster

パンフレット　Pamphlet

しおり　Bookmark

ブックカバー　Book Cover

ポスター　Poster

クリエイティブ　Media & Creative　209

だっち君　DACCHI KUN　　新聞社　Newspaper Company

CL, SB: 読売新聞東京本社　THE YOMIURI SHIMBUN　　CD: サトー克也　Katsuya Sato　　AD: 芝井洋二　Youji Shibai　　D: 鈴木 大（ADKアーツ）　Dai Suzuki (ADK Arts Inc.) / 荒井由香里（ADKアーツ）　Yukari Arai (ADK Arts Inc.)　　CW: 河野洋平　Yohei Kawano　　CM Planner: 山田高之　Takayuki Yamada　　CM Production: ガレージフィルム　Garage Film Inc.　　DF: ADKアーツ　ADK Arts Inc.　　Agency: アサツー ディ・ケイ　ASATSU-DK INC.　Japan

Concept

だっち君ファミリーは、読売新聞の夕刊販売促進のために生まれたキャラクター。そのため、夕焼けのオレンジをキーカラーとし、夕方から活躍し始める「コウモリ」をモチーフに、かわいくデザイン。「だっちボール」、「だっちまくら」など、毎年行われるキャラクターグッズプレゼントキャンペーンが好評。大人気のため、現在は夕刊の枠を越え、読売新聞のマスコットとして活躍するようになった。

The DACCHI KUN family are characters created for promoting sales of the Yomiuri Shimbun's evening edition. The motif therefore is a bat known for its nocturnal activity, based on a key color of sunset orange and a cute design. The free character goods campaign conducted annually such as Dacchi Ball and Dacchi Makura (pillow) are popular. The family's extreme popularity has transcended them beyond the evening edition and they are now Yomiuri Shimbun mascots.

Profile

だっち君ファミリーは「よみかきの森」に住んでいるコウモリの家族。お父さんの「であーる」、お母さんの「ざます」、弟の「だっちょ君」の4人家族。

The DACCHI KUN is a family of bats who live in "YOMI-KAKI-NO-MORI", the forest of reading and writing. The family has four members: DEAARU, the father bat, ZAMASU the mother bat and brothers DACCHI and DACCHO.

ポスター　Poster

POP

TVCM

フライヤー　Flyer

枕　Pillow

どんぶり　Rice Bowl　　ネッククッション　Neck Cushion

ナビーくん　Navi-kun　新聞社　Newspaper Company

CL, SB: 産経新聞社 SANKEI SHIMBUN CO., LTD.　CD: 石田康成 Yasunari Ishida　I: 石田孝文 Takafumi Ishida　DF: 石田図工室 ISHIDA ZUKOSHITSU, LLC.
Production: 電通西日本 DENTSU WEST JAPAN INC.　Japan

Concept
"テレビナビ"という誌名から、テレビ業界のあれこれをナビゲートするキャラクターを設定した。誌面の単なるアイコンではなく、さまざまな芸能人・業界人と絡めるよう、アクティブに動き、よくしゃべるキャラクター作りを心がけた。造形的にはなじみ深い"犬"をモチーフに。頭からスッポリとロゴ入りのTシャツをかぶったその姿は、犬というよりもちょっと不思議な生物の印象が強いが、可愛い路線ではなく、少し引っかかりのある性格と姿によって、読者と親密になることを狙った。

A navigator character was created in keeping with the magazine's title and role as a guide to everything television. Not just a decorative icon, Navi-kun is a proactive, talkative character who chats with TV insiders and celebrities. Though the dog design is a familiar one, with his head barely poking out of a snug-fitting logo T-shirt, Navi-kun looks less a dog and more some alien creature. Something about him makes you look twice, making him a character to which readers can relate.

Profile
テレビ雑誌「月刊テレビナビ」のマスコット犬、ナビーくん。身長27cm、体重10kg、犬種はナビーグル犬。迷子だったところをテレビナビ編集部に拾われる。以降はテレビナビのTシャツを着用し、抜群の嗅覚と「やるナビ！」の精神で面白い番組や人物を見つけるナビゲート役に。

The Navi-kun mascot of monthly TV guide "Gekkan TV navi" is a homeless "naveagle" dog taken in by the magazine's editorial staff. Dressed in the magazine's T-shirt, with a keen nose and can-do attitude he helps readers navigate their way around the TV schedule in search of interesting programs and people.

ブックマーク & カレンダー　Bookmark & Calendar　　　　月刊テレビナビ　Monthly TVnavi

ポストカード　Postcard

メモ　Note Pad

ラジ男　Rajio　ラジオ局　Radio Station

CL: エフエム香川　FM KAGAWA. INC　　I: 広田桂子　Keiko Hirota　　SB: ポレポレーション・スタジオ　polepoletion. STUDIO　Japan

Concept

「エフエム香川」開局20周年を記念して制作されたイメージキャラクター。キャンペーンを盛り上げるため、"ラジオ"や"FM香川"を感じさせる、可愛らしく、かつインパクトのあるキャラクターになるよう心がけた。基本形をシンプルにしてコスチュームを着替えさせることで、さまざまな音楽ジャンルや番組に対応できるよう配慮を施している。

Rajio was created to mark 20 years of FM Kagawa. The idea was to design an appealing, memorable character readily associated with radio and FM Kagawa, and special care was taken to make the character adaptable to various types of music and programs, by using different costumes on the same basic form.

Profile

名前はラジ男。讃岐生まれの讃岐育ちで、発明と機械いじりが趣味の男の子。黒タイツと自作のラジオチューナー付きヘッドフォンを身にまとい、得意の欽ちゃん走りで駆け抜ける。讃岐育ちなので、うどんが大好物。

Born and raised in Sanuki (now Kagawa Prefecture), Rajio loves inventing and tinkering with machinery. Donning black tights and radio headphones, he rushes about with a skipping sidestep of the sort made famous by veteran comedian Kin-chan. His favorite food is the local Sanuki speciality: udon.

のぼり　Flag

ステッカー　Sticker

缶バッジ　Badge

封筒　Envelope

タイムテーブル　Time Table

ファンキーモンキーベイビーズ　FUNKY MONKEY BABYS　音楽事業 Music Industry

CL: ドリーミュージック DREAMUSIC　AD, D: 山本智恵子 Chieko Yamamoto　I: 寄藤文平 Bunpei Yorifuji　DF, SB: アンサー ANSWR　Japan

Concept
「FUNKY MONKEY BABYS」というユニット名にちなみ、サルをモチーフに、分かりやすく親しみやすいキャラクターを設定。

Using a monkey motif in keeping with the band's name, characters were created that were accessible and easy to understand.

Profile
3ピースのヒップホップユニット「FUNKY MONKEY BABYS」のキャラクター。メンバーの分身として、あらゆるメディアで活躍中!

Characters from the Funky Monkey Babys three-piece hip-hop unit, used widely across various media to represent the individual members of the trio.

携帯待受画面　Standby Display for Mobile Phone

ポストカード　Postcard　　　　　　　　　　　　　　　　　　　　　　　ステッカー　Sticker

スーパーボール　Super Ball　　　　　　　　　　　　　　　ピンバッジ　Pin Badge

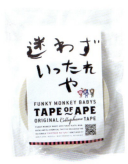

セロテープ　Cellophane Tape　　　　　　　　　　　　　リストバンド　Wrist Band

絆創膏　Plaster

コペット　copet　デザイン会社 Design Firm

CL, DF, SB: バタフライ・ストローク butterfly・stroke inc　CD: 田中 徹 Toru Tanaka　AD, D: 青木克憲 Katsunori Aoki　I: 久保誠二郎 Seijiro Kubo　Japan

イラストレーター、久保誠二郎氏のライフワークである「コペット」シリーズ。ペーパークラフトを思わせる直線的な表現にもかかわらず、フルポリゴンCGに勝る豊かな表情とドラマが楽しめる動物キャラクター。ターゲットに確実に印象づけることができる、強い訴求力をもったキャラクターである。

copet series of animal characters is the lifework of illustrator Seijiro Kubo. Despite their rectilinear surfaces and edges reminiscent of papercraft, they exceed full polygon computer graphics in their delightful expressions and drama. They are characters with strong appeal, able to make a distinct impression on their target market.

【エムブランド】
分譲マンション「エムブランド越谷 GAMO」のキャラクター。商品購買層であるファミリー層にとくに人気のある5つのキャラクターを起用した。「楽演ジャングリラ」というコピーにもあるように、にぎやかで愉快な生活を表現し、幅広い層に愛される存在になることを目指した。

<M-Brand>
The characters for the condominium M-Brand Koshigaya GAMO. The five characters particularly with families, the projected buyers, were utilized. Coupled with the copy "Jangri-La Jungle", they aim to express a lively and pleasant life, and to be endearing to a wide range of people.

チラシ　Flyer

ポスター　Poster

リーフレット　Leaflet

のぼり　Flag

≫ コペット copet

【コカ・コーラ】
サマーキャンペーンという性質上、リゾート・元気さ・楽しさといったキーワードをもとに制作。メインキャラクターのクーマのほか、夏らしい世界観を出すために、セイウチとペンギンがビーチでアクティブに夏を満喫する様子は、消費者に対し、ユーモアとインパクトを与えた。

<Coca Cola>
Expressing the qualities of a summer campaign, the characters were based on three keywords: resort, vitality, fun. To create a summery atmosphere, a walrus and penguin joined the main character, K~uMA, for an active summer at the beach, adding humor and impact for consumers.

フィギュア　Figure

ファン　Fan

ポスター　Poster

スピーカー　Speaker

TVCM

【numo】

「使用済み核燃料の地層処分」という事業内容を分かりやすく説明するナビゲーター役として動物キャラクターを制作。タレントとキャラクターの掛け合いのなかで内容を説明するという手法を使い、分かりやすくキャッチーに表現することを心がけた。

<numo>

An animal character was created to play the role of navigator, explaining the nature of the business of deep geological disposal of spent nuclear fuel in an easy to comprehend way. Using the approach of a dialogue between a celebrity and the character, care was taken to express the content in a simple, in a catchy way.

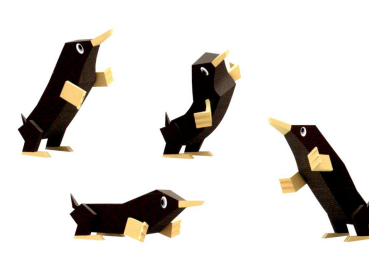

ポスター　Poster

新聞広告　Newspaper AD

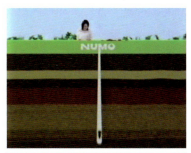

TVCM

にじぞう *niji-zou* デザイン会社 Design Firm

CL, DF, SB: バタフライ・ストローク butterfly・stroke inc.　　CD, AD: 青木克憲 Katsunori Aoki　　I: 林 修三 Shuzou Hayashi　Japan

Concept

グラフィックデザイナー兼イラストレーター、林修三氏のライフワークである「にじぞう」。キーワードはハッピー・子供・無邪気・平和・安らぎ……などで、"子供の無邪気さは多くの人を幸せにできる"という信念のもと、子供ならではの魂が力強く表現された状態を絵にしている。ファンタジックなストーリー性を取り入れることにより、子供時代にファンタジーと現実の境界線を自由に行き来して遊んでいたような大人たちを癒してくれるヒーリングキャラクター。

niji-zou is the brainchild of graphic designer and illustrator Shuzou Hayashi. Key words for niji-zou's design include happy, child, innocence, peace, and relaxation, and he is the visual representation of a child's spirit, based on a belief in the capacity of childhood innocence to bring happiness for many. With his ability to weave a story, niji-zou is a comfort to grownups who as children at play were able to move freely between fantasy and reality.

Profile

にじぞうは、幸福な世界の象徴。出会った人を大きく包み込む母親のような一面と、遊びに夢中になる子供のような一面を持っている。宇宙や月、雲と遊ぶこと、乗り物や傘に変身することが大好き。自然とも仲良しで、雨を降らせたり、花を咲かせたりすることが得意。

niji-zou symbolizes a happy world and is both a mother-like figure embracing everyone he meets, and a child absorbed in play. He enjoys cavorting with space, the moon and clouds, and changing into objects such as different forms of transport and umbrellas. A good friend too of the Earth, he specializes in making rain fall and flowers bloom.

ステッカー　Sticker

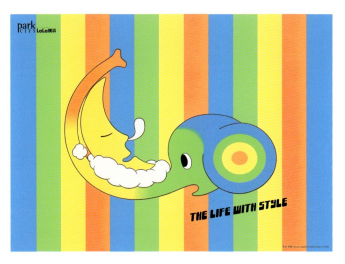

ポスター Poster

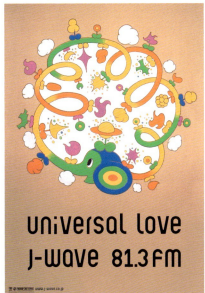

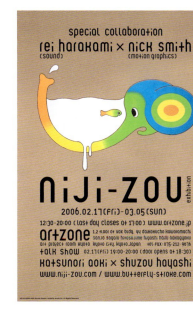

ポスター Poster

ウェブサイト Website

展覧会 Exhibition

展覧会 Exhibition

映像作品 Movie

クリエイティブ Media & Creative 221

6ちゃん roku-chan   デザイン会社 Design Firm

CL, SB, CD: 螢光TOKYO KEIKO TOKYO   AD, D: DESIGN BOY   P (Anthology): RiN   Japan

Concept
「将来、数字の絵本を作る」、というコンセプトのもと、その年々の数字をキャラ化し、全ての数字がキャラ化された時に話が完成するように企画した。従って来年は「8ちゃん」がデビュー予定。デザインについては、撮影で訪れたNYのMOMA美術館でダリの作品を見る機会があり、その有機的な曲線美にインスパイアされて描いたスケッチが元になっている。

Based on the idea of someday creating a "picture book of numbers", the plan calls for characterizing a number every year and when they are all complete the story too will finish. Consequently, 8-chan will debut in 2008. The design is based on sketches inspired by the beautiful organic lines seen in Dali's paintings upon visiting MoMA while in New York on a photo shoot.

Profile
クリエイティブブティック・螢光TOKYOのマスコットキャラとして誕生。制作された2006年の「6」をモチーフに。口から音符を吹き出すので楽器がモチーフとも言われている。現在は螢光TOKYOのウェブサイトで、2007年のキャラ「7ちゃん」と壮絶なバトルを繰り広げている。

Born as the mascot character for the creative boutique KEIKO TOKYO. Takes the number 6 – from 2006, the year it was produced – as its basic form, but because it has music notes flowing from its mouth, one might say it also images a musical instrument. Currently engaging in sublime battle with the 2007 character 7-chan on the KEIKO TOKYO website.

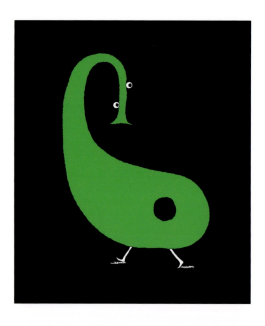

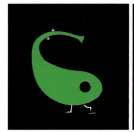 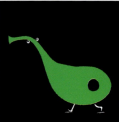 

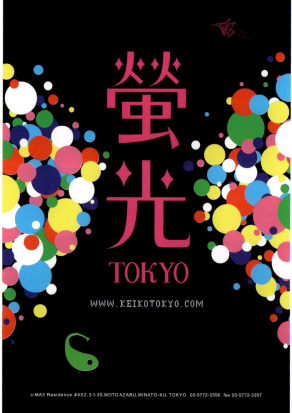

DM

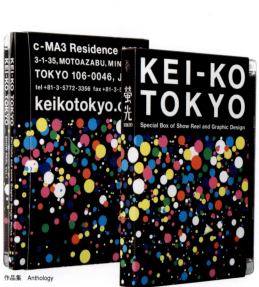

作品集 Anthology

企業広告 Company AD

封筒 Envelope

ドワーフ dwarf   キャラクター / アニメーション制作会社   Character & Animation Production

CL, SB: ドワーフ　dwarf inc.　Japan

Concept
dwarf inc.の企業キャラクター。キチンとしていないこと。落書きのような、ゆるさと自由さで、クリエイティブの楽しさを表現。「ドワーフ」とは小人のこと。デザイン時に小人モチーフのものをたくさん描き、肩の力を抜いて描いたものが現在のキャラクターとなった。なんの生き物かよくわからないところがポイント。

The company character for dwarf inc. Lax. Expresses the looseness, freedom, and creative pleasures of graffiti. A great many dwarfs were drawn in the process of designing this character; the one selected was drawn after loosening up and going with the flow. The main point is being an indefinable creature.

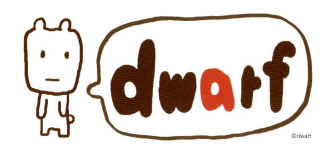

ステッカー　Sticker

ガムテープ　Gummed Tape

ガーデン・ノーム Garden Gnome   CM制作会社   Commercial Film Production Company

CL: SMITH AND JONES FILMS　CD, AD, D, I, SB: SWEDEN GRAPHICS　Sweden

Concept
スミス＆ジョーンズ・フィルムスのブランディング、ウェブサイト構築にあたり、ウェブ上に架空の世界をつくりあげ、生き生きとしたストーリーを与えた。

To put some life into the web site and help create a fictional world around the S&J web site and brand name.

Profile
ガーデン・ノームは短気なアマチュア科学者。

Garden Gnome is a ill-tempered, misunderstood, amateur scientist.

ウェブサイト　Website

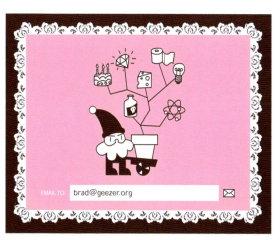

クリエイティブ　Media & Creative

1. **Just keep movin'** ファッション Fashion / CL: Graniph Japan I, DF, SB: Jeremyville Australia
2. **半額半蔵 Hangaku Hanzo** 映画配給(「半額半蔵」キャンペーン) Film Distributing Agency ("Hangaku Hanzo" Campaign) / CL: ソニーピクチャーズエンタテインメント Sony Pictures Entertainment Inc. I: 久保誠二郎 Seijiro Kubo SB: バタフライ・ストローク butterfly・stroke inc. Japan
3. **Anagadirri** 演劇 / 音楽 / パフォーマンス事業 Theatre & Music & Performance / CL: Anagadirri Productions D, DF, SB: Kjetil Vatne Norway
4. **Future Lion** 広告コンクール Advertising Competition / CL, DF: AKQA I, SB: Meomi Design Canada
5. **Ariane** 出版 Publishing / CL: Fil d'Ariane Guide Book DF, SB: Meomi Design Canada
6. **Berri, Nilla, Coco** オンラインマガジン Online Magazine / CL: Joypop DF, SB: Meomi Design Canada

Concept & Profile of Characters

056-2　中林歯科 キャラクター Character of NAKABAYASHI DENTAL CLINIC
コンセプト: "歯が元気！"をひと目見て分かるよう、歯に顔を描いてデザインした。
CONCEPT: To convey at a glance he has "healthy teeth", the character has been designed as a tooth with a face drawn on it.
プロフィール: 中林歯科のシンボルマークであり、マスコットキャラクターでもある。
PROFILE: The symbol mark and mascot character of NAKABAYASHI DENTAL CLINIC.

056-3　リフォーム・ワン キャラクター Character of Reform One
コンセプト: 住宅のリフォーム事業サービスを展開する際にロゴ・キャラクターともにデザイン。リフォームされた家が喜んでいるハッピーな様子に着目し、キャラクター化を行った。
CONCEPT: A logo and character were designed in conjunction with the expansion of services of a home remodeling business. This character personifies a remodeled home being a happy home.

056-4　ゴールドボーイズ GOLD BOYS
コンセプト: 新進気鋭の若きクリエイター集団「DEVILROBOTS」が手がける、TSUTAYA店頭やサイトで大暴れするやんちゃくれキャラ「GOLD BOYS」。
CONCEPT: Mischievous characters who break loose in TSUTAYA shops and website, designed by the up-and-coming creative group DEVILROBOTS.
プロフィール: 兄やん（ANI-yan）はGOLDの長男。おと坊と遊ぶのが日課。おと坊（OTO-bow）は、兄やんの弟。お風呂が大好き。ニヤ（Nya）はGOLD団の飼いネコ。特技は爪研ぎとネコだまし。
PROFILE: ANI-yan is the gang's big brother. His daily task is to play with his younger brother OTO-bow, who loves to take baths. Nya is the GOLD's spy cat. His special talents are sharpening his claws and the "cat clap" (a sumo technique used to deceive one's opponent).

056-5　ダブル子ちゃん Double-ko-chan
コンセプト: 2枚以上DVDを購入すると通常より安価で購入できる「TSUTAYA RECORDSなら、2枚で￥2,500」という定番コーナーの定番キャラクター。購入するDVDの枚数により頭にかぶっている帽子のとんがりの数が異なる。アカデミー賞のシーズンにはドレスアップしたり、季節によって衣装を変更することもある。
CONCEPT: The character for TSUTAYA RECORDS' standard "two for ￥2,500" corner. The number of peaks on the hat she wears changes to reflect the number of DVDs purchased. She dresses up during Academy Award season, and changes her garb with the four seasons as well.
プロフィール: 夢見るOL。好きなDVDを2枚購入。
PROFILE: An office clerk with a dream. Buys her favorite DVDs two at a time.

056-6　Ogosagi
コンセプト: ユーザーになる可能性のある幅広いターゲットにアピールする、シンプルで楽しいキャラクター。
CONCEPT: Simple, fun & appealing to wide target group of possible users.
プロフィール: 新しいコミュニケーションデバイスの機能を紹介し、説明するのを助けてくれる小さなヘルパーたち。
PROFILE: Little helpers. They help to introduce & explain the functions of a new communication device.

104-3　わいもぐら Waimogura
コンセプト: 商品である「わいも！」と「もぐら」を掛け合わせた造語、「わいもぐら」というネーミングからインスピレーションを受けてデザインした。
CONCEPT: The name Waimogura is an amalgamation of the product name Waimo! and "mogura" (mole). The design takes its inspiration from the name.
プロフィール: コイケヤの新商品カップスナック「わいも！」のマスコットキャラクター。
PROFILE: The mascot character for Koikeya's new product cup snack "Waimo!" His name is Waimogura.

104-4　Cloud 9 Airplane
コンセプト: 雲はトイレットペーパーの柔らかさを表している。飛行機は空のコンセプトを強調している。
CONCEPT: The clouds relate to how soft the toilet paper is. The airplane reinforces the sky concept.

104-5　Robochan
コンセプト: Robochanという米ニューメキシコのソフトウェア会社の依頼により、ブランディング、パッケージ、ソフトウェアに使用する楽しくて愛嬌のあるロボットキャラクターを制作した。
CONCEPT: Robochan is a software company based in New Mexico, US. They approached us about designing a fun, amiable robot character that they can use for their branding, packaging and software.
プロフィール: この会社と同様に、Robochanもキュートでスマート。
PROFILE: Like the company he represents, Robochan has to be cute and smart.

118-1　ダルテくん Darute-kun
コンセプト: 「アルテ高崎」応援のため、地域活性化の一貫として制作を行った。サッカーボールと、高崎名物であるダルマを融合させてキャラクタライズ。ネーミングはサポーターからの公募で決定した。
CONCEPT: Produced to generate support for ARTE TAKASAKI as part of a systematic program to reinvigorate the area. Darute-kun personifies the fusion of a soccer ball and one of Takasaki's noted products, the Daruma (Bodhidharma) doll. His name was selected in an open competition from suggestions by supporters.
プロフィール: 日本フットボールチーム「アルテ高崎」のキャラクター。名前はダルテくん。
PROFILE: Mascot character for the Japanese football team ARTE TAKASAKI. His name is Darute-kun.

118-2　スターマちゃん Miss STARMA
コンセプト: 「ホワイトスター高崎」を応援するため、地域活性化の一貫として制作を行う。フワフワした可愛らしい「雲」をキャラクター化することに着目。ホワイトスターの飾りを頭に付け、女性らしさを演出した。
CONCEPT: Produced to generate support for WHITE STAR Takasaki as part of a coherent program to reinvigorate the area. We focused on making a cute and fluffy "cloud-like" character. She wears a white star hair ornament as a feminine touch.
プロフィール: 女子サッカーチーム「ホワイトスター高崎」のイメージキャラクター。
PROFILE: The image character for the girls soccer team WHITE STAR Takasaki. Her name is Miss STARMA.

118-3　丼丼 DONDON
コンセプト: 茨城ゴールデンゴールズの監督、萩本欽一さんのイメージから、人気者である動物「パンダ」をマスコットとした。「GOLDEN GOLDS」の頭文字「GG」を目にし、萩本さんの顔の特徴であるタレを表現。「欽ちゃん走り」もデザインに取り入れた。
CONCEPT: The mascot was imaged after the Ibaraki GOLDEN GOLDS manager Kinichi Hagimoto and the ever popular panda. The GOLDEN GOLDS's initials GG form his droopy eyes, expressing one of Hagimoto's distinguishing features. He also characterizes Hagimoto's distinctive "Kin-chan run".
プロフィール: 野球チーム「茨城ゴールデンゴールズ」のマスコットキャラクター。名前は「丼丼」。
PROFILE: DONDON is the mascot character of the baseball team, the Ibaraki Golden Golds.

118-4　Fire Fest
コンセプト: 消火栓が消防署を表している。
CONCEPT: The fire hydrant represents Fire Department.

118-5　Clock
コンセプト: アイオワ州ステートフェアという毎年行われるお祭りのアイコンとなるキャラクター。
CONCEPT: Supporting icons for the annual Iowa State Fair.

142-1　Grumpy
コンセプト: ミネソタ州ミネアポリスにある、グランピーズ・バーというアートなレストラン＆バーの依頼により、怒っているけどかわいいキャラクターを制作。販促ツールおよびバー店内で販売するTシャツ、ライター、ボタンなどに採用した。
CONCEPT: Grumpy's Bar, an "artsy" restaurant and bar located in Minneapolis, MN approached us to create some angry but cute characters they can use for promotion and on merchandise that can be sold at the bar, including t-shirts, lighters, and buttons.

142-2　機長さん＆キャビンアテンダントさん Mr. Captain & Miss Flight Attendant
コンセプト: 架空の航空会社という設定のもとに展開し、70年代のアメリカを思わせるようなデザインに仕上げた。
CONCEPT: Developed on the idea of an imaginary airline and designed to be reminiscent of 1970s America.
プロフィール: アクタラスカンパニーのオリジナルキャラクター。キャラクター名は、機長さん＆キャビンアテンダントさん。
PROFILE: Original characters for actrus company inc. Their names are Mr. Captain & Miss Flight Attendant.

142-3　Lucy & Matt
コンセプト: 眼鏡をかけさせることで、「見る」という言葉を強調している。
CONCEPT: The eyes with glasses reinforces the word "look".
プロフィール: Lucyはお下げ髪で、Mattはキャップをかぶっている。
PROFILE: Lucy has pigtails and Matt has a cap.

142-4　Spencer
コンセプト: 犬のSpencerと骨はペットショップのテーマを表している。
CONCEPT: The dog Spencer and his bone work with the pet store's theme.

142-5　B-Flat
コンセプト: 覚えやすいキャラクターが店のアクセントとなっている。
CONCEPT: A memorable character is a high note for the store.
プロフィール: ハッピーな音符が、Bフラットミュージックの賛美を表現している。
PROFILE: This happy musical note signs the praises of B-Flat Music.

178-1　エコてつ君 Ecotetsu-kun
コンセプト: 「鉄道でエコ」キャンペーンのキャラクターとして、駅構内や車内のポスター他、リーフレット、

>> Concept & Profile of Characters

WEBサイトなどで使用される。「鉄道は環境にやさしい乗り物である」ということを、親しみやすいキャラクターをメッセンジャーに仕立てて表現。物語性が感じられるインパクトのある絵柄で、環境貢献や鉄道に乗ることの楽しさを伝えている。
CONCEPT: Used on posters in stations and trains, leaflets, and websites as the "Eco by rail" campaign character. Designed to be an endearing character and bearer of the message "the railway is an environmentally friendly mode of transportation." He conveys the fun of riding the train and helping the environment through impactive design that's narrative in nature.
プロフィール：2005年10月1日生まれ。身長4m、体重1.7トン。趣味は鉄道模型作りと沿線ウォーキング。好きな食べ物は駅弁で、「人にやさしく地球にやさしく」が座右の銘。「こんにちは。僕エコてつ君。チーム・マイナス6%の一員だよ。鉄道は環境にやさしい乗り物なんだ。みんなヨロシクね!!」
PROFILE: Born: October 1, 2005. Height: 4m; weight: 1.7 t. His hobbies are building model trains and walking along the railroad tracks. His favorite food is station lunches, and his motto is "people-friendly, Earth-friendly". "Hi, I'm Eco Tetsu-kun, a member of Team Minus 6%. Remember, the railway is an environmentally friendly mode of transportation!!!"

178-2 Adrienne
プロフィール：Adrienneは女の子に対する楽天的な気分を表現している。
PROFILE: Adrienne represents optimism for girls.

178-3 Beaverdale
コンセプト：ビーヴァーデイルという町の名前から生まれたビーヴァーのキャラクター。
CONCEPT: The beaver character plays off the town name: Beaverdale.

178-4 ウインドブラザーズ Wind Brothers
コンセプト：群馬名物として知られる、空っ風の妖精をイメージした。兄弟仲良く、群馬の文化について話し合っている設定に。
CONCEPT: Imaged as elf of Gunma's famed dry winds. The pair are premised on two brothers who get along well chatting about Gunma's culture.
プロフィール：名前は、ウインドブラザーズ。2004年、群馬県下で行われたイベント「ぐんま文化の日2004」のマスコットキャラクター。
PROFILE: The mascot characters for the Gunma Prefectural office event, Gunma Culture Day 2004. Their name is the Wind Brothers.

178-5 キャプテンわん CAPTAIN-WAN
コンセプト：「ハマスポどっとコム」は、総合スポーツコミュニティサイト。老若男女に親しまれやすく、「横浜らしい」キャラクターとなるよう、横浜のポピュラーなイメージである「港」から、港→海→自由に海原を巡るパイレーツと連想していき、パイレーツというキャラクター設定とした。性別、年齢等にとらわれず、かわいらしく、人間に最も愛され、かつスポーツサイトらしく活動的なイメージを持つ「犬」をモチーフとしたが、犬種はあえて限定せず、雑種としている。
CONCEPT: Hamaspo.com is an all-sports website. To make the character Yokohamaesque and readily endearing to men and women, young and old, Yokohama's popular image of a port led to associations of the sea and finally a pirate, who moves freely about the seas. And to keep him free of a defining age or sex he was made man's best friend, a charming dog befitting of the activities of sports website, and consciously made not a specific pedigree but rather a mixed breed.
プロフィール：キャプテンわんは、犬の姿で横浜に現れたパイレーツだが、犬の性格を受け継いでおり、大勢の仲間と走ったり、遊んだり、スポーツするのが大好き。港町横浜を拠点に、老若男女、競技種目問わずスポーツを通してコミュニティに顔を出し、ともに楽しみ、仲間意識を育むのにひと役買ってくれる。
PROFILE: CAPTAIN-WAN is a canine pirate. Having the personality of a dog, he likes to run about with his many friends, play, and do sports. With the port city of Yokohama as his base, he plays the role of fostering team spirit in men and women, young and old, by enjoying sports together with the community.

224-2 半額半蔵 Hangaku Hanzo
コンセプト：「半額半蔵」というキャンペーンタイトルにちなみ、忍者をモチーフに躍動感・スピード感・強さを意識して制作。アイキャッチとして強いイメージを持たせることで、他社との差別化を図り、インパクトの強いキャラクターに仕上げた。
CONCEPT: In keeping with the "Hangaku Hanzo" campaign title (from Hanzo Hattori, a famous real-life ninja) a ninja figure was chosen to convey dynamism, speed and strength. Eyecatching images were created to set the company apart from competitors and maximize impact.
プロフィール：ソニーピクチャーズエンタテインメントのキャンペーン「半額半蔵」のキャラクター。可愛いのに力強い、忍者の男の子。
PROFILE: Cute but tough ninja character from Sony Pictures Entertainment "Hangaku Hanzo" half-price DVD campaign.

224-3 Anagadirri
コンセプト：すっきりとモダンでありながら遊び心のあるキャラクター。演劇、音楽と子供たちにつながりをもつキャラクターとなっている。
CONCEPT: A character that would be clean and modern, but still be playful. Connecting to theatre/music and to children.
プロフィール：ラバー製のアヒルがパフォーマーになる。まじめだけど面白い。
PROFILE: The rubber duck turned performer. Serious but funny.

224-4 Future Lion
コンセプト：AKQAのFuture Lionコンクールのためのマスコット。キュートさと凄みを兼ね備えたキャラクター。
CONCEPT: AKQA approached us to design a mascot for their Future Lion competition, a character that can be cute but deadly at the same time.
プロフィール：この若いライオンは、広告業界において、限界を押し広げることもいとわない、勇敢で大胆な若手クリエイターたちを表している。
PROFILE: This young lion was designed to represent future creatives in the field of advertising: brave, daring & willing to push the boundaries

224-5 Ariane
コンセプト：『Le Fil d'Ariane』は、フランスのナンシー市の見どころを紹介する年刊ガイドブック。ナンシーはアールヌーボーの発祥の地として知られていることから、アールヌーボーのスタイルとオリジナルのドローイングを融合させ、現代的で親しみやすいイラストに仕上げた。ビジュアル・アイデンティティ（キリンのAriane）のリデザイン、ガイドブックの表紙デザイン、中面のイラストを手がけたほか、Tシャツやステッカーなどの宣伝ツールも制作した。
CONCEPT: Le Fil d'Ariane is an annual guidebook that hi-lites the city of Nancy, France. Nancy is known to be the 'birthplace' of Art Nouveau, so we enjoyed interplaying this artistic style with our own drawings, creating illustrations that are contemporary and personable to the city. We were asked to redesign their visual identity (the giraffe Ariane), design the cover of their guide, and provide illustrations for the many sections. We also designed various marketing materials such as t-shirts and stickers.
プロフィール：Arianeは、フランスのナンシーに住んでいるキリンの女の子。この街のツアーガイドで、すばらしい芸術、文化を紹介したり、その他のイベントなどを案内している。
PROFILE: Ariane is a young female giraffe who lives in Nancy, France. She is the "tour guide" to the city, showing visitors all the wonderful art, culture, activities and events they can partake in.

224-6 Berri, Nilla, Coco
コンセプト：Joypopの依頼により、「Tokyo á la Mode」というオンラインマガジンのキャラクターを制作。このサイトは北アメリカの人びとに日本の文化、ファッション、アートなどを伝えている。3人の女の子キャラクターはそれぞれ、このマガジンで取り上げられる各ジャンルを表している。
CONCEPT: Joypop approached us to design a set of characters for their online magazine called "Tokyo á la Mode" a site dedicated to bridging Japanese culture, fashion & art to a North American audience. We decided to create three girls, one to represent different fashion types and the different interest areas covered by the magazine.
プロフィール：Berri、Nilla、Cocoはオンラインマガジンの「アラモード」という名前にちなんで、アイスクリームのフレーバー名からとっているが、同時に、フルーツ、ゴシックロリータ、リュクスという日本の3つのファッションスタイルをも表現している。3人はそれぞれ興味の対象が違っていて、Berriはファッション、Nillaはカルチャーやライフスタイル、Cocoはアートやメディアに興味を持っている。
PROFILE: Berri, Nilla & Coco play off the magazine's name by representing three flavours of ice cream. But they also represent three Japanese fashion styles: Fruits, Gothic Lolita & Lux. Each girl has her own special interests. Berri loves fashion, Nilla is interested in culture and life style while Coco is into art and media.

※ 一部、コンセプト＆プロフィールを記載していない作品がございます。
Please note that some concept & profile has been omitted.

Index

Clients

A	actrus company inc. アクタラスカンパニー	142
	AEON Co., Ltd. イオン	124
	AICHI TELEVISION BROADCASTING CO., LTD. テレビ愛知	194
	Ajinomoto Co., Inc. 味の素	064
	All Nippon Airways Co., Ltd. 全日本空輸	039
	Anagadirri Productions	224
	AQUA	224
	ARTE TAKASAKI 日本フットボールリーグ・アルテ高崎	118
	Asahi Broadcasting Nagano Co., Ltd. 長野朝日放送	199
B	Beaverdale Business Coalition	178
	Benesse Corporation ベネッセコーポレーション	026, 055
	B-Flat Music	142
	Bone-A-Patreat	142
	butterfly・stroke inc バタフライ・ストローク	216, 220
C	Cable West Inc. ケーブルウエスト	032
	Central Union of Agricultural Co-operatives 全国農業協同組合中央会	172
	CHICHIYASU CO., Ltd. チチヤス	088
	CHUBU Electric Power., Inc 中部電力	020
	Cleaty Service CO., LTD クレアティー・サービス	056
	Cloud 9	104
	Coop Sapporo 生活協同組合コープさっぽろ	169
D	DyDo DRINCO ダイドードリンコ	087
	DREAMUSIC ドリーミュージック	214
	Des Moines Fire Department	118
	dwarf inc. ドワーフ	223
E	East Japan Railway Company 東日本旅客鉄道	160, 167
	EPSON SALES JAPAN CORPORATION エプソン販売	093
	Executive Committee of the 2009 National Sports Festival and the National Sports Festival for the Disabled in Niigata トキめき新潟国体・トキめき新潟大会実行委員会	176
	EZAKI GLICO CO., LTD 江崎グリコ	084
F	FIELDS CORPORATION フィールズ	110
	Fil d'Ariane	224
	FM KAGAWA. INC エフエム香川	213
	Fourseeds corporation フォーシーズ	034
	Fuji Television Network, Ink. フジテレビジョン	116
G	Glico Nyugyo グリコ乳業	061
	GMO Internet, Inc. GMOインターネット	029
	GOLDEN GOLDS 茨城ゴールデンゴールズ	118
	Graniph Japan	224
	Grumpy's Bar	142
	GUNMA Pref. 群馬県	178
H	Hawks Town mall ホークスタウンモール	135
	Heineken	082
	Hokkaido Broadcasting Co.,Ltd 北海道放送	190
	Hokuto Corporation ホクト	062
	Hudson soft Co., Ltd ハドソン	099
I	Innovatie Netwerk	158
	Iowa State Fair	118
	Iwate Asahi TV Co., Ltd. 岩手朝日テレビ	199
J	JA Zen-Noh Fukuren JA全農ふくれん	174
	Japan Department Stores Association 日本百貨店協会	155
	Japan Post 日本郵政公社	152
	Joypop	224
K	KAGOME CO., LTD. カゴメ	085
	Kagoshima Broadcasting Corporation 鹿児島放送	198
	KANRO CO., LTD. カンロ	075
	Kansai Economic Federation 関西経済連合会	164
	KDDI	021, 054
	KEIKO TOKYO 螢光TOKYO	222
	Kintetsu Corporation 近畿日本鉄道	164
	KITAJIMA 北島	078
	Kobunsha Co., Ltd. 光文社	206
	KOIKEYA Co., Ltd. 湖池屋	104
	Kyodo Milk Industry Co., Ltd. 協同乳業	076
L	LAWSON ローソン	136
	Lazona kawasaki plaza ラゾーナ川崎プラザ	130
	LEXMARK International k.k. レックスマークインターナショナル	094
	Lion Corporation ライオン	101
	Look Mum	142
M	Magmag, Inc. まぐまぐ	033
	Matsumoto 100th anniversary Project Executive Committee 松本市市制施行100周年記念事業実行委員会	156
	Matsushita Electric Industrial Co., Ltd. 松下電器産業	092, 096
	MdN Corporation エムディエヌコーポレーション	205
	Meiji Seika Kaisha, Ltd. 明治製菓	066, 067, 087
	Meitele メ〜テレ（名古屋テレビ放送）	195
	Metro Properties Co., Ltd. メトロプロパティーズ	129
	Mister Donut Business Group, Duskin CO., LTD ダスキン ミスタードーナツ事業本部	137
	Mitsubishi Electric Corporation 三菱電機	090
	Mitsubishi UFJ Asset Management Co., Ltd 三菱UFJ投信	040
	Mitsui Fudosan Residential Co.,Ltd 三井不動産レジデンシャル	046
	MITSUI LIFE INSURANCE COMPANY LIMITED 三井生命保険	038
	MOMIJI BANK もみじ銀行	045
	MORI BUILDING CO., LTD. 森ビル	128
N	NAGANO BROADCASTING SYSTEM CO.,Ltd 長野放送	197
	NAKABAYASHI DENTAL CLINIC 中林歯科	056
	Napster Japan, Inc. ナップスタージャパン	030
	National Council on Mt. Fuji World Heritage 富士山を世界遺産にする国民会議	147

	National Sports Festival and National Sports Festival for Disabled Bureau ゆめ半島千葉国体実行委員会（千葉県国体・全国障害者スポーツ大会局） …………… 177		Seven & i Holdings Co., Ltd.　セブン＆アイ・ホールディングス ……………… 127

National Sports Festival and National Sports Festival for Disabled Bureau
ゆめ半島千葉国体実行委員会（千葉県国体・全国障害者スポーツ大会局） …………… 177
National Treasure-Hikone Castle 400th Anniversary Executive Committee
国宝・彦根城築城400年祭実行委員会 …………………………………………………… 157
NESTLE JAPAN LTD.　ネスレ日本 ……………………………………………………… 080
NEXT Co., Ltd.　ネクスト ………………………………………………………………… 048
NHK …………………………………………………………………………………… 203, 205
NHK BOOK　NHK出版 …………………………………………………………………… 204
NHK ENTERPRISES　NHKエンタープライズ ………………………………………… 115
NHN Japan ………………………………………………………………………………… 031
NIKKEI HUMAN RESOURCES　日経HR ……………………………………………… 053
NIKKEI Inc.　日本経済新聞社 …………………………………………………………… 115
NIPPON TELEVISION NETWORK CORPORATION　日本テレビ放送網 ・ 180
Nissan Motor Co, Ltd.　日産自動車 ……………………………………………… 101, 102
Nissay Asset Management Corporation　ニッセイアセットマネジメント …… 054
NISSIN FOOD PRODUCTS CO., LTD.　日清食品 …………………………………… 073
Nisshin Seifun Group Inc.　日清製粉グループ ………………………………………… 058
Nomura Real Estate Urban Net Co., Ltd.　野村不動産アーバンネット …… 041
NTT DoCoMo Tohoku, Inc.　エヌ・ティ・ティ・ドコモ東北 …………………… 050
NTT DoCoMo, Inc.　エヌ・ティ・ティ・ドコモ ……………………………………… 022
NTT East　NTT東日本 …………………………………………………………………… 024
NTT Resonant Inc.　エヌ・ティ・ティ レゾナント …………………………………… 035

O OHK　岡山放送 …………………………………………………………………………… 186
Oita Asahi Broadcasting Co., Ltd　大分朝日放送 …………………………………… 201
Osaka City Environment Bureau　大阪市環境局 …………………………………… 175
Osaka Municipal Transportation Bureau　大阪市交通局 ………………………… 163
Otsuka Beverage Co., Ltd.　Crystal Geyser Ladies Golf Tournament
大塚ベバレジ　クリスタルガイザーレディスゴルフトーナメント ……………………… 117
OTSUKA PHARMACEUTICAL CO., LTD.　大塚製薬 ……………………………… 083

P P&G ………………………………………………………………………………………… 085
pal system　パルシステム生活協同組合連合会 ……………………………………… 170
PARCO CO., LTD.　パルコ ……………………………………………………………… 126
PASMO Co.,ltd.　パスモ ………………………………………………………………… 162
Petroleum Association of Japan　石油連盟 …………………………………………… 175
Pizza Hut（Kentucky Fried Chiken Japan., Ltd.）
ピザハット（日本ケンタッキー・フライド・チキン） …………………………………… 035
POPLAR PUBLISHING CO., LTD.　ポプラ社 ………………………………………… 208
President Chain Store corporation ……………………………………………………… 120

Q Q.P. Corporation　キユーピー …………………………………………………………… 104

R RECRUIT CO., LTD　リクルート ………………………………………………… 051, 052
Robochan LLC …………………………………………………………………………… 104
ROBOT MUSEUM　ロボットミュージアム …………………………………………… 111

S SAKURA, Inc　桜 ………………………………………………………………………… 086
SAKURAYA CO., LTD　さくらや ……………………………………………………… 134
SANKEI SHIMBUN CO., LTD.　産経新聞社 …………………………………… 115, 212
SEGA TOYS CO., LTD.　セガトイズ …………………………………………………… 103
Sendai City　仙台市　環境局リサイクル推進課 ……………………………………… 148

Seven & i Holdings Co., Ltd.　セブン＆アイ・ホールディングス ……………… 127
Shibasakiekimae dermatological clinic　柴崎駅前皮膚科 ………………………… 055
Shin-etsu Broadcasting Co., Ltd.　信越放送 ………………………………………… 201
SHINJUKU MITSUKOSHI ALCOTT　新宿三越アルコット ……………………… 135
Shizuoka Pref.　静岡県 …………………………………………………………………… 144
Sony Pictures Entertainment Inc.　ソニーピクチャーズエンタテインメント … 224
SMITH AND JONES FILMS ……………………………………………………………… 223
Swisscom …………………………………………………………………………………… 056
SYUTOKEN SINTOSHI TETSUDO CO.　首都圏新都市鉄道 ……………………… 167

T Television Nishi-Nippon Corporation　テレビ西日本 ………………………………… 196
Television Osaka INC　テレビ大阪 …………………………………………………… 188
Television Saitama Co., Ltd.　テレビ埼玉 …………………………………………… 184
Tempstaff Co., Ltd　テンプスタッフ …………………………………………………… 042
THE ASSOCIATION OF JAPANESE PRIVATE RAILWAYS
日本民営鉄道協会 ………………………………………………………………………… 178
The Hokkaido Shimbun Press　北海道新聞社 ……………………………………… 202
The National Association of Commercial Broadcasters in Japan
日本民間放送連盟 ………………………………………………………………………… 168
The Okinawa Electric Power CO., Inc　沖縄電力 …………………………………… 014
THE YOMIURI SHIMBUN　読売新聞東京本社 ……………………………………… 210
TM Co., Ltd. ……………………………………………………………………………… 056
Tohato Inc.　東ハト ……………………………………………………… 068, 070, 072, 074
Tokyo Gas Co., Ltd.　東京ガス ……………………………………………………… 016, 019
TOKYO METROPOLITAN RACING ASSOCIATION　特別区競馬組合 ……… 106
TOKYO WOMEN'S MEDICAL UNIVERSITY YACHIYO MEDICAL CENTER
東京女子医科大学附属　八千代医療センター ………………………………………… 049
TOKYU CARD INC.　東急カード ……………………………………………………… 036
Toshiba Corporation　東芝 ……………………………………………………………… 100
Toyama Light Rail co., ltd.　富山ライトレール ……………………………………… 166
TOYOTA MOTOR CORPORATION　トヨタ自動車 ………………………………… 089
TOYOTA CAROLLA (Volkswagen DUO Takamatsu)
トヨタカローラ（フォルクスワーゲンDUO高松） …………………………………… 137
TSUTAYA Co., Ltd. ……………………………………………………………………… 056

U Urban Explorers Festival ………………………………………………………………… 112

W Wacom Co., Ltd.　ワコム ………………………………………………………………… 098
WHITE STAR Takasaki 2007　ホワイトスター高崎 2007 ………………………… 118
WIN FOOD SYSTEM　ウィン・フードシステム ……………………………… 138, 140

Y Yamaguchi Asahi Broadcasting Co, Ltd.　山口朝日放送 …………………………… 192
YAMAHA MOTOR CO.,LTD　ヤマハ発動機　プール事業部 ……………………… 114
Yokohama Sports Association　横浜市体育協会 …………………………………… 178
Yomiuri Telecasting Corporation　読売テレビ ……………………………… 182, 200, 207
YOSHINOYA Co., Ltd.　吉野家 ………………………………………………………… 132
You Grow Girl …………………………………………………………………………… 178
yoyogi zeminar　代々木ゼミナール …………………………………………………… 028

Submitters

	310k 112, 158	
A	Adel Corporation アデル 092	
	AD-PASCAL Inc. アド・パスカル 198	
	AICHI TELEVISION BROADCASTING CO., LTD. テレビ愛知 194	
	Akihito Suzuki Design Office 鈴木章人デザイン事務所 175	
	All Nippon Airways Co., Ltd. 全日本空輸 039	
	ANSWR アンサー 214	
	Asahi Broadcasting Nagano Co., Ltd. 長野朝日放送 199	
	asahi seihan printing co., ltd. アサヒ精版印刷 200, 207	
B	BUILD creativehaus Inc. ビルド・クリエイティブハウス 064, 184	
	butterfly・stroke inc. バタフライ・ストローク	
	.... 031, 052, 053, 074, 098, 099, 103, 110, 216, 220, 224	
C	Central Union of Agricultural Co-operatives	
	全国農業協同組合中央会 172	
	CHUBU Electric Power., Inc 中部電力 020	
	CINQ DIRECTIONS INC. サンクディレクションズ 056, 080, 104, 134	
	Coop Sapporo 生活協同組合コープさっぽろ 169	
D	DyDo DRINCO ダイドードリンコ 087	
	DAIKO ADVERTISING INC 大広 096	
	Daiko Brand Design Inc. 大広ブランドデザイン 076	
	Dairy Fresh デイリー・フレッシュ 029, 118, 126	
	DENTSU EAST JAPAN INC. 電通東日本 050	
	DENTSU INC. 電通	
	016, 024, 028, 030, 039, 041, 061, 120, 124, 132, 136, 147, 160, 162, 184	
	DENTSU INC. KANSAI tokyoroom	
	電通関西支社「TOKYOROOM」 106, 138, 140	
	DENTSU KYUSHU INC. 電通九州 078, 174	
	DENTSU WEST JAPAN INC. 電通西日本 045	
	DENTSU WEST JAPAN INC. OKAYAMA 電通西日本 岡山支社 186	
	DENTSU WEST JAPAN INC. TAKAMATSU 電通西日本 高松支社 137	
	design service デザインサービス 026, 116	
	DEVILROBOTS 056	
	dmp Co., Ltd ディー・エム・ピー 148	
	doppo inc. ドッポ 088	
	dwarf inc. ドワーフ 203, 223	
E	East Japan Railway Company 東日本旅客鉄道 167	
	Executive Committee of the 2009 National Sports Festival and the	
	National Sports Festival for the Disabled in Niigata	
	トキめき新潟国体・トキめき新潟大会実行委員会 176	
	EZAKI GLICO CO., LTD 江崎グリコ 084	
F	Fourseeds corporation フォーシーズ 034	
	FUJI TELEVISION NETWORK, INC.	
	フジテレビジョン 美術制作局 CG・タイトル部 049	
	Furi Furi Company フリフリカンパニー 103	
G	General Press ゼネラル・プレス 170	
	GYROWALK Inc. ジャイロウォーク 111	
H	HAKUHODO Inc. 博報堂	
	.... 058, 062, 068, 070, 072, 073, 089, 093, 117, 152, 155, 206, 208	
	Hokkaido Broadcasting Co.,Ltd 北海道放送 190	
	HOKKAIDO HAKUHODO 北海道博報堂 202	
I	IC4 DESIGN 046	
	Idea アイディー 200	
	IPLANET Inc. アイプラネット 090	
	Iwate Asahi TV Co., Ltd. 岩手朝日テレビ 199	
J	Jeremyville 224	
K	KDDI 021	
	KEIKO TOKYO 螢光TOKYO 222	
	KesselsKramer 082	
	Kjetil Vatne Norway 224	
L	LIGHT graphics Inc. 056	
	Lion Corporation ライオン 101	
M	Magmag, Inc. まぐまぐ 033	
	Maniackers Design 055, 056, 104, 118, 142, 178, 205	
	Matsumoto 100th anniversary Project Executive Committee	
	松本市市制施行100周年記念事業実行委員会 156	
	Meiji Seika Kaisha, Ltd. 明治製菓 066, 067, 087	
	Meitele メ〜テレ（名古屋テレビ放送）........ 195	
	Meomi Design 104, 142, 224	
	Metro Properties Co., Ltd. メトロプロパティーズ 129	
	Mister Donut Business Group, Duskin CO., LTD	
	ダスキン ミスタードーナツ事業本部 137	
	Mitsubishi UFJ Asset Management Co., Ltd 三菱UFJ投信 040	
	MITSUI LIFE INSURANCE COMPANY LIMITED 三井生命保険 038	
	MORI BUILDING CO., LTD. 森ビル 128	
	mountain mountain マウンテンマウンテン 054, 085, 115, 205	
N	NAGANO BROADCASTING SYSTEM CO.,Ltd 長野放送 197	
	National Sports Festival and National Sports Festival for Disabled Bureau	
	ゆめ半島千葉国体実行委員会（千葉県国体・全国障害者スポーツ大会局）........ 177	
	National Treasure-Hikone Castle 400th Anniversary Executive Committee	
	国宝・彦根城築城400年祭実行委員会 157	
	NEXT Co., Ltd. ネクスト 048	
	NHK BOOK NHK出版 204	
	NIPPON TELEVISION NETWORK CORPORATION 日本テレビ放送網 180	
	Nishioka Pencil Co.,Ltd 西岡ペンシル 130, 144	
	NISSAN MOTOR CO, LTD. 日産自動車 101	
	Nissay Asset Management Corporation ニッセイアセットマネジメント 054	
	NTT DoCoMo, Inc. エヌ・ティ・ティ・ドコモ 022	
	NTT Resonant Inc. エヌ・ティ・ティ レゾナント 035	
O	Oita Asahi Broadcasting Co., Ltd 大分朝日放送 201	
	Osaka Municipal Transportation Bureau 大阪市交通局 163	
	OTSUKA PHARMACEUTICAL CO., LTD. 大塚製薬 083

P	Petroleum Association of Japan　石油連盟	175
	Pizza Hut (Kentucky Fried Chiken Japan., Ltd.)	
	ピザハット（日本ケンタッキー・フライド・チキン）	035
	polepoletion. STUDIO　ポレポレーション・スタジオ	086, 213
R	RECRUIT CO., LTD　リクルート	051
	RE-PORT CO.,LTD　リ・ポート	114
	Romando Co., Ltd.　浪漫堂	094
S	SANKEI SHIMBUN CO., LTD.　産経新聞社	115, 212
	Sayles Graphic Design	104, 118, 142, 178
	sean shono　ショーン・ショーノ	135
	Seven & i Holdings Co., Ltd.　セブン＆アイ・ホールディングス	127
	Shimazu Enviromental Graphics　島津環境グラフィックス	166
	Shin-etsu Broadcasting Co., Ltd.　信越放送	201
	SWEDEN GRAPHICS	223
	SYUTOKEN SINTOSHI TETSUDO CO.　首都圏新都市鉄道	167
T	tapetentiere	056
	tarout　タロアウト	085, 102
	Television Nishi-Nippon Corporation　テレビ西日本	196
	Television Osaka INC　テレビ大阪	188
	Tempstaff Co., Ltd　テンプスタッフ	042
	THE ASSOCIATION OF JAPANESE PRIVATE RAILWAYS	
	日本民営鉄道協会	178
	The National Association of Commercial Broadcasters in Japan	
	日本民間放送連盟	168
	The Okinawa Electric Power CO., Inc　沖縄電力	014
	THE YOMIURI SHINBUN　読売新聞東京本社	210
	Tokyo Gas Co., Ltd. GAS SCIENCE MUSEUM	
	東京ガス がすてなーに ガスの科学館	019
	Tokyu Agency Inc.　東急エージェンシー	036
	Toshiba Corporation　東芝	100
V	visiontrack　ヴィジョントラック	075, 135
Y	Yamaguchi Asahi Broadcasting Co, Ltd.　山口朝日放送	192
	YELLOW DOG STUDIO　イエロードッグスタジオ	055, 164
	Yokohama Sports Association　横浜市体育協会	178
	Yomiuri Telecasting corp　読売テレビ放送	182
Z	ZOOM Design Inc.　ズームデザイン	032

Character Design Today
キャラクターデザイン・トゥデイ

Jacket Design

Art Director
佐野研二郎　Kenjiro Sano

Designer
岡本和樹　Kazuki Okamoto

Designer
松村大輔　Daisuke Matsumura
佐藤美穂　Miho Sato

Editor
宮崎亜美　Ami Miyazaki

Writer & Interviewer
鈴木めぐみ　Megumi Suzuki

Editorial Assistance
白倉三紀子　Mikiko Shirakura

Translator
パメラ・三木　Pamela Miki
白倉三紀子　Mikiko Shirakura
ヴァルタニアン・アイヴァン　Ivan Vartanian

Photographer
藤本邦治　Kuniharu Fujimoto

Publisher
三芳伸吾　Shingo Miyoshi

2007年10月8日　初版第1刷発行

PIE BOOKS
2-32-4, Minami-Otsuka,
Toshima-ku, Tokyo 170-0005 Japan
Tel: +81-3-5395-4811
Fax: +81-3-5395-4812
e-mail: editor@piebooks.com
　　　　sales@piebooks.com
http://www.piebooks.com

発行元　ピエ・ブックス
〒170-0005　東京都豊島区南大塚2-32-4
編集　TEL: 03-5395-4820　FAX: 03-5395-4821
　　　e-mail: editor@piebooks.com
営業　TEL: 03-5395-4811　FAX: 03-5395-4812
　　　e-mail: sales@piebooks.com
http://www.piebooks.com

印刷・製本　株式会社サンニチ印刷

©2007 PIE BOOKS
Printed in Japan
ISBN978-4-89444-634-2 C3070

本書の収録内容の無断転載、複写、引用などを禁じます。
落丁、乱丁はお取り替えいたします。